D1280894

275 Helps For Winning the Lost

SOUL
WINNING [101]

including illustrations and sermons

FRANK R. SHIVERS

Published by
HILL PUBLISHING
Sumter, South Carolina

Published in Sumter, South Carolina, by Hill Publications.

Unless otherwise noted, Scripture quotations are from the King James Version.

Cover design: VConcepts
Editor: Dan Hazlett

Library in Congress Cataloging-Publication Data

Shivers, Frank R., 1949 –
    Soulwinning 101: 275 Helps In Winning the Lost/ Frank Shivers
    Includes biographical references
    ISBN # 1-878127-05-5
    Contact information: www.camplongridge.com

Library of Congress Control Number:
2005927703

Printed in the United States of America

To those whose passion it is to win souls
and train others to do so,
as well as to those I mentor
for both their work in the harvest field
and their incomparable encouragement.

CONTENTS

A father and son were fishing when the son fell into the water and began to drown. Struggling for life he cried to his father, "Throw me a rope." The father hurriedly cut the rope attached to the anchor of the boat and threw it to his son. However it was too short. The son cried, "Dad, the rope is too short. Throw me a longer rope." The dad frantically but unsuccessfully looked for another rope. The last words this father heard from his son were, "Dad the rope is too short; throw me a longer rope." In a day in which ten thousand Southern Baptist Churches failed to win and baptize one soul last year[1] and in which it takes 43 Southern Baptists an entire year working together to win and baptize one soul and when 92 percent of Southern Baptists will die without witnessing to another person,[2] God is truly crying out to evangelists, pastors, missionaries, student ministers, music leaders, teachers, children and youth workers, and layman at large to throw out a longer rope in soulwinning. Sadly most believers must confess that they either have failed to throw out the rope of soulwinning or have done so with passionless inconsistency. It's time that Christians "strengthen the stakes and lengthen the cords" rescuing as many souls from the plight of eternal darkness and damnation as possible.

Estimated Average of Souls that Die and go to Hell

> 1.68 per second
> 101 per minute
> 6048 per hour
> 145 thousand per day
> 53 million per year
> 3.7 billion per average lifetime (70 years)[3]

My heart pounds in agreement with C.H. Spurgeon, who declared, "Beloved, we must win souls, we cannot live and see men damned: we must have them brought to Jesus. Oh! then, be up and doing and let none around you die unwarned, unwept, uncared for."[4] All believers are called to this task, minister or layman; educated or illiterate; refined or unrefined; extroverted or introverted; male or female; spiritually mature or new convert; abilities or inabilities; famous or infamous; wealthy or poor; professor or student. L.R. Scarborough wrote, "Every Christian is called in the hour of salvation to witness for Jesus Christ. Nothing in heaven or on earth can excuse him from it. God gives no furloughs from this heaven-born obligation."[5]

This book is intended to be merely a tool to sharpen the saint's ability to witness more fluently, passionately, consistently and effectively. As with any evangelism instruction, the key is personal adaptation. Saul's armor could not fit David, and

FOREWORD

Billy Sunday's cannot fit most believers. It's imperative for the Christian to find and wear *soulwinning armor* that fits personally and comfortably.

It is my prayer that the Holy Spirit will consume believers with renewed determination and passion for souls as they read this book and that they will be encouraged to throw out longer ropes to the unsaved. May every Christian resolve that no man with whom he has contact will ever say, "I looked on my right hand, and beheld, but there was no man that would know me: refuge failed me; no man cared for my soul." (Psalm 142:4)

Frank Shivers
Columbia, South Carolina

THE SOULWINNER

The soulwinning man is disappearing from the land,
it's high time more believers join his soul-rescuing band.
200,000 die lost each and every day,
while ninety-six percent of Christians never lift their hand.
Oh fellow believer will you not take a stand
and tell the lost of Jesus in obedience to His command.

Sermons, studies and songs on soulwinning are plenteous is true
but those who actually "practice what they preach" are extremely few.

God calls from above; lost souls in brokenness and despair call from without;
the Holy Spirit calls from the heart within; and the eternally damned call from
Hell below compelling the saved to immediately GO.

Soulwinophobia resist at the start,
refusing to allow fear and Satan's intimidations strike through your heart.

Preparation to engage in this biblical task one must make
to avoid making some major theological and practical mistakes.
Learn how to get into a witness is a must
then master a method in which you can trust.
There are the Four Spiritual Laws, F.A.I.T.H., the Colors of Salvation and the
Roman Road to name a few,
the key is finding a plan comfortable with you.

However, a plan, Bible and know-how too
will not suffice if a passion for souls does not possess you.
Be thou consumed over the sinners damnable plight
until winning them to Jesus becomes your primary delight.
Resolve as the Apostle Paul to rest neither day nor night
knowing by your labor sinners will be brought into the Light.

Upon presenting the gospel message of "repentance and faith"
don't neglect with urgency to draw in the net.
This part of the witness is the most crucial do realize
for man's decision about heaven or hell in it resides.
It is at this point of the witness some soulwinners fail
due to lack of instruction in knowing how to compel.

Rely upon the Holy Spirit in the witness from beginning to end
for He alone can bring conviction of righteousness, judgment and sin.
Pray before you go, and in the witness too,
that He will anoint with power so souls will be won through you.

Fearlessly engage in this solemn task
never cowering down regardless of price.
Fear not inability, nor the possibility of failure
for Jesus the great soulwinner lives in you and is your enabler.

Don't be remiss to neglect evangelism on its knees,
talk to God about man before you talk to man about his salvation need.

Procrastinate not a day longer for the day of leisure is past,
cast off all excuse and witness while time doth last.

Throw out a longer rope to those drowning in sin,
increasing your effort their souls to win.
Roll up your sleeves for this work and do it "Now"
telling sinners the gospel message of the "who, why, when and how."

Discipline thyself to tell one soul a day
and in a year's time 365 witnesses will be made.

The moment a soul is won to Christ follow-up instruction you should impart,
this will give the new believer a footing so he will not easily depart.
Urge him immediately to share his decision of faith
and also to write down this spiritual birth date.

What a joy it will be in heaven to see a Brandon, Mary or Josh,
who God saved miraculously through us!

The crown of rejoicing in heaven the soulwinner will receive
in the presence of Jesus for all to see.
To take this crown and lay it at His feet
will bring rapturous joy that nothing else can compete.

So don't get used to boys and girls dying and going to Hell,
do what you can to save them from that eternal peril.

Frank Shivers

ONE

The Compulsion Factor In Soulwinning

Our main business, brethren, is to win souls.[1]   *C.H. Spurgeon*

Years ago in Kentucky resided two families, one of which had the only radio for miles. This family heard that a tornado was heading straight for their neighbor's house so the father sent his son Merle to give warning. Merle darted out the door to do just that but a bird landed on a limb and he stopped to throw a stone at it. He missed. He then started running to fulfill his mission again when the bird flew back to another limb close to him. This time his rock was right on target and the bird fell to the ground. As he picked up the bloody bird he heard a rushing sound coming from the direction of the Renfro family's home in the valley—the family he was to warn. He looked toward it just in time to see their four bodies thrust to death. He rushed back to tell his father what had happened. In the midst of the story his father noticed blood on his hands and asked him what that was. Merle told him it was the blood of the bird he killed. His father replied, "No, son that's not the blood of the bird you killed. It is the blood of the Renfro family you failed to warn."[2] Most believers are guilty of throwing stones at birds while people all around them die and go to Hell. And their hands are wringing wet with their blood! Look at your hands. Do you see the blood of a friend, an acquaintance, a stranger, or a family member dripping from them? God states that one day believers will be held accountable for those to whom they had the chance to witness and didn't (Ezekiel 33: 7-9). That is unalterable. A Christian can determine no one else's blood will be "required at our hand" though.

Are you guilty of throwing stones at birds while people perish? Though well intentioned as Merle, are you ever distracted from actually making face-to-face presentations of the gospel? Satan doesn't care how well intentioned believers are to witness to a doomed soul as long as they never quite get around to it. God sees through the empty excuses of Christians for not soulwinning as Merle's dad saw through his for not obeying. He has clearly commanded the saved to warn the entire world of impending Divine judgment upon sin and to realize man's only way of escape is through Jesus Christ (Matthew 28: 18-20).

The Christian should engage in soulwinning evangelism in response to four calls.

The Call from above: Christ on His throne in Heaven calls us to be soulwinners. He declares, "Ye shall be witnesses unto me both in Jerusalem (home area) and in all Judea (state) and in Samaria (across America) and unto the uttermost parts of the earth (everywhere else)" (Acts 1:8); "I have chosen you, that you should go and bring forth fruit" (John 15:16) and "Follow me and I will make you fishers of men" (Matthew 4:19). The command is crystal clear and believers have no option but to obey.

The Call from around: Broken, bleeding, bound and blind souls are crying out for help. Their body language and lifestyle are but a plead for you to tell them of Him who alone can make the eternal difference in their life.

The world's great heart is aching,
aching fiercely in the night,
And God alone can heal it,
and God alone give light.
And the men to bear the message,
and to preach the living Word,
Are you and I my brother,
and all others who have heard.
                                        - unknown

The Call from within: In the heart of the saved is the voice of the Holy Spirit pleading, "Go and tell of Calvary's love and Jesus' desire to save from sin." Indeed with Paul the saint cries, "The love of Christ constraineth me" to go and tell. God plants within the soul of all He saves the desire to reproduce. In fact the person who has no desire to tell is not "born of Him" (Matthew 10: 32-33). W.A. Criswell said, "The first impulse of a born-again Christian is to win somebody to Jesus. If we lose this drive, we are untrue to the Holy Spirit within us and we deny the great will of God for us."[3] I can understand how a person may work hard at soulwinning never to win a soul (though highly unlikely), but I will never understand how a person who claims to know Christ could never witness. It just doesn't mesh with what scripture teaches. In the Bible record after record is given about how those who Jesus saved immediately began to go and tell. Among these were Philip, Andrew, and the woman at Jacob's Well. The saved cannot but speak out loud for their Savior. He places within the saved soul a "divine heartburn" for the lost. Do you hear this call from within the citadel of your own heart to go and tell?

The Call from below: A call comes ringing loud and clear from the torment and darkness of Hell for the saved to be a witness. Luke 16 gives the record of a man who died and went to Hell. In verses 27-28 the man cries from Hell to Abraham in Heaven, "I pray thee therefore father, that thou wouldest send him to my father's house; for I have five brothers; that he may testify unto them, lest they also come to this place of torment." This man begged from Hell for someone on earth to warn his brothers lest they die in their sin and end up there with him. Do you hear such pleas from Hell begging you to witness to a son, a daughter, a spouse, or a friend?

A passion for souls must overwhelm us or we will never be serious about soulwinning. There are ten things that can enhance one's passion for souls.

Study the Savior. Jesus is the matchless soulwinner. We can learn from His example and be fueled with His burning passion for the damned. Jesus began His work as an evangelist by winning Andrew and sending him out as a soulwinner. Next He won Phillip and dispatched him to win Nathaniel. Following that Jesus for three years in sermon, personal encounters and Bible teaching dealt with lost man. He witnessed to the likes of Nicodemus, Zaccheus, Bartimaeus, the woman at the well, the Pharisees, publicans, priests, soldiers, children, and even Kings. Day and night His heart burned for the lost. He witnessed to all classes of people. He refused to let racial or cultural barriers impede His witness.[4] He refused to let man or schedule or opposition douse that burning flame for the lost. Scripture records nineteen personal soulwinning encounters of Jesus. He didn't just tell us to do it; He did it! To have a passion for souls like Jesus the soulwinner must do four things He did.

The soulwinner must see as Jesus saw. What did Jesus see? Matthew 9:36 states, "When He saw the multitude, He was moved with compassion on them, because they fainted, and were scattered abroad, as sheep having no shepherd." What do you see when you look at athletes, bankers, waitresses, waiters, and mechanics? Do you see just people or do you see souls for whom Jesus died and who stand in desperate need of what only He can give them? Do you see them as Jesus sees them – "as sheep without a shepherd," condemned, lost and hurting? Jesus saw man diseased (sin) in need of forgiveness. Jesus saw man dejected ("fainted") in need of hope. Jesus saw man deserted ("as sheep without a shepherd"). Jesus saw man doomed. He looked at these people and saw their end. Do you see sinners as Jesus sees them? We should look at sinners through the lenses of Christ our Savior and be inflamed with a burden for them as He manifested.

The soulwinner must feel as Jesus felt. As Jesus looked upon the multitude He was moved with compassion (v 36). If we are going to impact our world, change our schools and win our friends and acquaintances, we must not only see as Jesus saw but also feel as Jesus felt for the lost. A famous surgeon was asked, "Do you fear a day when your hands will no longer be able to operate?" He replied, "No, I fear the day when my heart no longer feels the suffering of those I operate on." Believer, that's the day we must fear! Fear the day when your heart becomes callous and indifferent to those dying and going to Hell around you.

The soulwinner must pray as Jesus prayed. No doubt if we see as Jesus sees and feel as He felt for the lost we will pray as He prayed for them. He exhorts, "Pray the Lord of the harvest that He will send forth laborers into His harvest" (v 38). We are to pray for the lost and also for the willingness of saints to share Jesus with them. Stephen Olford said, "Before you talk to man about God, talk to God about man." Develop a prayer list for the lost and pray incessantly for their salvation.

Finally, if believers are to have a burden for souls as Jesus *the soulwinner* must *do as Jesus did.* He planned to win souls. His entire life was purpose driven to that end. He never lost sight of His goal to bring people face to face with their sin and need of God. To enhance your passion for souls, you must be as purpose driven as our Lord. You must plan to win souls. You must make that a priority of your life.

Study Soulwinners. Go to school on the great soulwinners of history by reading the biographies of D.L. Moody, Billy Sunday, William Booth, John Wesley, Horatius Bonar, Charles Finney, Billy Graham, Robert M. McCheyne, John R. Rice, John Hyde, and others. Read to discover what they did to keep the fire burning in their heart for the souls of lost man. One great soulwinner's method to keep his heart aflame for souls was to go witnessing even when he lacked the desire. He said talking to souls about Christ always fueled his soulwinning passion. Another said it helped to look at "strangers and friends" as family who needed Christ. He looked at a girl as his sister, a boy as his brother, a man as his father, etc., which prompted him to be even more concerned for their spiritual well being. Read to dissect the inward man; let his tearful eyes, compassionate heart, resolved determination, thundering and pleading voice and soul aflame incite your passion for souls. Feel the "fire" that burned in the hearts of great soulwinners by pondering deeply their statements about winning souls.

George Whitefield, a Methodist evangelist, said, "O Lord, give me souls or take my soul." He also said to the people of his day, "I am willing to go to jail for you, I am willing to die for you, but I am not willing to go to heaven without you."

John Wesley, a Methodist evangelist, told his "preacher boys," "You have nothing to do but to save souls. Therefore, spend and be spent in this work. It is not your business to preach so many times but to save as many souls as you can."

R.G. Lee said " Look on soulwinning as a business, not an incidental matter; as work not play; as time well spent, not wasted; as a privilege, not a boresome duty."[5]

William Burns declared, "The thud of Christless feet on the road to Hell is breaking my heart."

George W. Truett preached, "If one is born again, that one is concerned that somebody else may be saved. "If any man have not the spirit of Christ, he is none of His." And the spirit of Christ is the spirit of compassionate anxiety that lost people may be saved."

Charles Finney declared "Contemplate much the guilt and danger of sinners, that your zeal for their salvation may be intensified. Also deeply ponder and dwell much upon the boundless love and compassion of Christ for them. So love them yourself as to be willing to die for them. Guard against every temptation that would abate your interest in it. Believe the assertion of Christ that He is with you in this work always and everywhere, to give you all the help you need. 'He that winneth souls is wise,' and, 'If any of you lack wisdom, let him ask of God, that giveth to all men liberally, and upbraideth not; and it shall be given him. But let him ask in faith.' Remember, therefore, that you are bound to have the wisdom that shall win souls to Christ."[6]

The missionary Phillip Armstrong declared, "I am promising everything I have to our Lord to be used where he chooses. I'll never be satisfied with anything else now, even if it means burying myself in the heart of heathendom - literally as well as figuratively. Yes I'll go, gladly! I have to."

Charles Haddon Spurgeon, a great pastor and soulwinner, said, "Even if I was utterly selfish and had no concern but for my own happiness, I would choose if I might to be a soulwinner." Spurgeon also said, "If sinners be damned, at least let them leap to Hell over our bodies. And if they will perish, let them perish with our arms about their knees, imploring them to stay. If Hell must be filled, at least let it be filled in the teeth of our exertions and let not one go there unwarned and unprayed for."

Petra Malena "Malla" Moe asked, "What are we here for, to have a good time with Christians or to save sinners?"[7]

C. T. Studd said, "Some want to live within the sound of church or chapel bells: I want to rent a rescue shop within a yard of Hell."

Dr. Sharp of Charles Street Church, Boston, before his death said, "I would rather have one young man come to my grave and affirm, 'the man who sleeps there arrested me in the course of sin and led me to Christ,' than to have the most magnificent obelisk that ever marked the place of mortal remains."

Keith Green said, "The World is tired of hearing 'praise the Lord,' they want to see it."[8]

David Brainerd said of himself, " I cared not how or where I lived or what hardships I went through so that I could gain souls for Christ. While I was asleep, I dreamed of these things; and when I awaked, the first thing I thought of was this great work. I longed to be a *flame of fire,* continuously burning and glowing in the service of God and building up Christ's kingdom to my latest, my dying moments."[9]

D.L. Moody, the great evangelist, said, "I look upon the world as a wrecked vessel, it's ruin coming nearer and nearer. God has given me a lifeboat and said, 'Moody, save all you can.' "

John MacArthur stated, "Most people do not come to Christ as an immediate response to a sermon they hear in a crowded setting. They come to Christ because of the influence of an individual."[10]

A. W. Tozer commented, "The testimony of the true follower of Christ might be something like this: The world's pleasures and the world's treasures henceforth have no appeal for me. I reckon myself crucified to the world and the world crucified to me. But the multitudes that were so dear to Christ shall not be less dear to me. *If I cannot prevent their moral suicide, I shall at least baptize them with my human tears.* I want no blessing that I cannot share. I seek no spirituality that I must win at the cost of forgetting that men and women are lost and without hope. If in spite of all I can do they will sin against the light and bring upon themselves the displeasure of a holy God, then I must not let them go their sad way unwept. I scorn happiness that I must purchase with ignorance. I reject a heaven I must enter by shutting my eyes to the sufferings of my fellow men. I choose a broken heart rather than any happiness that ignores the tragedy of human life and human death. Though I, through the grace of God, in Christ, no longer lie under Adam's sin, I would still feel a bond of compassion for all of Adam's tragic race, and I am determined that I shall go down to the grave (and) up into God's heaven mourning for the lost and perishing."[11]

John R. Rice said, "One who does not win souls is guilty of a list of sins which block revival, deaden the churches, grieve the Spirit of God, cause Christians to miss the joy and manifestation of the Holy Spirit, and damn millions of souls!"[12] Rice continues, "Evangelists sometimes become "Bible teachers" because their love for Christ has grown cold. And Christians everywhere content themselves with the mere outward forms of worship and giving and praying and reading and doing "church work" when they ought to be winning souls. Oh, the trouble is , they are guilty of the sin of little love for Christ. For "if a man love me he will keep my words," Jesus said. Do you love Christ? If so, then you will win souls. If you make a small effort to win souls, then your love is small. If you make none, then how can you say you love Him at all?"[13]

Oswald Chambers said, "We are not saved to be 'channels only,' but to be sons and daughters of God. We are not turned into spiritual mediums, but into spiritual messengers; the message must be part of ourselves."[14]

Dietrich Bonhoeffer wrote, "When Christ calls you, He bids you come and die."

Billy Sunday said, "Go out and work. The trouble is a lot of you take it too easy.

You rub elbows with people, and never a prayer goes from your lips. You never have a drop of sweat go down your face trying to keep people out of perdition. No wonder you sit there with a curl on your lip when someone is trying to preach."[15]

W.A. Criswell said, "We are found to find others; we are won to win others and we are saved to save others."

Bill Bright said, "Success in witnessing is simply sharing Christ in the power of the Holy Spirit and leaving the results to God."[16]

Horatius Bonar wrote, "We take for granted that the object of the Christian ministry is *to convert sinners and to edify the body of Christ.* No faithful minister can possibly rest short of this. Applause, fame, popularity, honor, and wealth - all these are vain. If souls are not won, if saints are not matured, our ministry itself is vain."[17]

Vance Havner said, "The solution for a sick church is to put it on a soulwinning diet" and "The tragedy of today is that the situation is desperate but the saints are not."[18]

Adrian Rogers stated, "We will either evangelize or fossilize; we will either go and grow or we will decay and die. Where there is no vision the people perish. Where there is no passion the church perishes."[19]

Freddie Gage said, "We've got enough preachers, what we need is more reachers."[20]

Billy Graham declared, "...when I present the simple message of the Gospel of Jesus Christ, with authority, quoting from the very Word of God – He...drives it supernaturally into the human heart."[21]

Concerning the Christians' hesitancy to witness, Paul Little wrote, "We're like the enthusiastic coach, inspiring his team in the locker room, "Here we are undefeated, untied, unscored upon....and ready for our first game!" We've never risked spoiling our record by going out to face the opposition. And our record will continue to be a perfect blank as long as we continue to avoid the necessary contacts."[22]

Ron Dunn said, "The ultimate of the Spirit filled life is sharing Jesus with others."[23]

William Booth wrote "As when a man from shore, seeing another struggling in the water, takes off those outer garments that would hinder his efforts and leaps to the rescue, so will you who still linger on the bank, thinking and singing and praying about the poor perishing souls, lay aside your shame, your pride, your cares about other people's opinions, your love of ease, and all the selfish loves that have kept you back for so long, and rush to the rescue of this multitude of dying men and women? Does the surging sea look dark and dangerous? Unquestionably it is so. There is no doubt that the leap for you, as for everyone who takes it, means difficulty and scorn and suffering. For you it may mean more than this. It may mean death. He who beckons you from the sea, however, knows what it will mean – and knowing, He still calls you and bids you come. You must do it! You cannot hold back. You have enjoyed yourself in Christianity long enough. You have had pleasant feelings, pleasant songs, pleasant meetings, and pleasant prospects. There has been much of human happiness, much clapping of hands and shouting of praises – very much of heaven and earth. Now then, go to God and tell Him you are prepared as much as necessary to turn your back upon it all, and that you are willing to spend the rest of your days struggling in the midst of these perishing multitudes, whatever it may cost you."[24]

Study Sin. Study its guilt, contagion, and tragic consequences. Get upset over what sin does in lives of people. Grasp how it breaks the very heart of God regardless who it is that commits it. Understand there is no limit as to what man can do in its vice grip. Study what sin is (I John 5:17, James 4:17, Genesis 6:5, I John 3:4, Deuteronomy 9:7, Ephesians 5:11, Romans 3:23, Proverbs 30:12, Hebrews 3:13, Galatians 5:1). Study the Savior's view of sin (Deuteronomy 25:16, Job 10:14, Revelations 18:5, I Kings 16:2, Habakkuk 1:13, Isaiah 13:11, Matthew 27:46). Study sin's consequences (Romans 6:23, Psalms 38:3, Job 20:11, I Corinthians 6:9, 10, Romans 6:23, Jude 13, 2 Peter 2:14, Ezekiel 16:52).

Study Sinners. Grasp the real condition of the sinner as revealed in scripture. According to Luke 19:10 he is lost, according to John 3:16 he is perishing, according to Ephesians 2:1 he is dead in trespasses and sins, and according to John 3:18 he is condemned. As a soulwinner, burn in your heart the reality of man's condition – his restlessness, emptiness, meaninglessness, insignificance, loneliness, hurting and his being just a heartbeat away from Hell. You may be the only witness they receive. What if you don't go and tell? Remembering what it was like to be lost will inflame one's heart to win souls.

A man was listening to disgruntled fishermen who were discussing their fruitless day of toil in fishing. Looking into their empty baskets, he said, "You should make a deeper study of the subjectivity of the fish." By this he meant these men ought to study more carefully what fish eat; what a fish is likely to nibble at; when a fish is prone to eat and what keeps fish from eating. I suggest that fishers of men take this same advice and study sinners to discover what will win them to Christ.[25]

Study Scripture. Digest what scripture states about the sinner's judgment and eternal punishment. Muse over such teaching until your heart burns for souls. Paul declared

"Knowing therefore the terror of the Lord, we persuade men; but we are made manifest unto God; and I trust also are made manifest in your consciences" (2 Corinthians 5:11). The Psalmist said, "It was when I mused the fire burned" (Psalms 39:3). The same will be your experience. Study Revelation 21:8, Luke 16: 19-31.

Study Supplication. The soulwinner should review how Abraham prayed for the lost of Sodom (Genesis 19: 22 – 33) and the prayers of the saints of old who were winners of men. He should study these prayers to learn how to pray incessantly, passionately and continuously for the lost as George Mueller, who prayed forty years for two men to be saved; one was saved prior to his death and the other shortly thereafter.

Set my soul afire Lord, for Thy holy word, Burn it deep within me,
Let your voice be heard;
Millions grope in darkness, in this day and hour, I will be your witness,
Fill me with Thy power.

Set my soul afire Lord, for the lost in sin, Give to me a passion as I seek to win;
Help me not to falter, never let me fail,
Fill me with Thy Spirit,
Let Thy will prevail.

Set my soul afire Lord, in my daily life, for too long I've wandered
In this day of strife;
Nothing else will matter but to live for Thee,
I will be your witness as you live in me.

Set my soul afire, Lord, set my soul afire,
Make my life a witness of Thy saving power.
Millions grope in darkness, waiting for Thy word,
Set my soul afire, Lord, Set my soul afire.
Gene Bartlett

Feel the passion for souls in a prayer by Horatius Bonar and be stirred to win souls: "Lord, let that mind be in us that was in Thee! Give us tears to weep; for, Lord, our hearts are hard toward our fellows. We can see thousands perish around us, and our sleep never be disturbed; no vision of their awful doom ever scaring us, no cry from their lost souls ever turning our peace into bitterness. Our families, our schools, our congregations, not to speak of our cities at large, our land, our world, might well send us daily to our knees; for the loss of even one *soul* is terrible beyond conception. Eye has not seen, nor ear heard, nor has entered the heart of man, what a soul in hell must suffer forever. Lord, give us bowels of mercies! What a mystery! The soul and eternity of one man depends upon the voice of another!"[26]

R. A. Torrey faced a day in which he felt his heart turn cold toward lost souls. He wrote, "I was so deeply disturbed that I had so little love for souls; that I could meet men and women who were lost and be so little concerned about it; that I could preach to them and had so little inclination to weep over them. I went alone with God and prayed, "O God give me a love for souls." Little did I realize how much the answer to that prayer involved. The next day there came into my Bible class a man who was the most distressing picture of utter despair I ever saw. At the close of my Bible class I walked down the aisle. I saw him in the last seat. His face haunted me. I was burdened. I could not lose sight of him. I cannot tell the pain I had for hours and days as I cried to God for his salvation, but I had the joy of seeing him profess to accept Christ. Love for souls is one of the costliest things a man can have, but if we are to be like Christ, and if we are to be successful in His work, we must have it. But don't pray for it unless you are willing to suffer."[27]

Study Sermons. The reading or hearing of sermons upon the subject of soulwinning by great soulwinners will add wood to the fire of one's heart for souls. In research for this book my burden for souls was increased as I waded with giant soulwinners through their writings upon this subject. Upon the shelf of every soulwinner should be three great volumes: *Great Preaching on* Soulwinning (Sword of the Lord Publishers); *Spurgeon's Sermons on Soulwinning* (Kregel Publications) and Horatius Bonar's *Words to Winners of Souls* (P & R Publishing) .

Mediate upon these words of C. H. Spurgeon's sermon, *What Have I Done?:* "Are there not many Christians now present who cannot recollect that they have been the means of the salvation of one soul during this year? Come, now; turn back. Have you any reason to believe that directly or indirectly you have been made the means this year of the salvation of a soul? I will go further. There are some of you who are old Christians, and I will ask you this question: Have you any reason to believe that ever since you were converted you have ever been the means of the salvation of a soul? It was reckoned in the East, in the time of the Patriarchs, to be a disgrace to a woman that she had no children; but what disgrace it is to be a Christian to have no spiritual children – to have none born unto God through his instrumentality! And yet, there are some of you here that have been spiritually barren, and have never brought one convert to Christ; you have not one star in your crown in heaven. Come, Christian, what have you done?"[28] What minister dare preach such a sermon to his congregation? It is he who loves God, his people and lost souls to the degree he risks all to awaken all saints to their gross neglect of winning souls.

Study Saints. Fellowship with saints ablaze with passion for the unsaved will pour fuel upon the flame for souls in one's life. Listen to their soulwinning stories. Feel their heartbeat for souls. Catch the urgency of soulwinning from their countenance and conversation. Warm your heart for the eternally damned by the fireplace of their souls. Soulwinning is contagious.

Study Songs. The hymns of the church are rich with evangelistic theology and soulwinning inspiration. Study them, sing them, and pray them, and they will inflame your heart for lost souls. Fifteen hymns I suggest for this purpose are, *Throw Out the Life-Line; Rescue the Perishing; Do You Really Care?; Jesus Saves; Tell the Good News; Must I Go and Empty-handed?; Bringing in the Sheaves; Bring Them In; Let the Lower Lights Be Burning; The Ninety and Nine; Jesus Calls Us; The Regions Beyond; People Need the Lord; Each One Reach One;* and *Send the Light.* Another classic example of a mission hymn that may incite soul passion is Lanny Wolfe's *My House is Full but My Field is Empty.*

My House is Full but My Field is Empty

There is peace and contentment in my Father's house today,
Lots of food on His table and no one turned away.
There is singing and laughter as the hours pass by,
But a hush calms the singing as the Father sadly cries,

My house is full, but my field is empty,
Who will go and work for Me today.
It seems my children want to stay around my table,
But no one wants to work my field,
No one wants to work my field.

Push away from the table.
Look out through the windowpane,
Just beyond the house of plenty
Lies a field of golden grain.
And it's ripe unto harvest,
But the reapers, where are they?
In the house,
Oh, can't the children hear the Father sadly say,

My house is full, but my field is empty,
Who will go and work for Me today.
It seems my children want to stay around my table,
But no one wants to work my field,
No one wants to work my field.

MY HOUSE IS FULL (BUT MY FIELD IS EMPTY) Words and music by Lanny Wolfe. © 1977 Lanny Wolfe Music. All rights controlled by Gaither Copyright Management. Used by permission.

Steady Sow. There is nothing like sowing seeds (soulwinning) to inflame one's passion for souls. The testimony of faithful soulwinners is that the more they go and tell the more their heart is stirred for the lost. Perennially sow in season, out of season; when it's convenient or inconvenient; when you feel like it or don't feel like it; in times of joy or sorrow; in persecution or praise; in times of fruitfulness or barrenness.

Bill Bright stated that a Christian ought to witness for seven reasons: the constraining love of Christ; the command of Christ; the lost condition of man; benefits received by those won; benefits received by those who witness; its tremendous privilege, and because the Holy Spirit empowers the believer to witness.[29]

In his inaugural address at the Pastor's College Conference shortly before his death, C.H. Spurgeon once again reminded the church of her primary purpose: "Oh, for a church of out-and-out believers, impervious to the soul-destroying doubt which pours upon us in showers!

Yet all this would not reach our ideal. *We want a church of a missionary character*, which will go forth to gather out a people unto God from all parts of the world. A church is a soul-saving company, or it is nothing. If the salt exercises no preserving influence on that which surrounds it, what is the use of it? Yet some shrink from effort in their immediate neighborhood because of the poverty and vice of the people. I remember a minister who is now deceased, a very good man he was, too, in many respects: but he utterly amazed me by a reply, which he made to a question of mine. I remarked that he had an awful neighborhood round his chapel, and I said, 'Are you able to do much for them?' He answered, 'No, I feel almost glad that we keep clear of them; for, you see, if any of them were converted, it would be a fearful burden upon us.' I knew him to be the soul of caution and prudence, but this took me aback, and I sought an explanation. 'Well,' he said, 'we should have to keep them: they are mostly thieves and harlots, and if converted they would have no means of livelihood, and we are a poor people, and could not support them!' He was a devout man and one with whom it was to one's profit to converse; and yet that was how he had gradually come to look at the case. His people with difficulty sustained the expenses of worship, and thus chill penury repressed a gracious zeal, and froze the genial current of his soul. There was a great deal of common sense in what he said, but yet it was an awful thing to be able to say it. We want a people who will not forever sing:

'We are a garden walled around
Chosen and made peculiar ground;
A little spot enclosed by grace,
Out of the world's wild wilderness.'

It is a good verse for occasional singing, but not when it comes to mean, 'We are very few, and we wish to be.' No, no brethren! We are a little detachment of the King's soldiers detained in a foreign country upon risen duty; yet we mean not only to hold the fort, but to add territory to our Lord's dominion. We are not to be driven out; but, on the contrary, we are going to drive out the Canaanites; for this land belongs to us, it is given to us of the Lord, and we will subdue it. May we be fired with the spirit of discoveries and conquerors, and never rest while there yet remains a class to be rescued, a region to be evangelized!

We are rowing like lifeboat men upon a stormy sea, and we are hurrying to yonder wreck, where men are perishing. If we may not draw that old wreck to shore, we will at least, by the power of God, rescue the perishing, save life, and bear the redeemed to the shores of salvation. Our mission, like our Lord's, is to gather out the chosen of God's from among men, that they may live to the glory of God. Every saved man should be under God, a savior: and the church is not in a right state until she has reached that conception of herself. The elect church is saved that she may save, cleansed that she may cleanse, blessed that she may bless. The world is the field, and all the members of the church should work therein for the great Husbandman. Wastelands are to be reclaimed, and forests broken up by the plough, till the solitary place begins to blossom as the rose. We must not be content with holding our own: we must invade the territories of the prince of darkness."[30]

TWO

The Content Factor In Soulwinning

The soulwinner's message is simply the plan of salvation as revealed in the Word of God .[1] E.M. Harrison

A magazine carried a cartoon during the 1960 Olympics depicting a marathon runner rushing into the palace of a King. Fatigue and anguish was written all over his face. As he fell before the King he was shown looking up to him saying, "I have forgotten my message." I fear many believers when they go soulwinning have forgotten their primary message. The message the King of Kings has charged the believer to tell the eternally damned is not one dealing with baptism, church membership, tithing, doing right, religious reform or "quit your meanness" but "Ye must be born again."

Paul Little stated that the soulwinner's message must include and evolve around five truths: (1) Jesus Christ, who He is; (2) Jesus diagnosis of human nature; (3) the fact and meaning of the crucifixion of Jesus Christ; (4) the fact and meaning of the resurrection of Jesus Christ and (5) the how of becoming a Christian.[2]

Charles Finney wrote, "No directions should be given that do not include a change of heart, a right heart or vigorous obedience to Christ. In other words, nothing is proper which does not imply actually becoming a Christian. Any other direction that falls short of this is of no use. It will not bring a sinner any nearer the kingdom, but will lead him to put off doing the very thing which he must do in order to be saved."[3] Horatius Bonar commented, "The one true goal or resting-place where doubt and weariness, the stings of a pricking conscience, and the longings of an unsatisfied soul would all be quieted, is *Christ Himself.* Not the church, but Christ. Not doctrine, but Christ. Not forms, but Christ. Not ceremonies, but Christ. Christ the God-man, giving His life for ours; sealing the everlasting covenant, and making peace for us through the blood of His cross; Christ the divine storehouse of all light and truth. '*In whom are hid all the treasures of wisdom and knowledge*' (Colossians 2:3); Christ the infinite vessel, filled with the Holy Spirit, the Enlightener, the Teacher, the Quickener, the Comforter, so that '*of his fullness have all we received, and grace for grace*' (John 1:16). This, this alone is the vexed soul's refuge, its rock to build on, its home to abide till the great temper be bound and every conflict ended in victory."[4]

John MacArthur stated, "The call to follow Christ must always be grounded in submission to Him in repentant faith for salvation from sin – not to achieve some earthly benefit."[5]

C. H. Spurgeon wrote, "Give the people every truth, every truth baptized in holy fire…But the great truth is the cross, the truth that 'God so loved the world that he gave his only begotten son that whosoever believeth in him should not perish, but have everlasting life.' Brethren, keep to that. That is the bell for you to ring. Ring it, man! Ring it! Keep on ringing it."[6]

The soulwinner's appeal must be doctrinally sound regarding the *Why, Who, Way* and *When* of salvation. The *Why*: Man has violated God's law. He has broken the Ten Commandments and every other law of God. James the Apostle stated that if one is guilty of breaking one part of the law he is guilty of breaking it all. (James 2:10) This violation of God's law brings severe consequences, the separation from God presently and eternal separation from God in Hell. (Romans 6:23) Spurgeon stated, "No man will ever put on the robe of Christ's righteousness until he is stripped of his fig leaves, nor will he wash in the fount of mercy till he perceives his filthiness. Therefore, my brethren, we must not cease to declare the Law, its demands, its threatenings, and the sinners multiplied breaches of it."[7] It is the Law that shows man his sinfulness and thus his need of Jesus Christ. Spurgeon again weighed in on the role of the Law in conversion when he declared, "Lower the Law and you dim the light by which man perceives his guilt; this is a very serious loss to the sinner rather than gain; for it lessens the likelihood of his conviction and conversion...They will never accept grace till they tremble before a just and holy Law. Therefore the Law serves a most necessary purpose, and must not be removed from its place."[8] God uses the Law to convict and the Cross to convert. John MacArthur stated, "Until a person acknowledges his basic sinfulness and inability to perfectly fulfill the demands of God's Law, he will not come repentantly to seek salvation. Until he despairs of himself and his own sinfulness, he will not come in humble faith to be filled with Christ's righteousness. A person who says he wants salvation but refuses to recognize and repent of his sin deceives himself. Grace means nothing to a person who does not know he is sinful and that such sinfulness means he is separated from God and damned. It is therefore pointless to preach grace until the impossible demands of the Law and the reality of guilt before God are preached (and I add shared by the soulwinner)."[9] C. H. Spurgeon added, "Open up the spirituality of the law as our Lord did and show how it is broken by evil thoughts, intents, and imaginations. By this means many sinners will be pricked in their hearts. Old Robbie Flockart used to say, 'It is of no use trying to sew the silken thread of the gospel unless we pierce a way for it with the sharp needle of the law.' The law goes first, like the needle, and draws the gospel thread after it; therefore, preach concerning sin, righteousness, and judgment to come."[10]

The *Who*: In that "all have sinned and fallen short of the glory of God," all must be saved (Romans 3:23). And all may be saved who desire to be (Romans 10:13). The preacher must make clear that God's offer of reconciliation through the death of His son on the Cross is not for a chosen few but for the "whole world." (John 3:16) It has been said that the blood of Jesus is sufficient to save the whole world but only efficient to save those souls who come to Him in faith and repentance. Each person to whom the soulwinner speaks must without doubt know that the Father waits with open arms to receive them regardless of the "far country" of sin in which they live. No man is beyond the hope of salvation.

The *Way:* Man's problem with God can only be remedied through the blood Jesus spilt upon the Cross. "Without the shedding of blood there is no remission" (Hebrews 9:22). The Apostle Paul states, "But God commendeth his love toward us, in that, while we were yet sinners Christ died for us. Much more then, being now justified by his blood, we shall be saved from wrath through him" (Romans 5:8-9). This reconciliation of sinful man to holy God instantaneously occurs the moment he repents of sin and receives Jesus Christ by faith into his life (Acts 20:21). Man's sin was so bad it necessitated nothing short of God's only son's death upon a Cross to make possible its forgiveness. Jesus was, is and will always be man's only hope of salvation (John 10:9). The whole basis of soulwinning is the death, burial and resurrection of Jesus Christ. The soulwinner must endeavor to make that primary in his appeal. The soulwinner has no discretionary authority from God to alter the way in which a sinner must come for salvation. He must not lower the bar or raise the bar higher than God has placed it in scripture; to do so would result in damnable heresy being espoused and false converts being produced! Spurgeon stated, "If the professed convert distinctly and deliberately declares that he knows the Lord's will, but does not mean to attend to it, you are not to pamper his presumption, but it is your duty to assure him that he is not saved. Do you imagine that the gospel is magnified, or God glorified by going to the worldings and telling them that they may be saved at this moment by simply accepting Christ as their Savior, while they are wedded to their idols and their hearts are still in love with sin? If I do so, I tell them a lie, pervert the gospel, insult Christ, and turn the grace of God into lasciviousness."[11] The soulwinner must clarify to sinners what it means to repent (Acts 20:21), to embrace Jesus as both Lord and Savior (Acts 16:31) and to calculate the cost involved in being His follower (Luke 14: 28-30). Shallow appeals yield unsaved souls still.

The *When.* The soulwinner, along with the Apostle Paul, must with passion and urgency plead with the unsaved to come to Christ saying, "Behold, now is the accepted time; behold, now is the day of salvation" (II Corinthians 6:2).

A railroad crossing employee had the responsibility of warning drivers of incoming trains by waving a lantern at the crossing. One night a train collided with a vehicle and lives were lost. This employee was taken to court accused of gross neglect in not giving a warning. The prosecutor at the trial asked if he waved a lantern at the crossing and he testified that he did. Upon his acquittal he yet was distraught. His attorney believing he was just feeling bad for what happened tried to calm him by asking, "You were at the Crossing in time to warn of the incoming train correct?

He answered, "Yes, I was." You waved your lantern at the Crossing did you not? He again replied, "Yes, I did." Then what is troubling you. The man answered, "It is true I was at the Crossing and that I was waving my lantern, but my lantern was not lit." Soulwinners must be certain that there is oil in their lantern (Biblical Truth about how one is saved) as they seek to warn the lost or else their effort is meaningless and eternally futile. O Christian, wave the Gospel Lantern constantly and keep "ringing the bell" warning the lost of their impending doom and need of Jesus Christ.

THREE

The Character Factor In Soulwinning

What you are thunders so loud in my ears that I cannot hear what you say.[1]
Ralph Waldo Emerson

What does it take to be an effective soulwinner?

1. It takes conversion.
E. M. Harrison stated, "The basic, indispensable prerequisite of a soulwinner is an experience with Jesus Christ that can be stated in terms of *first person, singular number, possessive case.* 'Blessed Assurance, Jesus is mine,' 'The Lord is my Shepherd,' 'My Lord and my God.' Without this experience, one's efforts at soulwinning are doomed to failure." C.H. Spurgeon declared, "God will not use dead tools for working living miracles."[2] L.R. Scarborough wrote concerning the soulwinner, "He must have looked at Christ through eyes of repentance and faith and have accepted Him as Lord and Master. He must know the way over which he would lead others."[3] John Wesley once said, "What a dreadful thing it would be for me if I should be ignorant of the power of the truth which I am preparing to proclaim."[4] I fear the reason why many "believers" are ineffective in soulwinning or neglect it altogether is due to a false hope. They yet are in their sin in need of the New Birth. C. H. Spurgeon declared, "Fish will not be fishers. We cannot be fishers of men if we remain among men in the same element with them."[5] Jerry Long, Minister of Evangelism and Outreach at Shandon Baptist in Columbia, South Carolina, testified that a lady attending an evangelism training program designed to equip believers to win people to Jesus acknowledged though a church member she was unsaved. This servant gladly led her to a saving relationship with Christ. If a person does not have a testimony, he does not have a Savior.

2. It takes cleansing.
Ralph Connors wrote of two rival university football teams in Canada. On one of these teams was a player by the name of Cameron. He was agile, strong and quick on the field. His team was assured victory merely by his playing in that big game. However, the night before the game he broke training rules and got drunk. The next day instead of being the help of his team, he was there hurt and they lost. That game went down in the annals of that school's record books as a game they had ever right to win but lost because Cameron was unfit. Concerning your opportunities to win a soul to Christ, how often is it written in God's record books that you failed because of being spiritually "unfit?"

The second prerequisite to effective soulwinning is purity of heart. It has been said that God can use a tall vessel and a small vessel, a weak vessel and a strong vessel but He cannot use and will not use a dirty vessel. Dr. L. R. Scarborough,

past president of Southwestern Baptist Seminary, said, "Holiness must be on the
skirts of God's priests today." John Hyde ("Praying Hyde," who won four souls
a day to Christ for much of his life) declared, "Holiness precedes soulwinning."
Scripture commands, "Be thou clean that bear the vessels of the Lord." You and I
who have been entrusted with the eternal treasure of salvation that the entire world
needs must stay clean morally and mentally. Nothing will sap one's desire to
witness like sin. Nothing will rob of power in witnessing like sin. Nothing will
cause fruitlessness in soulwinning effort like sin. Murray Downey underlines this
point stating that in soulwinning it is more important to be clean than to be cleaver.[6]

The Psalmist asked a question of the soulwinner, "Who shall ascend unto the hill
of the Lord and who shall dwell in His holy presence?" Then he answers it for
him, "He that hath clean hands and a pure heart." (Psalms 24: 3-5) Paul exhorts
the soulwinner, "Wherefore come out from among them, and be ye separate saith
the Lord, and touch not the unclean thing; and I will receive you" (II Corinthians
6:17). John reminds the soulwinner, "Love not the world, neither the things that
are in the world" (I John 2:15). The writer of Hebrews exhorts the soulwinner,
"Let us lay aside every weight, and the sin which doth so easily beset us" (Hebrews
12:1). Paul reminds the soulwinner that his "body is the Temple of the Holy Ghost"
(I Corinthians 6:19). Indulgence in sin, the condoning of sin in ones life kills ones
influence with the lost and "quenches" the Holy Spirit's power from flowing
through their life. If the saved are to impact lost friends for Christ and others it is
imperative that though they be in the world that they never become like the world.
Soulwinners must stay pure and clean before the Lord ever determining to be a
Romans 12: 1-2 Christian. D. L. Moody said, "Present yourself useable to God
and He will use you."

Henrietta Mears said that a Christian should be like a lifeguard at the beach. People
know who he is and where his lifeguard stand is but pay him little attention until
someone in the water begins to drown. As Christians if we live a holy life letting
people know where we "stand" then in times of trouble or hurt some will come to
us.[7] This is one reward of living a clean and holy life before all men.

3. It takes communion.
John Piper said, "The aroma of God will not linger on a person who does not
linger in the presence of God…without prayer the God of our studies will be the
unfrightening and uninspiring God of insipid academic gamesmanship."[8] The
London pastor C. H. Spurgeon said, "The longer I live, the more sure do I become
that our happiness in life, our comfort in trouble, and our strength for service – all
depend upon our living near to God, nay, dwelling in God, as the lilies in the
water…I would rather spend an hour in the presence of the Lord than a century in
prosperity without Him."[9] Prayer and soulwinning are intricately linked. Prayer
spurs soulwinning. Prayer supports soulwinning. Prayer strengthens soulwinning.

Prayer sustains the soulwinner. The apostle Paul knew what it was to pray for the unsaved. He declared, "Brethren, my heart's desire and prayer to God for Israel is, that they might be saved." (Romans 10:1) The soulwinner must be a man of earnest, passionate and consistent prayer. L.R. Scarborough remarked, "A prayerless Christian is a powerless Christian and a powerless Christian is never a soulwinning Christian. Prayer conditions power. Prayer makes possible power. And power is essential in winning men to Christ."[10] God said, "Ask of me and I will give thee the heathen for an inheritance" (Psalms 2:8). The winning of souls according to this verse is linked to prayer. James stated, "You have not because you ask not" (James 4:2). The soulwinner must claim souls on his knees before to them he urgently pleads. He should have a prayer list of names of the unsaved and faithfully pray for their conversion. He may title this list *My Most Ten Wanted,* providing a space beside each name for the date of entry, a scriptural promise to claim, dates of personal contact, and date of conversion. In soulwinning it is good to remember the words of Sidlow Baxter, "Man may shun our appeals but he cannot escape our prayers."

Prior to viewing the birth of my daughter the doctor said, "Watch real close, preacher. You can get a sermon out of this," and, boy, did I! As my wife travailed in excruciating birth pains to birth Stephanie, I recalled that the prophet Isaiah declared, "Not until Zion travails will she bring forth children"(Isaiah 66:8). How the soulwinner needs to travail in spiritual pains through intense prayer for the lost until they are birthed into God's eternal family. David Brainerd gave the church the secret of reaching the unsaved when he exhorted, "Travail, travail, travail until you prevail, prevail, prevail." Travail in prayer for the unsaved before talking to them about Christ. Travail for the unsaved as you go soulwinning. Travail for the unsaved after the visit. Prayer can be the means of tearing down strongholds and setting the captive free. Never underestimate its power. "With God all things are possible" (Mark 10:27) – no man is beyond the reach of God, not even the chief of sinners whose life is dedicated to the persecution and eradication of Christians. Just ask the Apostle Paul. "With great soul wrestling, souls are won." Alvin I. Reid told of a picture he saw in a pastor's study that depicted a man prostrate on the floor praying. The caption, in large letters declares, MAKE WAR ON THE FLOOR.[11] The soulwinner must make war on the floor in prayer for the unsaved to enlighten the mind of the lost to the Truth of Christ, his soul to personal sin that he will see the need of Christ, and alter his will so that he will say yes to Christ. Prayer blasts satanic strongholds in the sinners' life granting deliverance from the blindness of the flesh, the pride of life and the shackles of sin (2 Corinthians 10:4). R. A. Torrey declared, "It is doubtful if even a single soul is born again without travail of soul on the part of someone."[12] C.H. Spurgeon declared, "Let us never venture to speak for God to men, until we have spoken for men to God."[13]

Casting Crowns, a contemporary Christian singing group, surely voices the soul winner's prayer for unsaved friends and acquaintances in its song "Here I Go Again."

Father, hear my prayer
I need the perfect words
Words that he will hear
And know they're straight from You
I don't know what to say
I only know it hurts
To see my only friend slowly fade away

So maybe this time I'll speak the words of life
With Your fire in my eyes
But that old familiar fear is tearing at my words
What am I so afraid of?

'Cause here I go again
Talkin 'bout the rain
And mulling over things that won't live past today
And as I dance around the truth
Time is not his friend
This might be my last chance to tell him
That You love Him
But here I go again, here I go again

Lord, You love him so, You gave Your only Son
If he will just believe; he will never die
But how then will he know what he has never heard
Lord he has never seen mirrored in my life

This might be my last chance to tell him
That You love him
This might be my last chance to tell him
That You love him
You love him, You love him

What am I so afraid
What am I so afraid
What am I so afraid of?
How then will he know
What he has never heard

C.H. Spurgeon prayed for the unsaved, "O sword of the Lord, pierce them through, that carelessness may be slain, that their souls may live. O Thou who are as a polished shaft hidden in the quiver of the eternal, go forth today to smite to the heart the proud, the self-righteous, and those that will not stoop to ask mercy at Thy hands: but as for the humble and the contrite, look upon them; the broken-hearted and the heavy-laden do Thou relieve, and such as have no helper do Thou succour. Bring up the sinner from the prison house, let the lawful captive be delivered. Let the mighty God of Jacob lead forth His elect, as once He did out of Pharaoh's bondage. The Red Sea is already divided that they may march through it. The Lord saved multitudes – He knoweth them that are His. Accomplish their number and let Jesus so be rewarded, though Israel be not gathered."[14]

Praying for the Soulwinning Visit

1. Pray for personal safety in driving to the home.
2. Pray for peace to reign in the home prior to the visit.
3. Pray for receptivity of the Gospel.
4. Pray for a conducive atmosphere to present the Gospel.
5. Pray the witness will be divinely protected from distractions and interruptions.
6. Pray that satanic strongholds will be demolished and "every thought will be led captive to the obedience of Christ" in the life of the sinner. (II Corinthians 10:4-5)
7. Pray for the sinner's clear understanding of the Gospel message.
8. Pray for immediate recall of scripture to refute excuses.
9. Pray that the person will experience the conviction of the Holy Spirit regarding sin, judgment and righteousness: realize the danger of delaying a decision for Christ and receive Jesus as Lord and Savior.
10. Pray for Holy Spirit enabling to share the best possible witness for Christ.
11. Pray in behalf of the person who rejects Christ that the Word sown in the witness will not be "devoured by the birds of the air" but in time will bear fruit unto eternal life. (Matthew 13:4)

David Brainerd's journal bears this entry, "I withdrew for prayer, hoping for strength from above. In prayer I was exceedingly enlarged, and my soul was as much drawn out as I ever remember it to have been in my life. I was in such anguish, and pleaded with so much earnestness and importunity, that when I arose from my knees I felt extremely weak and overcome. I could scarcely walk straight; my joints were loosed; the sweat ran down my face and body; and nature seemed as if it would dissolve."[15] Charles Finney wrote in his autobiography "It loaded me down with great agony. As I returned to my room I felt as if I should stagger under the burden that was upon my mind; and I struggled and groaned and agonized but could not frame to present the case before God in words, but only in groans and tears. The Spirit struggled within me with groanings that could not be uttered."[16] Oh for a return to passionate intercessory praying for the unsaved as these saints of old!

4. It takes compassion.

E. J. Daniels wrote, "A passion for souls must possess us, overwhelm us, burden us, break us, or we will never be great soulwinners. This possessing passion is, in my opinion, the greatest need of every evangelist, pastor, teacher, church member, and soulwinner. The lack of it explains our lack of prayer and personal effort to win souls."[17] L .R. Scarborurgh did not mince his words when he said, "Many a minister is on a treadmill, marking time, drying up, not earning his salt, because he has no passion for souls and no power for effective service."[18] John R. Rice states of the soul winner that "He must go, he must bear precious seed, but the thing that so often lacking is the broken heart. Indeed, I make bold to say that it is the broken heart that drives one out, that makes him go. The broken heart will sow the seed that will bring forth fruit."[19]

The German philosopher and poet Heine in a time of distress stood before the statue of Venus of Milo and cried, "Ah, yes! I suppose you would help me if you could, but you can't. Your lips are still and your heart is cold."[20] I wonder how many hurting, lonely, troubled, doubting and discouraged people look to Christians saying the exact same thing. Sadly, many believers are unable to help them because they lack the compassion required. All too often believers' "lips are still and hearts are cold." Southey said, "No man was ever yet convinced of any momentous task who did not experience both the desire and the power to communicate it."[21] If you and I are earnestly convinced of man's desperate need of God it will be manifested in both our desire and our power to reach him.

Oh, for a passion for souls like that of Paul, who declared, "Brethren, my heart's desire and prayer to God for Israel is, that they might be saved" (Romans 10:1). Again, feel Paul's burden for the unsaved when he declared, "I say the truth in Christ, I lie not, my conscience also bearing me witness in the Holy Ghost, that I have great heaviness and continual sorrow in my heart. For I could wish that myself were accursed from Christ for my brethren, my kinsmen according to the flesh" (Romans 9: 1-3). Oh that the soulwinner might know the passion of a Jeremiah who wished his head were waters and his eyes fountain of tears so he could weep for Israel's restoration (Jeremiah 9:1). Oh, for a burden for souls like that of George Whitefield who said to the people of his day, "I am willing to go to jail for you. I am willing to die for you. But I am not willing to go to Heaven without you." O may a passion wail up within the soulwinner for souls like that of William Burns, who stated, "The thud of Christless feet on the road to Hell is breaking my heart." May a passion for souls possess the soulwinner like that of C. H. Spurgeon, who said, " My main business is the saving of souls. This one thing I do." With John Wesley may those who seek souls for the Savior declare, "I desire to have both heaven and hell in my eye."

Writing to ministers, Horatius Bonar stated, "The question, therefore, which each of us has to answer to his own conscience is, 'Has it been to the end of my ministry, has it been the desire of my heart to save the lost and guide the saved? Is this my aim in every *sermon* I preach, in every visit I pay? Is it under the influence of this feeling that I continually live and walk and speak? Is it for this I pray and toil and fast and weep? Is it for this I spend and am spent, counting it, next to the salvation of my own soul, my chiefest joy to be the instrument of saving others? Is it for this that I exist? To accomplish this would I gladly die? Have I seen the pleasure of the Lord prospering in my hand? Have I seen souls converted under my ministry? Have God's people found refreshment from my lips and gone upon their way rejoicing or have I seen no fruit of my labors, and yet am content to remain unblest? Am I satisfied to preach, and yet not know of one saving impression made, one sinner awakened?' "[22]

William Booth, founder of the Salvation Army, was once commended by the King of England for his good work. Booth wrote in the King's autograph album, "Your Majesty, some men's passion is for art, some men's passion is for fame, some men's passion is for gold. My ambition is the souls of men." Oh Christian is that your ambition? Oh, that the soulwinner may say with John Wesley that he is "out of breath pursuing souls."

C. H. Spurgeon in his sermon "When the Preacher Has No Burden for the Souls of Men" stated, "And what shall I say of the unfaithful preacher, the slumbering watchman of souls, the man who swore at God's altar that he was called of the Holy Ghost to preach the Word of God, the man upon whose lips men's ears waited with attention while he stood like a priest at God's altar to teach Israel God's law, the man who performed his duties half asleep in a dull and careless manner until men slept too and thought religion a dream?

What shall I say of the minister of unholy life whose corrupt practice out of the pulpit has made the most telling things in the pulpit to be one of no avail, who has blunted the edge of the sword of the Spirit and turned the back of God's army in the day of battle?

Ay, what shall I say of the man who has amused his audience with pretty things when he ought to have aroused their consciences, who has been rounding periods when he ought to have pronounced the judgment of God, who has been preaching a dead morality when he ought to have lifted Christ on high as Moses lifted the serpent in the wilderness?

What shall I say, brethren, of those who have dwindled away their congregations, who have sown strife and schism in the churches of Christ once happy, peaceful, and prosperous?

What shall I say of the men who out of the pulpit have made a jest of the most solemn things, whose life has been so devoid of holy passion and devout enthusiasm that men have thought truth to be fiction, religion a stage play, a prayer a nullity, the Spirit of God a phantom, and eternity a joke?

If I must perish, let me suffer anyhow but not as a minister who has desecrated the pulpit by a slumbering style of ministry, by a want of passion for souls. God knoweth how oftimes this body trembles with horror at the thought lest the blood of souls should be required at my hands."[23]   May every preacher and layman know this same passion for ministry and lost souls.

5. It takes Convictions.
The soulwinner must possess sound and strong convictions about the cardinal doctrines of the faith less he mislead those he seeks to help. He must possess a biblical and clear understanding of the doctrine of the Depravity of Man; the Deity of Christ; Hell; Heaven; Judgment; Justification; the Second Coming, Inspiration of Scripture, Eternal Security and the Great Commission.

Billy Sunday was asked what the secret of his success was in reaching souls. It is said that in walking over to a window and looking upon the masses of people on the street he declared, "They are going to Hell! They are going to Hell! They are going to Hell!" He went on to say, "If there is a secret to my winning so many souls, it is because I really believe that men without Christ are going to Hell."[24] The soulwinner must have a deep conviction that men without Christ are indeed going to Hell.

The soulwinner not only must hold to biblical convictions but know how to use the scripture in witnessing. It is through the Word of God the Holy Spirit convicts of sin, judgment and unrighteousness. The Word of God is a hammer that can break the hardest heart (Jeremiah 23:29), a sword that can pierce the soul asunder (Hebrews 4:12), a fire that can purge the deepest sin (Jeremiah 23:29), a Light that can expose the deepest darkness (Psalms 119:130), and a roadmap that can show the way (Psalms 119:105; 133). The Holy Scripture is a living book for He who inspired its every word is fully alive anointing and blessing it to His eternal purposes and mans best end. A young ministerial student asked Spurgeon how to defend the gospel successfully. He replied, "How do you defend a lion? You don't. You just turn him loose."[25] Lewis Drummond stated, "But is one justified in having such confidence in the gospel? The answer is an emphatic yes, because it is the Good News about God from God. Its source and its content are divine. This is why confidence in the power of the message is most reasonable and an important part of our theology of evangelism." Drummond continued, "This clearly implies that we need not rely on human ingenuity, psychological manipulations, dramatics, or any mere human invention to convince people of the truth and relevance of the message. God will speak for Himself through His Word. The Holy Spirit will press home the truth (John 16: 7 – 11)."[26]

6. It takes confidence.

"Without faith it is impossible to please the Lord (Hebrews 11:6)." In soulwinning, the saint must exhibit faith believing the Lord to honor and bless his efforts. L.R. Scarborough declared that faith "...puts iron in the blood and steels in the soul for battle. It made a Moses laugh at Pharaoh, as well as at the barriers of the sea and desert. It bridged swollen Jordans and demolished Jericho's for a Joshua, and held back setting suns that victory might crown his day while fighting God's battles. It took the rage out of the lions' dens and made them safe places for a Daniel. It made heroes like John the Baptist, Paul, Luther, Knox and thousands of others. With it weaklings are conquerors, and without it giants are pygmies. It is a divine necessary for all who would win souls."[27]

The gospel is the power of God to all that believe. In soulwinning you are sharing that power. Donald S. Whitney stated, "Sharing the gospel is like walking around in a thunderstorm and handing out lightening rods. You don't know when the lightning is going to strike or who it will strike, but you know what it's going to strike—the lightning rod of the gospel. When it does, that person's lightning rod is going to be charged with the power of God and he or she is going to believe."[28]

My pastor, Dick Lincoln, told the story of an employee of the North American Mission Board whom he thought to possess a poor self-image based upon his mannerisms and method of preaching. This man stunned him in testifying how it had been his joy to witness to executive corporate officers on air flights. Lincoln responded, "I never would have thought that of you based upon your poor self-image." The man answered, "I may have a poor self-image but I have a great God-image."[29] In soulwinning it certainly is an asset to have a healthy self-image but most important the believer must have a great God-image. Listen to Paul when he declared, "Not that we are adequate in ourselves to consider anything as coming from ourselves, but our adequacy is from God, who also made us adequate as servants..." (2 Corinthians 3: 5 –6 ASV). God will enable every believer who places his confidence and dependence in Him to be an "adequate" witness regardless of personal deficiencies.

7. It takes Counsel.

Soulwinning is an art that must be taught or caught. The believer who desires to be a great soulwinner will do well to attend witnessing training courses offered in their church; accompany skilled soulwinners as they witness, and read books upon the subject.

Experienced soulwinners should mentor others in soulwinning as Paul did young

Timothy through personal instruction, role play and actual witnessing. Roy Fish said, "The church must return to the principle of multiplication if we are to make the impact on this lost world our Lord would have us make." This work of multiplication involves the training of those won to win others. Suppose you were the only Christian alive and that over a six-month period you won one person and trained him to win and train others. Now there are two Christians. Suppose each of you over the next six months wins and trains one, making the number saved and trained to witness now four. If each of these wins and trains one over the next six months, the number increases to eight. If this procedure continued for 16 years, the number won to Christ and trained to witness would be 4, 294, 967, 296![30] As a pastor, evangelist or teacher who might be a person the Lord would have you personally disciple in soulwinning?

8. It takes Constancy.
Soulwinning requires patience and persistence. The winning of some demands multiplied visits and relentless praying. Too many battles have been lost at the eleventh hour due to the soulwinner's giving up. Elmer Towns declared, "Research tells us people hear the gospel 3.4 times (the law of three hearings) before they accept Christ. Usually they are stepping closer to salvation each time they hear the gospel."[31] This same research[32] also revealed that it takes an average of 7.6 meaningful contacts by a Church to get a prospect to visit.[33]

Paul advised that the believer proclaim the gospel, "in season and out of season" (perennially), when it is convenient and inconvenient; when it is favorable or unfavorable to do so (2 Timothy 4:2).

9. It takes the Control of the Holy Spirit.
A person with a third grade education can be just as a powerful soulwinner as a seminary professor. Why? It is because the power in witnessing is not in man's intellectual ability or technique or even experience but in the indwelling power of the Holy Spirit in him. "This *is* the word of the LORD unto Zerubbabel, saying, Not by might, nor by power, but by my spirit, saith the LORD of hosts" (Zechariah 4:6). Jesus declared, "It is the Spirit that quicketh, the flesh profited nothing" (John 6:63). To the degree the soulwinner is empty of self and filled with the Holy Spirit will be the measure of success he will experience in witnessing. R. A. Torrey declared, "The Holy Spirit is given to the individual believer for the definite purpose of witnessing for Christ."[34] Scripture states, "But ye shall receive power, after that the Holy Ghost is come upon you: and ye shall be witnesses unto me both in Jerusalem, and in all Judea, and in Samaria, and unto the uttermost part of the earth" (Acts 1:8). It is of the Holy Spirit whom Jesus declared, "Nevertheless I tell you the truth; it is expedient for you that I go away: for if I go not away, the Comforter will not come unto you; but if I depart, I will send him unto you. And when he is come, he will reprove the world of sin, and of righteousness, and of

judgment: Of sin, because they believe not on me; Of righteousness, because I go to my Father, and ye see me no more; Of judgment, because the prince of this world is judged. I have yet many things to say unto you, but ye cannot bear them now. Howbeit when he, the Spirit of truth, is come, he will guide you into all truth: for he shall not speak of himself; but whatsoever he shall hear, *that* shall he speak: and he will shew you things to come. He shall glorify me: for he shall receive of mine, and shall shew *it* unto you" (John 16: 7-14). In this passage Jesus states that the Holy Spirit is the believer's *Paraclete*, one called along side of to help and plead their cause. The soulwinner who is infilled with the Holy Spirit never witnesses alone because He is ever "along side" pleading His case. It is the Holy Spirit who through the soulwinner *"convicts of sin,"* that is "presents or exposes facts, to convince of the truth." "The mighty working of the Holy Spirit is necessary to convince and convict people of their desperate plight."[35] Someone has written, "If all the angels and saints in heaven, and all the godly on earth, should join their wills and endeavors and unitedly exert all their powers to regenerate one sinner, they could not effect it; yea, they could do nothing toward it. It is an effect infinitely beyond the reach of finite wisdom and power."[36]

Dick Anthony wrote:
> No Power of my own, I have no power of my own.
> I confess to you, Holy Spirit, I have no power of my own.
> So I claim the promise of God's Word and I yield myself to Your control.
> For I need your Holy Filling, Yes, I want your Holy Filling,
> I expect your Holy Filling.
> For I have no power of my own.

David Brainerd understood the soulwinner's utter dependence upon the Holy Spirit for he wrote in his journal "I was exceeding sensible of the impossibility of doing anything for the poor Heathen without special assistance from above; and my soul seemed to rest on God, and leave it to him to do as he pleased in that which I saw was his own cause."[37] Martin Luther said, "We are His vessels and instruments, powerless either to receive or give unless He Himself gives and receives."[38]

L. R. Scarborough wrote that the Holy Spirit has promised to go before us (Isaiah 45:2), behind us (Isaiah 58:8), beneath us (Deuteronomy 33:27), with us (Matthew 28:20), within us (John 14:17), upon us (Acts 1:8), and all around us (Matthew 3:11). He has promised to hold us with the right hand of his righteousness (Isaiah 41:10) and never to let us fall (John 10:27-28; Jude 24).[39] John R. Rice wrote, "Soulwinning can only be done as people are endued with power of the Holy Spirit. 'Ye shall receive power after, after that the Holy Ghost has come upon you: and ye shall be witnesses unto me...' (Acts 1:8). No congregation is endued with the power of the Holy Spirit as an institution but only as individuals present are filled with the Spirit. Those who are won to Christ must come as individuals, and those who win souls to Christ must do it as individuals."[40]

Addressing the two reasons why Christians do not witness, Bill Bright stated, "First, the average Christian is living a defeated, impotent, fruitless, carnal life. He is not walking in the fullness and control of the Holy Spirit. Second, the average Christian has never been trained to communicate his faith in Christ effectively. He has never learned how to begin a conversation about Christ, how to explain the gospel simply and clearly, and how to lead a person to make a decision to receive Christ by faith."[41]

It is the Holy Spirit who surely orchestrates soulwinning encounters. He led Philip to leave the metropolis of Jerusalem to go to a desert strip to witness to and win an Ethiopian treasurer to Christ. (Acts 8: 26-39) The Holy Spirit still is ever seeking to connect the saved with the lost so a witness may be given and a soul may be won. Soulwinners must ever be careful to constantly "walk in the Spirit" so as to be "led by the Spirit." It is absolutely futile to try to win souls apart from His presence and power being manifest in our lives.

A Spirit-filled man will be a zealous man both for God and souls. This will be his priority, pursuit and consuming passion. "A zealous man in religion is pre-eminently a man of one thing. It is not enough to say that he is earnest, hearty, uncompromising, thorough-going, whole-hearted, fervent in spirit. He only sees one thing, he cares for one thing, he lives for one thing, he is swallowed up in one thing: that is to please God. Whether he lives, or whether he dies – whether he has health, or whether he has sickness – whether he is rich, or whether he is poor – whether he pleases man, or whether he gives offence – whether he is thought wise, or whether he thought foolish – whether he gets blame, or whether he gets praise – whether he gets honor, or whether he gets shame – for all this the zealous man cares nothing at all. He burns for one thing; that one thing is to please God, and to advance God's glory. If he is consumed in the very burning, he cares not for it – he is content. He feels that, like a lamp, he is made to burn; if consumed in burning, he has but done the work for which God appointed him. Such a one will always find a sphere for his zeal. If he cannot preach, work, and give money, he will cry, and sign, and pray. . .If he cannot fight in the valley with Joshua, he will do the work of Moses, Aaron, and Hur, on the hill (Exodus 17:9-13). If he is cut off from working himself, he will give the Lord no rest until help is raised up from another quarter, and the work is done. This is what I mean when I speak of 'zeal' in religion."[42]

10. It takes Cultivation.
Paul instructed Timothy that the farmer who labors in the field will be a "partaker of its firstfruits" (2 Timothy 2:6). Farming is extremely hard and tiring work. Just

ask any farmer. He will testify that long before a harvest there must be the painstaking task of breaking up and preparing the soil; the sowing of the precious seed; the removal of obstacles to crop growth such as various insects; times of disappointment and set back and constant cultivation of the field through blading and watering. Paul's point to Timothy is that soulwinners are to work like farmers in the field of the world diligently preparing the soil of mans heart for the sowing of the "precious seed" (Psalms 126: 5 – 6). In Amsterdam '83 Billy Graham stated that witnessing was like a chain with several links all of which must be connected before true conversion occurs. Link A soulwinners share an initial introduction to the Christian faith to those who are completely ignorant. Link B soulwinners connect to what the soulwinners in Link A shared and lead the person a little closer to salvation. Link C soulwinners then connect to what Link B soulwinners shared and hopefully are able to draw the person into the net of salvation. Soulwinners (Link A and B) in this witnessing scenario simply are cultivating the soul for a harvest by Link C soulwinners. Granted this is not always the case in soulwinning because sometimes a person is saved by Link A or Link B soulwinners, but in most cases some measure of cultivation of the lost must be engaged to bring them to Christ.

While writing this book a friend shared with me how he won his barber to Christ. It took two long years of sowing the precious seed in her life. George Mueller cultivated the souls of two men through prayer for forty years. One of these men was saved prior to Mueller's death, the other shortly thereafter. The soulwinner must have a disposition of patience as the farmer trusting God that in "due season he will reap, if he faints not" - if he keeps cultivating the field (Galatians 6:9).

11. It takes Courage.

A holy boldness infused by the Holy Spirit must consume the soulwinner. The soulwinner must be courageous enough to witness to King or pauper, rich or poor, educated or illiterate, black or white regardless of cost or consequence. Boldness must possess a soulwinner like that of John the Baptist, who spoke the truth to King Herod about his adultery fearlessly; like that of Paul, who, after being stoned and left for dead for witnessing in Lystra, returned to that city declaring the gospel; like Martin Luther at the Council of Worms, who when asked to recant his stand on the Word of God replied, "Here I stand. I can do none other;" like that of Polycarp, who declared as he was about to be burned at the stake for his faith, "Eighty and six years have I served Him and He never did me any injury. How then can I blaspheme my King and my Savior?"; and like that of John Huss, who, before being burned at the stake for his stand for Christ, said, "In Thee, O Lord, do I put my trust; let me never be ashamed." May we stand shoulder to shoulder with Paul and look the world in the face and say, "I am not ashamed of the gospel for it is the power of God unto salvation to everyone that believeth; to the Jews first, and also to the Greek." (Romans 1:16) It is said that John Knox feared no face except the face of God. May that be so with the soulwinner.

London's great pastor and soulwinner C.H. Spurgeon said, "A successful soulwinner must have (1) holiness of character, (2) spiritual life to a high degree, (3) humility of spirit, (4) a living faith, (5) thorough earnestness, (6) great simplicity of heart, (7) a complete surrender to God."[43]

Keys to D.L. Moody's Effectiveness[42]

Key #1: Commitment
Key #2: Willingness to take Risks
Key #3: Vision
Key #4: Sense of the Holy Spirit
Key #5: A high view of Scripture
Key #6: A Christ-Centered life
Key #7: Confidence in Young People
Key #8: Teachability
Key #9: Humility
Key #10: Love for Souls

FOUR

⇒━◆━⇐

The Caution Factor In Soulwinning

The other things we have to do may be called important by those around us, but there is nothing on earth more important to do than to win a person to Jesus Christ.[1] Bailey Smith

In soulwinning caution must be exercised not to say or do things that will hinder an effective witness. In this chapter I share 105 things that a soulwinner should avoid in the winning of souls to Christ.

1. Avoid halitosis.
The soulwinner will be extremely close in proximity to the sinner in his witness, making good breath imperative. Bad breath can kill a witness so prior to making a witness use a breath mint. The soulwinner should make it a habit to have a pack of breath mints in his pocket or automobile.

2. Avoid joking about spiritual matters.
Often it is Christ, the church, or minister that is the blunt of religious jokes, and thus such are always inappropriate especially in an effort to win the unsaved. Stay serious minded in your witness presentation. Charles Finney stated, "Levity will produce anything but a right impression. You ought to feel that you are engaged in very serious work which is going to affect the character of your friend or neighbor and probably determine his destiny of eternity."[2]

3. Avoid arguing.
Every book in my study on the subject of soulwinning emphasizes the must of the soulwinner not to enter into argumentation with the unsaved. The purpose of the visit is not to win a debate but to win a soul. D. L. Moody refused to argue in witnessing to those who didn't believe the Bible; he just kept on using scripture in talking to them. The saying goes in soulwinning "If you win your argument you may lose your man."[3] "Truth does not need a defender, nor theology or apologist. A great many times a quiet, gentle spirit wins where a brainy argument drives away."[4]

4. Avoid being distracted.
There will be times in which a witness could be interrupted by a ringing phone, crying baby, knock on the door or a question the person may ask. It's imperative the soulwinner have a "game plan" to handle such distractions when they arise so the witness may continue unhampered.

5. Avoid an unkempt appearance.
Appearance counts so the soulwinner should dress as neatly as possible. This

"neat as possible" will mean one thing to a mechanic witnessing as he works on a greasy engine or a painter as he tells of Christ as he paints and something else to a person visiting prospects with his church on Tuesday night outreach.

6. Avoid witnessing to a person of the opposite sex alone.
In soulwinning it is a must for men to witness to men and women to women in private one-to-one encounters. Mike Gallagher said, "Never put yourself in a position of being alone with a woman."[5] This is great counsel not just for the soulwinner but businessman.

A promising young evangelist made the mistake of counseling a young lady in a church office following a revival service. The girl's intention was impure and when the youthful evangelist rejected her advances she recoiled with anger and began spreading vicious untruth about him. Though innocent of her accusations, his ministry was pretty much destroyed. Two nights later at a private board meeting of the church the girl confessed to the lie she told, but then it was sadly too late for him to recover. This could happen to any evangelist, pastor, teacher or other soulwinner. The soulwinner must be alert to protect his reputation as he seeks to win souls.

7. Avoid pushiness.
The soulwinner ought to be persuasive but never pushy, always remembering a man convinced against his will is unconvinced still. He must not strong handle the gospel upon the sinner. Jesus never forced the gospel upon any person even if it meant watching them walk away from eternal life as was the case with the Rich Young Ruler (Luke 18:23).

8. Avoid being ill prepared.
Most witnesses are not planned, necessitating the soulwinner ever to be ready on the spare of the moment not only to share the plan of salvation but to have gospel material available to distribute. The soulwinner, therefore, should keep gospel tracts, Bibles, and follow-up booklets in a box in their automobile, book bag, desk, etc.

9. Avoid confusion with your witnessing partner.
A good witness degenerates into a poor one when the soulwinner and his partner interrupt each other. Prior to the visit, determine who will be the silent witness and who will make the actual witness. The silent witness must understand that his task is to pray as his partner presents the gospel; handle all interruptions and distractions and only join in the verbal witness should he be passed the ball. Dawson C. Bryan commented, "If your partner is leading in the interview and someone else in the family tries to talk to you, give a courteous short answer and turn to the conversation your partner is conducting. Do not let your conversation go any further."[6] On occasions when a family member or guest present is persistent in

talking to the silent witnessing partner, it is wise for him to ask to see something in another room or in the yard wherein the conversation can continue without interrupting the witness.

10. Avoid ridicule.
In door-to-door visitation, a pastor and I were refused an audience by a man. This pastor in response to this man's impoliteness vehemently said, "Then go to Hell." He was so wrong in saying that to this man. The soulwinner must ever be courteous to the sinner. C. H. Spurgeon preached, "We cannot always tell when we are driving poor souls away from Christ. Often when we think we are wooing we are driving them away; would we be winning to the Savior, some harsh expression of ours frightens sinners away from him."[7]

11. Avoid a No response.
The soulwinner should not ask questions that could prompt a "no" response. If the soulwinner asked John Doe at the outset of the visit, "John would you like to have your sin forgiven and become a Christian?" and he answered, "No, I do not," then it would present a tremendous uphill battle to have him say "Yes" later. Present your case to the "jury" before asking for a verdict.

12. Avoid empty talk.
The soulwinner must stay on task with his mission with each person he confronts. Smoothly and quickly he must get into the gospel presentation. Sad it is that oft a discussion about football or golf begins in a witnessing situation and time expires for the visit without the gospel ever being presented! Jesus in sending out the disciples to witness gave them this clear instruction "Salute no one in the way" (Luke 10:4). It was urgent business of which these disciples were embarked and no time was to be wasted with idle chat. That instruction yet needs heeding by the 21st Century soulwinner.

13. Avoid leaving a witness without extending an invitation.
The soulwinner should clearly present the "why" and "how" of salvation giving the person an opportunity to become a Christian before he departs. In witnessing encounters where the person seems to be unconcerned, the soulwinner should leave a tract that clearly indicates the how of salvation highlighted or circled encouraging the prospect to pray the prayer that is recorded should he decide later to be saved. C. E. Autrey stated, "It is possible for a life-changing decision to take place during one visit and often it does."[8]

14. Avoid discouragement.
The soulwinner should be confident in knowing that whether he succeeds in his witnessing effort or not he is successful in God's eyes. Jesus did not win every person unto whom He witnessed. Arthur Archibald stated, "No one fails in this

work except the one who does not make the attempt."[9] A Sunday School teacher asked her class of Junior boys to bring an object the following Sunday that would illustrate a scripture verse. One boy brought a salt shaker saying, "Jesus said, "Ye are the salt of the earth." A second boy brought a candle saying, "Ye are the Light of the world." The third boy brought a Bantam egg. The teacher confused asked, "Is that an egg?" The boy replied, "Yes, it is a Bantam egg." The teacher then asked, "And what scripture does it illustrate?" The boy said, "She hath done what she could."[10] Soulwinner, just do what you can do, the best you can, and leave the results to God.

15. Avoid egotism.
The soulwinner must exhibit a spirit of humility and meekness to the sinner in his endeavor to win him. Don't parade before the sinner as a pious Pharisee but as one who identifies with his spiritual need in compassion and love. A fisherman said, "Let the trout see the angler, and the angler will catch no trout."[11] Oswald Chambers writes, "Never water down the Word of God, but preach it in its undiluted sternness. There must be unflinching faithfulness to the Word of God but when you come to personal dealings with others, remember who you are - you are not some special being created in heaven, but a sinner saved by grace."[12]

16. Avoid prayerlessness.
The soulwinner ought to talk to God about the person he is about to see before the encounter, during the encounter, and following the encounter. The witness from start to finish must be bathed in prayer, yea much prayer. The prophet Isaiah declared, "Not until Zion travailed did she bring forth children" (Isaiah 66:8). Not until the soulwinner travails in spiritual birth pains through prayer before Holy God for lost man will such be birthed into the family of God. D.L. Moody encourages the soulwinner in saying, "If our hearts are with God, our prayer must be answered."[13] Martin Luther stated that prayer "is not a matter that is to be left to our choice, for if we are to do anything of eternal profitability we must pray."[14]

17. Avoid chewing gum.

18. Avoid "overlaying your case."
Lawyers must always be careful not to "overlay their case." The soulwinner must as well. Sensitivity to the leadership of the Holy Spirit as to what approach to use and the duration of a witness is imperative. Following a revival service, a friend of mine was approached by a student who desired to be saved. In his attempt to lead this young man to Christ he began sharing a witnessing booklet. The young man looked up at him and asked, "Do I have to hear all that before I get saved?" Obviously what he heard in the service had prepared his heart to be saved negating the need for a lengthy presentation.

19. Avoid forgotten promises.
The soulwinner should follow through on everything he tells a person he will do. If he tells him he will send him a Bible, he must send it. If he tells him he will pray for him, he must pray for him. The soulwinner should make a habit of writing down details of each witness to remind him of commitments he made to each.

20. Avoid a mechanical presentation of the gospel.
As a seminary student I recall hearing a sermon that had no doubt been preached so often it had become *routine* void of passion and power. Witnessing presentations can become like that sermon. Keep the presentation fresh and passionate guarding against it becoming mundane; business as usual.

21. Avoid religious terminology.
In soulwinning I learned to choose my words carefully following a witness to a young man who misunderstood what I meant in using the word "lost." He thought I meant to be physically lost and related a story about once being lost in the woods. Words such as "saved," " lost," "salvation," "justification," and "rapture" should be used cautiously in witnessing to the unsaved. Make a diligent effort to keep your witness clear and simple.

22. Avoid condemnation.
The role of the soulwinner to the sinner is one of compassion not condemnation. Avoid exhibiting a judgmental attitude toward the sinner. Don't look down on him. Embrace him with the love of Jesus and allow the Holy Spirit to use the scripture you share to do the reproving. John R. Rice wrote, "I never say, "You are a sinner." Instead I say, "Of course, you know that we are all poor sinners, and Christ died to save sinners like you and me." In the first place, it is true that I needed the same Savior as others do. It is also the courteous and considerate way to state the matter."[15]

23. Avoid plucking green fruit.
Some fruit is ripe for the harvest; other fruit is yet green necessitating fertilization before harvesting. The believer must be careful not to pick unripe fruit. The soulwinner must stay alert and discerning to the Holy Spirit's leadership in pressing or not for a decision. The story is told of a drunkard who confronted D.L. Moody saying, "I am one of your converts." Moody responded, "You must be one of mine for you sure are not one of the Lord's." Green fruit that is harvested prematurely is far more difficult to ripen for true conversion than it was in its original state. Don't bruise the fruit giving a false hope of salvation and making it harder to reach people.

C. H. Spurgeon wrote, "How can he be healed who is not sick? The old-fashioned sense of sin is despised, and consequently a religion is run up before the foundations are dug out. Everything in this age is shallow...men leap into religion and then leap out again."[16]

24. Avoid hurriedness.
R A. Torrey said, "One man with whom slow but thorough work has been done, and, who at last has been brought out clearly for Christ, is better then a dozen with whom hasty work has been done, who think they have accepted Christ when in reality they have not."[17] Phillip took time to sit down in a chariot with the Ethiopian Eunuch to ride with him a distance explaining the plan of salvation and this resulted in this eunuch's conversion and baptism (Acts 8: 29 – 38).

25. Avoid being offensive or belligerent.
J.W. Ellis wrote, "Sinners liked to be in Jesus presence. Not that He catered to their whims and fancies and evils! – but that in winning them He did not offend them. Where lesser religious leaders would cast stones, Christ was gentle and kind. Anyone can throw a rock; but it takes wisdom to win souls."[18] The soulwinner must graciously address personal sin in soulwinning without throwing stones of condemnation.

26. Avoid dishonesty.
The soulwinner must truthfully declare the scripture's teaching about salvation. He must not hedge one iota from it in order to "claim" a convert.

27. Avoid abruptness.
The soulwinner should not start with the "bang-bang" double question "Are you saved? Would you like to be?" at the outset of a witness. These questions ought to be reserved for the time of "net drawing" at the conclusion of the witness in most instances. Jesus in His approach to the Woman at Jacob's Well did not immediately say to her, "Lady, you need to be saved." He took time to ask her for a drink of water before proceeding with His witness (John 4:9-10).

Jesus' witness to Nicodemus was "bang-bang" forthrightly telling this religious leader he must be born again (John 3: 1 – 3). Nicodemus, however, was ready to receive such a witness due to his religious background. A "bang-bang" witnessing approach may be used when the soulwinner discerns a person is fruit ripe unto harvest due to a crusade or revival service attended or some other such factor.[19]

28. Avoid playing private detective.
This excellent point comes from the writing of J.W. Ellis.[20] The soulwinner should not pry into the sinners past or ask questions concerning it that could be humiliating. Point the sinner beyond their sin to Calvary where a gracious Savior poured out His blood to provide cleansing and eternal life.

29. Avoid witnessing to one person in a crowd.

In witnessing I have always found it most effective to talk to a person personally, without a spouse or other family member present. R. A. Torrey stated, "No one likes to open his heart freely to another on this most personal and sacred of all subjects when there are others present. Many will from pride defend themselves in a false position when several are present, who would fully admit their error or sin or need, if they were alone with you."[21]

30. Avoid witnessing to two people simultaneously.

Insure success to its maximum level by confronting one person at a time with the gospel. In cases where you must speak to two or three persons at the same time, address the witness first to the one deemed most ready for the gospel.

In speaking to two people at the same time always ask for a salvation decision first from the one that seems the most receptive.

31. Avoid quitting too soon.

I have heard great evangelistic sermons that failed to win souls primarily because the appeal of invitation was cut short. This happens in soul winning all too often as well. It is of utmost importance the soulwinner stay in tune with the Holy Spirit as to when to close a witness. To close it prematurely may cost a person his soul for all eternity!

32. Avoid Foul-up due to no Follow-up.

It is a crime against the new convert for the soulwinner to *save 'em and leave 'em* without providing guidance. The apostle Paul declared, "So everywhere we go, we tell everyone about Christ. We warn them and teach them with all the wisdom God has given us, for we want to present them to God, perfect in their relationship to Christ" (Colossians 1:28 NLT). Jay Kesler stated, "The man who has only spiritual dwarfs or stillborns to present to God will be ashamed. The Great Commission asked for more than just going and telling; it also said, 'Make disciples.' "[22] Chapter eight is devoted to this subject in detail.

33. Avoid belaboring the appeal.

The soulwinner must not share a witness too long or press an appeal to stringently. Upon the unsaved person's stating or indicating he is not ready to make a decision for Christ the soulwinner should desist in his appeal; politely close the witness and await another opportunity to win him to Christ. He must be careful to keep the door open for future witnessing encounters.

34. Avoid a sad disposition.

C.E. Matthews commented, "Any person who has lost the joy of salvation will be a failure at trying to win souls to Christ. A frown and a smile do not speak the same language. A complaining Christian is God's poorest advertisement for Christianity. On the other hand, the best advertisement for Christianity is a rejoicing, happy Christian, regardless of his lot in life."[23] Paul and Silas despite imprisonment and the possibility of death sang songs of praise to God and a jailer was converted. (Acts 16: 25 – 31) The witness no doubt would have ended differently had their disposition been the opposite.

Dr. Jowett commented, "Is that not rather a far fetched notion of an angler's equipment? I do not know a fisherman ought to be able to sing. Why should he require the gift of music? Because when the angler is depressed he cannot throw a light line. When a man is melancholy his throw is heavy. When his spirits are light and exuberant, he will be able to touch the surface of the water with the exquisite delicacy of a passing feather."[24] Likewise the soulwinner must be cheerful if he expects to win souls.

35. Avoid a waiting-to-be-led-to-a-witness mindset.
In my college days I recall a fellow student stating that the only soulwinning one was to do was that prompted by the Holy Spirit. Such an attitude is theologically flawed and opens the door to guiltless inactivity in soulwinning. The scripture clearly commands the believer to witness (Acts 1:8; Matthew 28: 18 – 20) inasmuch as it does for him to tithe, to be faithful to the church, and to live a holy life. The believer does not have to feel led of the Spirit to tithe or pray and neither does he have to feel led of the Spirit to talk to people about Christ. It should be an automatic.

Don't misunderstand me. Generally every Christian's job is to witness. No amount of praying or waiting on the leadership of the Spirit can alter this. However specifically there will be times when the Holy Spirit will certainly lead the soulwinner to talk to a person at a particular time and place such as with Phillip and the Ethiopian Eunuch (Acts 8). These specific and definite soulwinning encounters are "Divine Appointments" which God clearly orchestrates.

36. Avoid using the shotgun.
In soulwinning take your pistol (New Testament) not your shotgun (large Bible). C. E.Autrey warned, "The very sight of a large Bible under the arm of a visitor may prejudice the prospect immediately, or it may cause him to unnecessarily throw up his guard. No one appreciates religion on parade."[25] I prefer the use of a coat pocket New Testament that can be placed in my coat or back pocket until I am ready to seize the moment with the unsaved to make clear the way of salvation. The inexperienced soulwinner may find it most helpful to use a marked New Testament that leads him step by step through scripture in presenting the gospel.

37. Avoid asking the prospect "Are you a Christian?"
My experience teaches that most people in religious America really have no concept

of what it means to be saved or to be a Christian and are thus likely to say they are when in fact they aren't. J. W. Ellis said, "Don't ask a person if he is a Christian. You will never get truth of the heart. Too many embrace a false hope of salvation and thus a false security. The soulwinner must probe gently as he presents the gospel to ascertain the true condition." He went on to say that the soulwinner must find out if the person is born again without asking if he is. "Instead of asking a man if he is a Christian, ask him what he thinks a Christian is. Here is almost an infallible law: if you can find out what a man thinks he has to do to become a Christian, you will find out if he is a Christian."[26]

38. Avoid talking too much.

George Sweazey stated, "Two eager callers, who are full of things they want to say, may easily drown those they visit in a sea of words. People are not merely talked into a decision – they must partly talk themselves into it."[27] The soulwinner should consciously provide opportunities for the lost to speak without feeling they are barging in on a lecture. The soulwinner must not feel as if he has to tell the unsaved everything from A to Z in his effort to win them.

39. Avoid overlooking children.

C.H. Spurgeon said, "Some hinder the children because they are forgetful of the child's value. The soul's price does not depend upon its years. God forgive those who despise the little ones. Will you be angry with me if I say that a boy is more worth saving than a man? It is infinite mercy on God's part to save those who are seventy; for what good can they now do with the flag-end of their lives? When we get to be fifty or sixty we are almost worn out and if we have spent all our earthly days with the devil, what remains for God? But these dear boys and girls....is something to be made out of them. If now they yield themselves to Christ they may have a long, happy and holy day before them in which they may serve God with all their hearts."[28] Robert M. McCheyne stated, "Jesus has reason to complain of us that He can do no mighty work in our Sunday School because of our unbelief."[29]

The argument of some is that children ought not be evangelized but left alone. The Christian poet Coleridge was told that a child should wait until grown to choose his "religion." Coleridge, without verbal response, led the man into his garden. "Looking around the bare ground he said quietly, "I have decided not to put out any flowers and vegetables this year, but wait till August and let the garden decide for itself whether it prefers weeds or strawberries!" The lesson he was teaching is obviously clear – just as nothing is required to raise a crop of weeds nothing is required to be done for a child to be lost and grow up in sinful disobedience.[30]

40. Avoid trying to duplicate your experience.
In soulwinning don't seek to get the sinner to have an experience of salvation like
your own. You may have cried; he may shout. Do not gauge the sincerity of a
person's decision based upon how he did or did not do what you did when you got
saved. God deals with each person individually and differently.

41. Avoid quoting scripture.
It is good for soulwinners to memorize texts that make plain the way of salvation.
However, in witnessing it is often best for the soulwinner to allow the prospect to
read the text with him.

42. Avoid failure to critique the presentation.
Critiquing one's witnessing presentation sharpens his Sword. The soulwinner
should ask, "What did I do that was not necessary? What did I fail to do? How
could the transition from the greeting at the door to the witnessing presentation
go smoother? Did I press too hard or was I too lax in pressing for a decision? Did
I utilize the best approach and method? What do I count as my greatest weakness
in the witness?"

43. Avoid being turned off by appearance.
The style of dress, hairdo, or wearing of body rings in uncommon places must not
deter the soulwinner from his mission to give all men everywhere the opportunity
to be saved. In visiting a dying teenage boy at a hospital, I was deeply saddened
by what his mother shared concerning a prior visit by a minister. Seeing a ring in
her son's ear, this minister commented on it and walked out never to return. These
types of ministers need to reread Paul's and James's admonition, "For there is no
respect of persons with God" (Romans 2:11) and "But if ye have respect to persons,
ye commit sin, and are convinced of the law as transgressors" (James 2:9).

44. Avoid using only the two-by-two approach.
Jesus sent the seventy out two-by-two to witness is true (Luke 10:1) but He
sanctioned one-to-one soulwinning by His own example. He witnessed to the
Woman at the Jacob's Well alone and also to Nicodemus. Both approaches to
soulwinning have value, so neither should be shunned. Personally I have won
more souls to Christ alone than with partners.

45. Avoid slothfulness.
Neither snow nor rain nor heat nor gloom of night stays these couriers from the
swift completion of their appointed rounds. (Inscription on the General Post Office,
New York City) This is the closest thing to a motto for the United Postal Service.
It would serve well to be the motto for the soulwinner. The soulwinner must ever
remember he is a courier for the King of the Universe and must faithfully dispatch
His summons to one and all regardless of the spiritual climate of the day or that of
his own soul.

46. Avoid being the 'Shell Answer Man' when you are not.

It's okay for the soulwinner when asked a question of which the answer is not known to say, "I am sorry, I don't know the answer to that but when I get one it certainly will be passed on to you." Don't try to answer questions of which you are not qualified to respond.

47. Avoid shrinking back.

Regarding soulwinning visitation, "Just do it." Don't shrink back. Don't turn back at the prospect's door and head for home. Lee Strobel stated, "Almost every day, we come to evangelistic turning points. We make choices whether to help rescue these people from danger or to walk the other way. We make spur-of-the-moment decisions whether to heroically venture into their lives and lead them to a place of spiritual safety, or merely hope that someone else will do it. We make split-second decisions all the time to play it safe or tilt the conversation toward spiritual topics, and many times we shrink back."[31] A retracing of our steps today would probably shockingly reveal just how many times in fact we chose to shrink back from a witness.

48. Avoid allowing the lost to monopolize the conversation.

It is of absolute necessity to the soulwinner who starts the witness to guide the conversation. At times the soulwinner will confront individuals who want to do all the talking. He must stick to the course and wrest control of the conversation back into his hands as tactfully as possible. The soulwinner must control the direction of the conversation, the time both he and the sinner talk, and most certainly its conclusion and appeal for a decision for Christ as the Holy Spirit directs.

49. Avoid hiding behind the excuse, "I don't know how."

It is not expected by God or man for the Christian to witness at the start thoroughly polished in presentation and technique. The blind man Jesus saved immediately gave testimony without any training period. He immediately testified "...whether he be a sinner *or no*, I know not: one thing I know, that, whereas I was blind, now I see." (John 9:25). The adulterous woman converted at Jacob's Well left her water pot immediately, entered into the town broadcasting, "Come, see a man, which told me all things that ever I did: is not this the Christ?" (John 4:28). This woman had no instruction in soulwinning, but that didn't stop her from telling others of Christ. She had no prior experience yet," ... many of the Samaritans of that city believed on him for the saying of the woman, which testified, He told me all that ever I did" (John 9:39).

Don't let books on soulwinning intimate you or cause you to develop *soulwinophobia.* You can win souls apart from instruction from man. You possess enough knowledge and power to lead a soul to Christ if you have been saved. Books like this simply are intended to serve as "iron sharpeth iron" (Proverbs 27:17), enabling the soulwinner to witness better and more effectively.

50. Avoid violating confidences.

The soulwinner must be tight lipped concerning sins that may be confessed in a witnessing encounter. "Let him know, that he which converteth the sinner from the error of his way shall save a soul from death, and shall hide a multitude of sins" (James 5:20). God covers the repentant sins with the blood of Christ and forgets them. The soulwinner must do the same.

51. Avoid feeling satisfied.

W.B. Riley stated, "The man who is satisfied in soulwinning is stultified in spiritual interest."[32] How can the soulwinner ever be satisfied with either his labor or fruit when so many need to be rescued from the grip of sin and Satan. Paul certainly wasn't satisfied with his soulwinning effort for he cried, "I say the truth in Christ, I lie not, my conscience also bearing me witness in the Holy Ghost, that I have great heaviness and continual sorrow in my heart. For I could wish that myself were accursed from Christ for my brethren, my kinsmen according to the flesh" (Romans 9: 1-3). The soulwinner should rejoice much in the work of soulwinning but never grow satisfied and complacent.

52. Avoid gullibility.

My soulwinning experience has revealed that often a person will profess they are a Christian when they are not. Don't be gullible to assume all that tell you they are saved are in fact saved. Barna research reveals that fifty percent of all adults argue that anyone who "is generally good or does enough good things for others during their life will earn a place in Heaven."[33] To authenticate the genuineness of salvation ask the person to share their conversion testimony. Remember that the most difficult part of soulwinning is getting a person to realize he is lost so they can see his need to be saved. Sinners must loosen their grip upon false hopes to see their utter need of the only true hope in Jesus Christ.

53. Avoid "Tip Toeing through the Tulips."

James Tomkins claimed fellow golfer George Long failed to warn him with the traditional "Fore" when hitting a wayward shot that hit him in the right eye knocking him out of a golf cart. Long testified in court that he did yell out a warning. The jury returned a verdict of not guilty.[34] The soulwinner must be careful to shout out warning to the sinner of the judgment that will be his lot if he continues to live in defiance of God's law. This shout of "Fore" must not be whispered so as not to disturb or scare sinners but blasted to gain their attention and alert them of the urgency of salvation. The soulwinner will stand before the Judgment bar of God to give an accounting of his soulwinning effort. It will be indeed sad for some to hear the Lord state on that day, "You gave a warning to John and Susan but it was so low key they didn't hear it or believe it and now their blood will I require at thy hand."

"Son of man, I have made you a watchman for the house of Israel; therefore hear a word from my mouth, and give them warning from me: When I say to the wicked, You shall surely die, and you give him no warning, nor speak to warn the wicked from his wicked ways, to save his life, the same wicked man shall die in his iniquity; but his blood will I require at your hand. Yet, if you warn the wicked, and he does not turn from his wickedness, nor from his wicked way, he shall die in his iniquity; but you have delivered your soul" (Ezekiel 3: 17 – 19). As the Lord's watchman it is essential that sounding forth from our lips to the unsaved is a clear, certain and compelling call to repentance and faith in Christ Jesus.

Charles Finney exhorted, "Bring up the individual's particular sins. Talking in general terms against sin will produce no results. You must make a man feel that you mean him."[35] C. H. Spurgeon said, "The man whom God means to be a laborer in his harvest must not come with soft and delicate words, and flattering doctrines concerning the dignity of human nature, and the excellence of self-help, and of earnest endeavors to rectify our lapsed condition, and the like. Such mealy-mouthedness may God curse, for it is the curse of this age. The honest preacher (soulwinner) calls a sin a sin, and a spade a spade, and says to men, "You are ruining yourselves; while you reject Christ you are living on the borders of hell, and ere long you will be lost to all eternity. There shall be no mincing of the matter, you must escape from the wrath to come by faith in Jesus, or be driven for ever from God's presence, and from all hope of joy." Our sickle is made on purpose to cut. The Gospel is intended to wound the conscience, and to go right through the heart, with the design of separating the soul from sin and self, as the corn is divided from the soil."[36]

54. Avoid telling the "convert" he is saved.
I like to ask the person who prays the sinner's prayer, "What did you just ask Jesus to do for you?" Upon their response I then ask, "Did you mean what you asked Him to do in your life?" Next I share with the person a text like Revelation 3:20 asking, "Did you open the door of your heart to Jesus inviting Him to become your Lord and Savior"? Upon their response I then ask, "Based upon the word of God what happened when you did?" Use of this approach leads the convert to affirm his salvation, not the soulwinner. It is the Holy Spirit not the soulwinner who must authenticate genuine salvation in the heart for it is "The Spirit itself beareth witness with our spirit, that we are the children of God" (Romans 8:16).

55. Avoid speaking out of line.
Silence is Golden. Silence certainly is golden in times of soulwinning when the Holy Spirit clearly forbids the soulwinner to share a witness. It is for a Divine purpose. Brother Andrew, God's Smuggler, shares about a girl who became a Christian because he didn't share the gospel with her when he had the perfect opportunity. This Spirit-led unwillingness on his part seized this girl's heart with

fear causing her to think she was moving past the hope of salvation prompting a decision of salvation. Scripture teaches that "the Lord ordereth the steps of a good man" and I add his tongue also (Psalms 37:23). The soulwinner must "walk in the Spirit" in order to "to be led by the Spirit" in witnessing encounters (Galatians 5:25, Romans 8:14).

56. Avoid controversial subjects such as politics.

C. H. Spurgeon commented, "If you are going to try to win people for Christ, always seek to break down everything that would separate…Or do you happen to belong to any political party? Do not bring that question in; you will not win souls that way; you will be more likely to excite prejudice and opposition."[37]

57. Avoid apologizing.

Those who share the gospel should never apologize. The believer is given Heavenly authority to tell all men of Jesus Christ. Paul stated, "And all things are of God, who hath reconciled us to himself by Jesus Christ, and hath given to us the ministry of reconciliation; to wit, that God was in Christ, reconciling the world unto himself, not imputing their trespasses unto them; and hath committed unto us the word of reconciliation. Now then we are ambassadors for Christ, as though God did beseech you by us: we pray you in Christ's stead, be ye reconciled to God (2 Corinthians 5: 17-20). Spurgeon wrote, "Ambassadors do not apologize when they go to a foreign court; they know their monarch has sent them, and they deliver their message with all authority of king and country at their back."

58. Avoid mistaking visitation for soulwinning.

It is good to do humanitarian deeds but that is not soulwinning; it is awesome to visit the elderly and care for the sickly but that is not soulwinning; it is great to invite people to church but that is not soulwinning and it is tremendous to visit hospitals and prisons teaching Bible studies but that is not soulwinning. Soulwinning is the express task of purposely and pointedly talking to a person about Christ seeking a salvation response or decision. Acts 1:8 can only be obeyed by actually going and telling not of one's great pastor , church or program (though this may be included) but of Jesus Christ who died, was buried and raised from the dead to secure man's redemption.

59. Avoid permanently shutting the door.

"Every communication must be crafted with the goal of ensuring that it's not the last one."[38] Michael L. Simpson commented, "The best way to do this is to make sure they know they are in charge of choosing how much information they receive. They must know you honor their choices at their level of willingness to engage, or they will feel pressured and threatened and trust will be broken."[39] I add that the door of opportunity to win them to Christ also may be irrevocably shut.

60. Avoid Short Cuts.

George E. Sweazey stated, "SHORT CUTS IN EVANGELISM NEVER WORK. That invariable rule must be learned soon and remembered often! There is no easy way to bring people to the Christian faith. Only those who are willing to do the most important work in the world in a conscientious, painstaking way will have-or deserve to have-success. Churches keep hoping they can hire a revivalist to do their evangelism for them. Or they send out half-trained members to ring doorbells and call it 'evangelistic visitation.' "[40] Nothing can substitute for a one-to-one presentation of the gospel. There is nothing!

61. Avoid just pulpit soulwinning.

Soulwinning in preaching is imperative and must be exercised. The minister, however, must be cautious not to allow soulwinning in the pulpit to replace personal soulwinning. Roland Q. Leavell wrote, "Indeed, if the pulpit evangelist is not also a personal evangelist, he is merely a pretender evangelist, and possibly an imposter evangelist."[41] Dean Inge, distinguishing public preaching from personal soulwinning, stated, "Preaching is like taking a bucket of water and throwing it over a number of open-necked bottles; whereas personal soulwinning is taking each bottle to the tap and filling it."[42] C.H. Spurgeon remarked, "Hand-picked fruit for me every time."[43]

C. E. Autrey wrote, "Great preaching has always had its place; but the most urgent need at home and abroad is not for a great pulpit ministry; but for preachers who can and will talk effectively with men heart to heart and one at a time about the Savior."[44] D.L. Moody regarded his pulpit soulwinning appeal only as preparatory to personal soulwinning. "To him, pleading with individual souls in the inquiry room was of more importance than his appeal before the great audiences. Moody knelt by, pleaded with, prayed for, and won personally seven hundred fifty thousand people to Christ."[45] Speaking to a group of young men, Moody commented, "Plenty of men are willing to preach to get on a platform, and preach and exhort, and to that kind of work; but workers are scarce who will labor with a drunkard, or deal with men one at a time."[46] Moody believing in the supremacy of personal soulwinning work stated, "We must have personal work – hand-to-hand work – if we are going to have results."[47]

62. Avoid talking in approaching a home.

Soulwinners, instead of talking to each when approaching a home, should silently pray and be observant of house décor, pets and toys, which may enhance the visit.

63. Avoid unnaturalness.

It has been said that in everything natural one ought to be spiritual and in everything spiritual one ought to be natural. This certainly applies to soulwinning. Use a relaxed conversation voice in the evangelistic presentation.

64. Avoid cramming the prospect's door.
In door-to-door visitation the soulwinner should knock on the door loudly five or six times and then take several steps back. One soulwinner states that a loud and long knock gives a psychological reaction that there is somebody important at the door contrasted to a soft knock that gives the impression that someone that is timid, scared and unimportant is at the door.[48]

65. Avoid delay.
The soulwinner must immediately submit to the Holy Spirit's prompting to make a witness. Procrastination could mean a sinner's eternal damnation. God always has the right to interrupt the Christian's schedule. C. H. Spurgeon stated, "When they heard the call of Jesus, Simon and Andrew obeyed at once without demur. If we would always, punctually and with resolute zeal, put in practice what we hear upon the spot, or at the first occasion, our attendance with the means of grace, and our reading of good books, could not fail to enlist us spiritually. Do not give place to the devil by delay! Haste while opportunity and quickening are happening in conjunction."[49]

66. Avoid giving up.
John MacArthur stated, "Don't give up on those who mock Christ when you share your faith. God is able to turn their hearts to saving faith in the most surprising ways."[50] Who of Paul's day would ever have thought he of all people would get saved but he did. G.S Dobbins writes, "Are we not prone to give up too easily? A successful insurance agent says that he sometimes makes as many as forty to fifty contacts before he at length sells his prospect a policy. Wise business and professional men cultivate "good-will" as they look many years ahead to future business."[51]

C. H. Spurgeon wrote, "I sometimes hear of persons getting very angry after a good sermon, and I say to myself, 'I am not sorry for it.' Sometimes when we are fishing the fish gets the hook into his mouth. He pulls hard at the line; if he were dead, he would not; but he is a live fish, worth the getting; and though he runs for a while, with the hook in his jaws, He cannot escape. His very wriggling and his anger show that he has got the hook and the hook has got him. Have the landing-net ready; we shall land him by and by. Give him more line; let him spend his strength, and then we will land him, and he shall belong to Christ forever."[52]

I yet can hear my father's instruction about fishing, "Hook him first, Son. Give him some line. Keep tension on the line. Don't let him get away. Let him run awhile. Now pull him in." That's great advice for catching men. Keep reeling off line to the sinner; if he is hooked he cannot get away.

67. Avoid pestering people.

The soulwinner should be careful not to pester a person about the gospel; it only makes it more difficult for the next soulwinning visit. Man must be willing to hear the gospel before he ever will consider applying its truth to his heart.

In witnessing to a family member, don't continuously nag about their need to be saved or attend church for such may only serve to drive that person further away from Christ. Pray for their salvation, speak to him/her of salvation when the Holy Spirit leads, ask others to make a witness, and live a consistent Christian life but don't nag.

68. Avoid criticizing soulwinners.

C. H. Spurgeon stated, "The great wisdom of soulwinners, according to the text (Proverbs 11:30), is proven only by their actual success in really winning souls. To their own Master they are accountable for the ways in which they work, not to us. Do not let us be comparing and contrasting this minister and that. Only children wrangle about incidental methods; men look at sublime results. Do these workers of many sorts and divers manners win souls? Then they are wise, and you, who criticize them, being yourselves unfruitful, cannot be wise, even though you affect to be their judges."[53]

69. Avoid failure to engage in Arrow Witnessing.

The soulwinner often will have only minutes with a lost soul, necessitating an arrow witness. This form of witness is a pungent gospel declaration compacted into one or more brief sentences. The soulwinner must redeem whatever opportunity he has to share Christ regardless of the time factor. God exhorts us to sow Gospel bread beside the waters - even the fast moving rivers. (Ecclesiastes 11:1)

70. Avoid a false assumption.

One thing I have learned in nearly forty years of soulwinning is to never assume a person is saved simply because of church membership, confirmation, baptism or the word of others. It is always right and expedient for the soulwinner to presume one is lost until told differently.

71. Avoid false guilt.

It is right for the Christian who fails to witness to experience guilt; after all Christians are explicitly commanded by God in scripture to evangelize. (Acts 1:8) However, failure to witness according to man- imposed methods, times and quota goals should not cause the believer to feel guilty. Methods, times and goals are helpful in soulwinning if wisely implemented but must never be legalistically binding.

72. Avoid Bait and Switch schemes.
"Right this minute, hundreds of well-meaning (and some not so well-meaning) church and parachurch leaders are promoting subtly dishonest schemes specifically designed to entice and fool folks into hearing the gospel and getting saved."[54] The soulwinner must ask sincerely "Is my method of witnessing though purposed to win a person to Christ unethical or deceiving?" The soulwinner must be upfront about the real purpose behind the free bottled water, dessert social, free car wash, pizza blast, or church census. God's representative must raise the *bar* higher than telemarketers.

In writing this book I received a classic *bait and switch* phone call. The representative for the company informed me that they would send my daughter a free proposal to consolidate her student loans without obligation. Although I should have known better, I bit the bait. In providing information requested this spokesperson only then informed me that a cost may be involved and that prompted an immediate termination to the conversation. This was a classic bait and switch scheme. We detest these in the business world and must avoid use of them in the church.

73. Avoid being impersonal.
Henry Ward Beecher said, "The longer I live, the more confidence I have in those sermons preached where one man is the congregation; where one man is the minister; where there is no question as to who is meant when the preacher says "Thou art the man!" Beecher's remarks clearly concerned preaching but may equally be applied to soulwinners. May he who seeks to win souls keep it personal, personal, personal.

74. Avoid impression of insincerity.
In reference to soulwinning, Alvin Reid commented that the lost "may not believe what you share but let there be no doubt you believe what you share."[55] The lost easily spot and are turned off by religious *fakes*. It has well been said, "A person doesn't care how much you know until they know how much you care."

75. Avoid neglect of eye contact.
In soulwinning encounters it's important to maintain eye contact while talking and listening to the prospect. Curtis Hutson stated, "Looking people in the eye helps communicate a clear message and demonstrates that we're interested in what others are saying to us."[56] At times in witnessing the soulwinner should say, "Is this making sense to you?" or "Look at me for a minute" to reconnect eye contact.

76. Avoid excuse of age.
C. H. Spurgeon wrote, "Oh that every one of you might "save some." Yes, my

venerable brethren, you are not too old for service. Yes, my young friends, ye young men and maidens, ye are not too young to be recruits in the King's service. If the kingdom is ever to come to our Lord, and come it will, it never will come through a few ministers, missionaries, or evangelists preaching the Gospel. It must come through every one of you preaching it – in the shop, and by the fireside, when walking abroad and when sitting in the chamber. You must all of you be always endeavoring to "save some." How many others have you brought to Christ? You cannot do it by yourself, I know; but I mean how many has the Spirit of God brought by you? How many, did I say? Is it quite certain that you have led any to Jesus? Can you not recollect one? I pity you, then! Your children are not saved, your wife is not saved, and you are spiritually childless. Can you bear this thought? I pray you wake from your slumbering and ask the Master to make you useful."[57]

The Psalmist stated, "The righteous shall flourish like the palm tree: he shall grow like a cedar in Lebanon. Those that be planted in the house of the LORD shall flourish in the courts of our God. They shall still bring forth fruit in old age; they shall be fat and flourishing." (Psalms 92:12-14) Aged Saint, claim this promise of thy God and embark upon the fields that are white unto harvest while it is yet day for "The night cometh when no man can work" (John 9:4). Determine that by the grace of God you will win more to Christ in the final quarter of life than in the previous three combined.

77. Avoid the attitude that soulwinning is a special talent.
Soulwinning is not a talent nor is it a gift but is an art that can and should be developed by every believer.

78. Avoid being a spiritual psycho.
Buddy Murphrey wrote, "Don't be hollering, jerking, shouting, etc. Exhibit a sane, sensible, pleasing disposition."[58]

79. Avoid entering a home at bad times.
No one likes to have a meal interrupted or be delayed in leaving for an appointment. In such situations leave Gospel and church literature and make arrangements for a later visit. Absolutely do not infringe upon people.

80. Avoid physically leaning on the sinner.
"Avoid intimate contact. One sinner said, "The first half-hour I was concerned about my heavy load of sin, but the last half-hour I was more concerned about the heavy Christian lying on me."[59]

81. Avoid letting the sin of yesterday keep you from witnessing today.
Paul refused to allow his great sins against the church, Christians and God prevent his soulwinning once becoming a born again believer. He declared, "Brethren, I

count not myself to have apprehended: but *this* one thing *I do*, forgetting those things which are behind, and reaching forth unto those things which are before, I press toward the mark for the prize of the high calling of God in Christ Jesus" (Philippians 3: 13-14). Paul determined not to let yesterday paralyze work for God today. Every believer must exhibit that same mind.

82. Avoid the "I can't" phrase.
Oswald Chambers stated, "When it is a question of God's almighty Spirit, never say, "I can't."[60] Believers certainly "can do all things through Christ which strengtheneth me" (Philippians 4:13), even confront the lost with the Gospel. "For with God nothing shall be impossible" (Luke 1:37). John MacArthur exhorted, "Start looking beyond the minutiae to the Eternal Christ, who can take even your weak faith and use you for His kingdom purposes."[61]

Chambers also remarked, "If Jesus ever commanded us to do something that He was unable to equip us to accomplish, He would be a liar. And if we make our own inability a stumbling block or an excuse to obedience, it means that we are telling God that there is something that He has not taken into account. Every element of our self-reliance must be put to death by the power of God. The moment we recognize our complete weakness and our dependence upon Him will be the very moment that the Spirit of God will exhibit His power."[62]

83. Avoid talking a sinner into it.
If you can talk a person into being "saved" somebody else can talk him out of it. A little boy inquired, "Why is it that when I open a marigold it dies, but when God does it lives." The reply came, "Because when God opens a marigold He opens it from the inside out." The soulwinner must never forget the lesson of the marigold as he seeks to "open mans heart" for salvation. Lewis Drummond stated, "Any form of evangelism that resorts to the manipulation of people, regardless of the motive is unworthy of the gospel. Even more tragically, such a use of evangelism can lead unsuspecting and honest inquirers into a shallow understanding that falls short of a genuine experience of salvation. Scriptural evangelism demands that the evangelist fill the presentation of the gospel with solid theological content. That price must be paid if God's approval of the work is to be expected, for people are rarely if ever genuinely converted by psychological maneuvering, persuasive oratory, or emotional stories devoid of the impact of the Holy Spirit. For the sake of those whom we would reach for Christ, authentic theology and evangelism must not be separated. We must avoid superficial "believeism." People deserve to hear the *full* truth of Jesus Christ and salvation."[63]

84. Avoid skipping the "burnt over stomps."
Occasionally in evangelistic meetings I am asked to see a man who has been

witnessed to unsuccessfully by every evangelist or pastor that has come into town for years. That's cool; I'm glad to do that in hopes that I might be able to build upon what the others shared and reel him in for Jesus! Fleshly tendency would have the soulwinner to "invest his time more wisely" neglecting a continued effort to win *burnt over stomps,* but such an attitude must be choked down or these will never be won. It has often been the case that when such a person is won the church and community breaks out into revival.

85. Avoid demeaning a church or denomination.
The focus of a soulwinner is not to attack the prospect's church but to win him to Christ. Keep the main thing the main thing: soulwinning. Biblical Truth has an amazing way of revealing theological flaws and heresy apart from a soulwinner's frontal assault.

86. Avoid failure to witness to family, friends, and relatives.
"The most winnable people are those who are closely related to us, **F**riends, **R**elatives, **A**ssociates, and **N**eighbors (*F.R.A.N.S).*"[64] The wife of a great evangelist said, "He won the world but let his own son die and go to Hell." Evangelism begins at home. It is horrendously wrong to win others without first endeavoring to win one's own family.

87. Avoid body-odor.

88. Avoid over concern for getting dirty.
I was asked to witness to a teenage boy once he got off the school bus one afternoon. I saw him walk into a hog pasture and I pursued. Right there in the midst of the stench, mud, and hogs I led that young man to Christ. This young man, now twenty-five years older, is still living for Christ and involved in the church. Don't mind getting dirty for Jesus if that's what it takes to win souls.

89. Avoid soulwinning when sick.
People don't want a stranger in their home who constantly is blowing his noise, sneezing or coughing. You don't either. "Do unto others as you would have them do unto you." Remain home and pray for others who visit.

90. Avoid parking on the lawn.
The first impression is the best impression so respect the prospect's yard by parking on the road or in the driveway.

91. Avoid letting climate of the day to deter soulwinning.
Jimmy Draper, using Paul's aggressive pursuit to reach the immoral society of his day, said, "One's environment should never be a deterrent for witnessing. The Gospel was born in a day just like ours – a heretic, immoral environment. The

Gospel exploded in that kind of culture."[65] A pastor who had begun to believe the day of door-to-door visitation was past excitedly shared with me the great results his church was experiencing in using that approach in reaching souls for Christ. Often the sinner's hardness of heart is blamed for the lack of soulwinning when in reality it is the saint's hardness of heart.

92. Avoid just talking soulwinning.
Sermons, songs and studies on soulwinning are a dime a dozen. Spurgeon cautioned, "There are some, whose knowledge of terms and phases, and whose extensive preparation, lead you to fear that they will exterminate the fishy race; but as their basket returns empty, they can hardly be so proficient as they seem. The parable hardly needs expounding: great talkers and theorizers are common enough, and there are few whose cultured boastfulness is only exceeded by their lifelong failure. We cannot take these for our examples...We must have sinners saved. Nothing else will content us: the fisherman must take fish or lose his toil; and we must bring souls to Jesus, or we shall break our hearts with disappointment."[66]

93. Avoid unclarity.
"It's so easy to be hard to understand, very easy. All you have to do is not know what you're talking about and nobody else will either."[67]

94. Avoid single hook fishing.
Fishermen often engage in trot line fishing to multiply the chance to catch fish. This method consists of fishing line with numerous baited hooks attached placed in the water between two anchors. The Christian ought to employ this method in fishing for souls. This trot line might bear the hook of a gospel tract; evangelistic movie; audio evangelistic sermon; evangelistic letter; evangelistic book and personal evangelism. As with fishing the soulwinner who utilizes this technique increases the likelihood of catching souls.

95. Avoid a know-it-all attitude.
Soulwinners should always be open and willing to learn from other soulwinners. Charles Finney advised, "Give your most intense thought to the study of ways and means by which you may save them (souls). Make this the great and intense study of your life."[68]

96. Avoid soulwinning ruts.
If what the soulwinner or church is doing to reach souls is ineffective then a change is necessary. Lewis Drummond rightly stated, "The church's reluctance to change, update itself, and speak relevantly to our day constitutes a serious problem for more churches than one. When we speak of the necessity for overturning tradition, the reference is essentially to outmoded approaches and

programs that fail to reach a changing mindset and culture. The gospel itself is unchanging...but every generation has the right to hear the Good News in a framework that addresses itself to them in their present sociological environment. This often implies change, perhaps drastic at times."[69]

97. Avoid "the deadening familiarity with the sublime."
The believer must guard against the deadening trap of the gospel becoming *old hat*. Lewis Drummond wrote, "We need to grasp the incredible depths of these realities, even though they seem so familiar to us. Remember, they are not familiar to the unbeliever; and when understood, they are revolutionary."[70]

98. Avoid unsound theology.
After a plea for missionaries, William Carey was told to sit down by a man who said that if God wanted to convert the heathen he would do it without Carey's help. He didn't sit down but aggressively and passionately sought to win the lost.[71] Neither the freedom of man's will nor the sovereignty of God negates the necessity of soulwinning. John Piper's comment about the evangelistic invitation is true of soulwinning, "...pleading with our listeners to make a response to our preaching is not at odds with a high doctrine of the sovereignty of God. When we preach, to be sure, it is God who effects the results for which we long. But that does not rule out earnest appeals for our people to respond."[72] C.H. Spurgeon stated, "Now the gospel is true, whatever else may be false. Whatever doctrine may or may not be of God, the gospel certainly is. The doctrine of sovereign grace is not contrary to the gospel, but perfectly consonant therewith. God has a people whom no man shall number, whom he hath ordained unto eternal life. This is by no means in conflict with the great declaration, "He that believeth on him is not condemned." If any man who ever lived, or ever shall live, believes in Jesus Christ, he hath eternal life. Election or no election, if you are resting upon the Rock of Ages you are saved. If you, a guilty sinner, take the righteousness of Christ, - if, all black and foul and filthy, you come to wash in the fountain filled with blood, - sovereignty or no sovereignty, rest assured of this, that you are redeemed from the wrath to come."[73]

99. Avoid attacking a sin.
In the devil's den expect to find drugs, beer bottles, pornographic magazines, and foul language. These things are but the symptom of the great sin of rejection of Jesus Christ as Lord and Savior. The soulwinner must remain focused on the chief need of the sinner and make clear the way and how of salvation. It is good to remember in soulwinning that fish are cleaned after they are caught.

100. Avoid contentment with empty baskets.
The soulwinner must ever guard against contentment with empty nets and useless hooks. The heart of any soulwinner who is not winning souls should be broken

asunder with pain and anguish until he does.

101. Avoid misuse of scripture.
A text that is used out of context as a proof-text is a pretext. As soulwinners we must be careful not to pull a text out of its biblical context to *prove* a point for which it has no real theological bearing. Revelation 3:20 may be used in soulwinning with theological integrity. When sharing this text, state that though its context deals with God's invitation to His church it nonetheless depicts His heart for the unsaved.

102. Avoid fishing in the same pond.
C. H. Spurgeon said , "We would do better if we went further afield. We are fools to waste time in the shallows of our churches, when the deep outside teems with waiting fish. Invite the often-invited, certainly, but do not forget that those who have never been invited as yet have not been hardened by refusals."[73]

103. Avoid being surprised.
Howard Ramsey declared, "Don't ever be surprised when a lost man acts like a lost man."[75] In no more important arena is such an expectation necessary than in witnessing. Expect profanity, defiance, and distain for God and realize it is but the consequence of man's Adamic nature.

104. Avoid missed opportunities due to their unlikely potential.
Charles G. Trumbull wrote, "No opportunity is so slight or trifling that it can safely be passed by. The "trifles" in this work, rejected of men, may become the cornerstone in life-buildings planned by the Master-Builder. If we admit of any opportunity that it is too trifling to use, we are sure to lose priceless opportunities. We are especially in danger of missing the opportunities that are close at hand – the commonplace, everyday openings; and in so doing to overlook the souls nearest to us who need our help. "It may be a small matter for you to speak the one word for Christ that wins a needy soul – a *small matter to you* but it is *everything to him.*"[76]

105. Avoid believing God will save the lost apart from human involvement.
Andrew Bonar declared that there will not be a redeemed soul in Heaven who has not a human thumb-mark upon it. He is biblically correct in making that assertion. Frankly put, if you and I fail to tell, men and women will die and go to Hell.

FIVE

The Coward Factor In Soulwinning

More people are amazed at our silence then offended at our witness.[1]
Alvin I. Reid

Many who feel that they cannot visit and fear to try, turn out to be the most effective visitors once they have gotten into it.[2] C.E. Autrey

Fear is a stifling, stultifying, scourging thing for soulwinners[3]. Roland Q. Leavell

For God gave us not a spirit of fearfulness; but of power and love and discipline. Be not ashamed therefore of the testimony of our Lord. Paul the Apostle

Fear. The Apostle Paul experienced it (I Corinthians 2:3). All believers do. It's not unnatural or unspiritual. The key is not to allow fear to paralyze and deter soulwinning efforts. Paul didn't. We mustn't. There are eleven types of fear that must be overcome for the believer to be an effective passionate soulwinner.

1. *The fear of fumbling the ball.* Do you fear that in sharing the gospel that someone will catch you ill prepared? Is it that you feel inadequate to tell others of Christ? This fear paralyzes soulwinning efforts. The solution to this fear is learning how to effectively share the gospel. Take time to work at learning how to be a master soulwinner like Jesus. Thomas Edison worked hard on inventing the phonograph. He had grave difficulty in perfecting the sound. He said, "I would speak into the machine the word 'specia,' and the hateful thing would answer back 'pecia.' I worked on that difficulty eighteen hours a day for seven months until finally I conquered it." If Edison valued the invention of such a machine that much how much more should believers value the winning of souls. Christians should be willing to go without sleep if need be to practice, study, practice, study how to win souls until they perfect the right "sound."[4] The knowing how of soulwinning produces a confidence that destroys the fear of fumbling the ball.

2. *The fear of execution.* This fear deals with one's ability to tell how one is saved. As a high school athletic trainer the coach surprised me when he informed me I would be dressing out for the homecoming football game. Obviously I was fearful as I hit the field that I would foul up but after the first play that fear banished. Similarly, the Lord has told every believer to dress out for soulwinning and for most that creates nervousness and fear. Rest assured, Trembling Heart, that once you knock on that first door and talk to that first person about Christ, fear will dissipate and the more you "stay on the field" the less fear will surface. The Lord has promised to be with your every step and immerse each soulwinning contact with the power of His Holy Spirit (Acts 1:8). Don't allow fear to keep you on the sideline. Jeremiah feared he could not do God's work due to his timidity,

but he did. Moses feared his lack of ability to deliver the Israelites out of captivity, but he did. You may fear dressing out and making that first contact, but this is possible by the Lord's grace. Many fears are only conquered through confrontation; they cannot be overcome simply by reading a book or receiving classroom instruction. Mark Twain is attributed with saying, "I know a man who grabbed a cat by the tail and learned 40% more about cats then the man who didn't."[5] Experience certainly is one of the soulwinner's greatest teachers and one of fear's greatest conquerors.

A skeptic had argued with and won out over every preacher for miles around his town. In this town was a blacksmith who loved souls. One night God laid the infidel upon the heart of the blacksmith so heavily he could not sleep for thinking and praying for him. That night as he was wrestling with God in prayer for this man's soul he begged God to send someone to witness to him who had the wisdom and power to win over his arguments and lead him to Christ. It was then the Lord spoke to him saying, "You go — go now at the midnight hour." He tried to plead with God to send someone more gifted in soulwinning because he felt he was no match for a man who talked down the ministers. The call of God was relentless saying, "Get up and go see the man and tell him about my love for him." At three o'clock in the morning the blacksmith finally went to this man's house awaking him out of sleep. Upon asking the blacksmith his purpose for coming he responded, "God has so disturbed me about your lost soul that I just had to get up and come over and beg you to be saved." This so shocked the infidel he forgot all about his arguments and was noticeably moved as the blacksmith shared scripture. At the invitation of the blacksmith to kneel with him to be saved; he fell to his knees and cried out to God for salvation. What the trained preachers could not do, the unlearned blacksmith did with his love and passion for this man.[6] Oh, soulwinner, doubt not that God will use you to win souls as with this blacksmith regardless of knowledge or experience. A soulwinner who has ability with availability will win souls but one who has ability without availability never will. Despite ability stay available and God will use you to win souls.

The famous evangelist D. L. Moody once was criticized for his method of winning souls. To that critic he kindly said, "I like my way of doing it better than your way of not doing it." A young boy was courting a beautiful young lady on the front porch swing of her home. He looked at her and said, "If I had a thousand lips I would kiss your rosy cheek; if I had a thousand eyes I would stare into your beautiful blue eyes; if I had a thousand arms I would embrace you so tight." The young girl looked at him and said, "Just use what you've got." In soulwinning don't harp on what you would do if you had the abilities of a Graham or Finney but rather "Just use what you've got."

3. *The fear of rejection.*
Jesus, the master soulwinner, was often rejected. John declared of Jesus, "He

came unto His own but His own received Him not" (John 1:11). Ultimately this rejection nailed Him to the Cross. The soulwinner risks personal rejection for both his righteous life and verbal witness. He must weigh this risk against man's eternal rejection by God if he fails to tell.

4. *The fear of failure.*

No person is a failure who attempts to win souls regardless of the outcome of such efforts. If you are faithful to sow the seed, the Lord counts you successful. Soulwinning is a win-win task, never win-fail. D.L. Moody exclaimed, "It's better to tell others about Jesus in a faltering way. . .than never to tell them at all."[7]

5. *The fear of turning some off.*

The fear of turning a person off to the gospel is always a possibility, one of which the soulwinner must be extremely cautious. This fear however must not prevent a witness. The gospel in and of itself (no fault of the soulwinner) will be a "turn off" to some. Paul stated, "Now thanks *be* unto God, which always causeth us to triumph in Christ, and maketh manifest the savor of his knowledge by us in every place. For we are unto God a sweet savor of Christ, in them that are saved, and in them that perish: To the one *we are* the savor of death unto death; and to the other the savor of life unto life" (2 Corinthians 2:14-16) and "For the preaching of the cross is to them that perish foolishness; but unto us which are saved it is the power of God" (2 Corinthians 1:18).

6. *The fear of your own hypocrisy.*

It may be that you stagger and struggle with witnessing due to a fear that those to whom you share the gospel may point to personal inconsistencies. The fear of people saying, "Here you are telling me how to live and yet you go to the same questionable places, watch the same obscene movies, and engage in the same disreputable activities as I do. Thank you, but no thank you" stops you from witnessing. Clean up your act and this fear will be history. The believer must first be different before he can make a difference. I deal with the need of purity of heart and life in soulwinning in Chapter Three, The Character Factor in Soulwinning.

7. *The fear of reaction by other saints.*

At one point in my ministry a fellow minister spoke despairingly of my witnessing of Christ to people in places like parks, restaurants, sports events pressing for a decision. I respected this servant of God and his condemnation at the first staggered me until I was overwhelmed with God's assurance that I was doing the right thing in the proper manner. As I have matured in the faith I can honestly say it doesn't bother me if a saint or sinner approves of my soulwinning efforts.

As a soulwinner you will have your critics. Ridicule goes with the territory. Stand firm in sure confidence that you are doing the greatest work on earth and refuse to allow any critic to discourage or sidetrack you from witnessing fervently and winning souls passionately. To the persecuted soulwinner Jesus declared, "Blessed are ye when men shall reproach you, and persecute you, and say all manner of evil against you falsely, for my sake. Rejoice, and be exceedingly glad: for great is your reward in heaven: for so persecuted they the prophets that were before you" (Matthew 5: 11-12). Soulwinners must have backbone not to allow the objections of others to hinder witnessing efforts.

Several years ago a prominent Southern Baptist pastor stated that passing out gospel tracts was "tacky evangelism." This saddened my heart because my personal experience had proved tracts were effective in winning souls to Jesus Christ. I shutter to think how many saints who were distributing tracts seeking souls for Christ stopped because of his remarks. I caution the soulwinner not to allow the conviction or opinion of other saints regarding soulwinning to alter his.

8. The fear of resentment.
W. D. Weatherford stated, "Many Christians fear to speak to another person about the Christ friendship lest it will be resented. This, however, assumes that we are forcing on others that which is not worth having. You do not fear to give a friend a beautiful Christmas present, sharing with him your blessing of life. But you do hesitate to share with him your experience with Him who made the Christmas and gave to it all its present significance. Instead of fearing to share with others, we should rejoice to do so."[8]

9. The fear of conversation with a stranger.
The introverted and timid personalities of some hold them back from soulwinning. These saints may want to witness but they just cannot stand the thought of approaching a stranger. Is there any hope for these to become vibrant and fruitful soulwinners? Can their disposition be altered?

In Exodus 3 - 4 the account of God's call to Moses to be Israel's deliverer is recorded. A frightened Moses responded to this call by stating "O my Lord, I am not eloquent, neither heretofore, nor since thou hast spoken unto thy servant: I am slow of speech and of a slow tongue" (Exodus 4: 10). Moses tried to excuse God's call to go to Pharaoh because of his "lack of fluent speech" and "eloquence." In fact he felt so inadequate for the task that he asked God for a replacement of which angered the Lord (v 13 -14). God responded to Moses, "I will be with your mouth and with his (Aaron's) mouth, and teach you what ye shall do" (v 15). In essence God told Moses, "I can transform your disposition and enable you to do this task effectively. I will make it easier for you by teaming you up with Aaron. You two together can get the job done."

If God can change the disposition of cowardly Moses into a courageous one He certainly can alter any man's in the same manner. As with Moses every believer has been called to go into spiritual Egypt to grant deliverance to the captives through the Lord Jesus Christ. Excuses about one's inabilities or shyness don't hold water. Christ will "be with your mouth…and teach you what you are to do" and even team you up with an "Aaron" if necessary. Soulwinners must confidently trust the Lord to perform this work in and through them.

In Numbers 22 God used a mule to communicate His message to Balaam and that mule's talking saved Balaam's life (Numbers 22:27 – 33). Obviously, if God can use a dumb mule to communicate His word He is more than able to use the most feeble and ignorant Christian to speak the gospel message saving the lost.

10. *The fear that converts will not go and grow.*
The soulwinner's priority is to reach unsaved men with the gospel. His next priority is conservation of converts. I have included in this book a chapter that details how to do effective follow up that when implemented will go a long way in insuring that those won will grow in the knowledge and grace of our Lord Jesus Christ negating this fear.

11. *The fear of false professions.*
No soulwinner, regardless how experienced and masterful in leading men to Christ, bats a thousand in harvesting genuine commitments. Jesus had His Judas, Phillip had his Simon Magus, and D. L. Moody had his drunk. The soulwinner certainly must take every step to insure decisions made are based upon genuine repentance and faith in the Lord Jesus Christ but then He must rest them in the hands of God. Don't despair in witnessing due to bitter disappointment with "decisions" experienced in the past. Learn from them but don't allow the fear of this happening again hinder soulwinning. In times when I am uncertain of a person's genuine desire to be saved I say, "If I left right now without you praying to receive Christ would that be okay with you?" Sinners who are convicted of sin and their need to be saved quickly object to my departure.

The Lord's command not to fear is the most repeated command in scripture. The saturation of the heart and mind with the *fear not* promises of God will incite holy boldness in the soulwinner. Personalize these promises using them as prayers claiming deliverance from hindering fear.

The Soulwinners "Fear Not" Promises

"And the LORD appeared unto him the same night, and said, I am the God of Abraham thy father: fear not, for I am with thee, and will bless thee, and multiply thy seed for my servant Abraham's sake." (Genesis 26:24)

"Be strong and of a good courage, fear not, nor be afraid of them: for the LORD thy God, he it is that doth go with thee; he will not fail thee, nor forsake thee." (Deuteronomy 31:6)

"And the LORD, he it is that doth go before thee: he will be with thee, he will not fail thee, neither forsake thee: fear not, neither be dismayed." (Deuteronomy 31:8)

"And the LORD said unto Joshua, Fear not, neither be thou dismayed: take all the people of war with thee, and arise, go up to Ai: see, I have given into thy hand the king of Ai, and his people, and his city, and his land." (Joshua 8:1)

"The LORD is my light and my salvation; whom shall I fear? the LORD is the strength of my life; of whom shall I be afraid?" (Psalms 27:1)

"Fear thou not; for I am with thee: be not dismayed; for I am thy God: I will strengthen thee; yea, I will help thee; yea, I will uphold thee with the right hand of my righteousness." (Isaiah 41:10)

"What time I am afraid, I will trust in thee. In God I will praise his word, in God I have put my trust; I will not fear what flesh can do unto me." (Psalms 56:3-4)

"They that sow in tears shall reap in joy. He that goeth forth and weepeth, bearing precious seed shall doubtless come again with rejoicing bringing his sheaves with him." (Psalms 126:5-6)

"For He himself has said, and the statement is on record, I will not, I will not cease to sustain and uphold you. I will not, I will not, I will not let you down. So that, being of good courage, we are saying, The Lord is my helper. I will not fear. What shall man do to me? (Hebrews 13:5-6 WEUSTNT)

What fear impedes your soulwinning efforts? What steps can you take to thwart them in order to be a soulwinner bringing friends, acquaintances, classmates, family members and strangers to Christ before the opportunity is forever gone?

The story is told about a master violinist who publicized that in an upcoming concert he would use an unusually expensive violin. People packed into the hall on that designated day to hear the great violinist play that expensive violin. The crowd applauded the violinist for a most excellent performance. He then startled everyone when he took the violin and threw it upon the floor stumping it to pieces and walked off the stage. A few moments later, the stage manager said to the crowd, "Ladies and gentlemen, the violin that was just destroyed was only a twenty-dollar violin. The maestro will now return to play on the advertised instrument." He did so and few could discern any difference between the two musical instruments. It's not the violin but primarily the violinist that makes the music. Most of us are twenty-dollar violins or less but the Master can use us to sound forth beautiful music touching many lives for His Glory and Honor.[9] Don't discount your usefulness and potential as a soulwinner for in the hands of God you become a mighty tool that He will use.

SIX

The Confrontation Factor In Soulwinning

Mass crusades, to which I have committed my life, will never finish the job; but one to one will.[1] *Billy Graham*

The winning of individuals by individuals in personal conversation is the main way to win souls.[2] *John R. Rice*

This chapter is intentioned simply to be one of "Helps to the soulwinner" on how to initiate a witness and make a soulwinning presentation. Thirty-two years in vocational evangelism has taught me that some authors and instructors of soulwinning unintentionally have made a task that ought to be enjoyably simplistic difficult and stressful. This certainly is not how God intended it nor how Jesus did it. Soulwinning to Jesus was a natural outflow of who He was and His love for the eternally damned. It must be the same for all who win souls.

In soulwinning one can expect to experience three "sound barriers," much like the sound barrier through which an airplane passes. Each can rattle the nerves and produce stress. The first "sound barrier" is moving the conversation from the physical realm to the spiritual. The second is boldly asking the sinner if he would be willing to receive Christ and the third is when the soulwinner presses for a decision on the spot. The soulwinner will face fear and hesitation with each of these "sound barriers" which will grow more intense the further the witness progresses necessitating a jet propulsion blast of Holy Spirit power to get through.[3]

The transition from front door to conversation to confrontation with the gospel requires studious preparation, sensitivity and discernment.

How to get into the witness?

1. Get into the witness by using FORM.
The letters of FORM acrostically can guide the soulwinner in his witness. He should inquire about one's Family, Occupation, Religious affiliation, and then proceed in sharing the gospel Message.

2. Get into the witness by using AIRS.
In witnessing to college students use the letter of AIRS acrostically to ask about their Academic major, Interests, Religious affiliation, and then Share with them the plan of Salvation.

3. Get into the witness by using Questions.

(1) "May I share with you the greatest discovery of my life?"

(2) "Have you come to that place in your life where you know with all certainty that you are going to Heaven when you die?" Follow up with asking, "May I have a few minutes to share from the Bible how you can know with complete assurance?"

(3) "If you were to stand before the Judgment Bar of God today and He asked "Why should I let you into my Heaven?" how would you answer?"

(4) "Where are you going?"
This is a good question to begin witnesses on buses, airplanes or trains. Follow up on this question by asking, "Where are you really going when you leave this life?" Most will either give you a blank look or honestly say, "I don't know." The door then is open to explain where those who know Jesus are going and where those who do not know Him are going.[4]

(5) "Has anyone ever taken the Bible and shown you what it teaches about how one is saved? May I?"

4. Get into the witness by using gospel tracts.
Gospel tracts are excellent door openers to a presentation of the gospel. Hand the unsaved the tract Where will you be five minutes after you die? asking "Have you ever thought about where you would go at death?" Tell the person you have seriously pondered this important question and now know its answer. Proceed to share a witness as to how you know and how they also can know their eternal destiny. Not all tracts are created equal so utilize wisdom in the selection of the gospel tracts you distribute. Probably every soulwinner has been fooled into picking up what appears to be a twenty dollar bill from the sidewalk or restaurant bathroom counter only to discover it's a gospel tract. This deceptive tract is a turn off to the very people the soulwinner is attempting to reach. The Truth should never be masqueraded in a lie.

"There is a way of offering a tract in the street which will insure its acceptance, and another way which will prejudice the receiver against it: you can shove it in a person's hand so roughly that it is almost an insult, or you can hold it out so deftly that the passer-by accepts it with pleasure. Do not thrust it upon him as if it were writ, but invite him to accept it as if it were a ten-pound note. Our fish need delicate handling. A certain painter, when asked how he mixed his colors, replied, "With brains, sir," and we must fish for the souls of men in like fashion. If you are to win souls, you must not be fools. Men will no more succeed in the Lord's business than they will in their own unless they have their wits about them. If Christ's work be done in a slovenly or churlish manner, it will answer no man's purpose, but prove labor in vain." [5]

5. Get into the witness by using a Current or Past Event.

The soulwinner could effectively use the comments of President George Bush about the death of the Columbia astronauts to open a witness. He said though these astronauts have not returned to earth, "We pray that they safely arrived at home." The soulwinner should then ask, "What do you think is necessary for a person to arrive safely at home (Heaven) at death?" Upon hearing their response the soulwinner then shares what the scripture teaches is necessary for one to enter Heaven.

Another effective witness starter especially to golfers is the unexpected and sudden death of PGA golfer Paine Stewart. Paine boarded a Lear Jet in Orlando, Florida, at 9:19 the morning of October 25, 1999. He died shortly afterwards. USA Today the next day carried a photo of Paine's Lear Jet escorted by US Fighter Jets. The caption read, "Final Flight." In sharing this story the soulwinner could then ask, "Have you ever thought about when you might take your Final Flight? What do you think one has to do to be ready for it? Paine Stewart was ready for his Final Flight for he made preparation years earlier by receiving Jesus Christ into his life as Lord and Savior. You can be ready for yours whenever and wherever it may occur by doing the same."

6. Get into the witness by using a Pencil and Eraser.

Seated near the prospect write a word on a piece of paper with a pencil and misspell it purposefully. As you begin to erase it casually say, "Isn't an eraser a wonderful thing? I am so grateful for the person who invented it. I guess everyone has made a spelling mistake necessitating the use of an eraser to blot it out so they could start new. But what man needs more than anything is an eraser that can blot out all his mistakes, errors and sins. I certainly do. How about you? The big question then is how can mans sin be erased so he can start new."[6] The soulwinner at this point then can move into a witness about God's Sin Eraser, the blood of the Lord Jesus Christ (I John 1:7; Acts 3:9).

7. Get into the witness by using a Silver Dollar.

The soulwinner using this approach shows a silver dollar to the prospect calling on him to pay attention to the word "Liberty" found on one of its sides. (1) Talk about the freedom in America this word represents and its great cost. (2) Tell of the freedom God has made possible for all people through the death, burial and resurrection of His son, the Lord Jesus Christ. Isaiah proclaims that Jesus came into this world to bring "liberty to the captive" (Isaiah 61:1).[7]

8. Get into the witness by using a Badge or Button.

Purchase a large bold colored button or badge and wear it on your coat, shirt or blouse. Upon an inquiry as to what it means respond in saying, "It is to remind me to give you this tract that tells of God's wonderful love and plan for your life."

9. Get into the witness by riding horseback on something the unsaved state.

The soulwinner should be alert to "door openers" the unsaved provide in conversation and immediately redeem them. I was taking my morning run when I was joined by another runner who told me it was his thirtieth birthday and that he had heard that "life begins at thirty." This immediately opened the door for a witness on what the Bible teaches about the beginning of real life. He received the message joyously and was converted.

Running an unfamiliar road I asked a farmer in the field the shortest direction to the town of Eastover. In thanking this man for his directions I asked if anyone had ever given him directions to Heaven to which he said no. This provided me with the opportunity to tell this man how one can enter Heaven.

I was at a restaurant mentoring a "preacher boy" and the waitress asked if he were my son. I replied that he wasn't my son but my brother in Christ. I told her if she was a Christian she was our sister. She wasn't but said her mother and pastor had been talking to her much about becoming one and just the night before she tried to pray about it. Realizing God was at work in this encounter I shared what was necessary for salvation, gave her a tract pinpointing the sinner's prayer, and instructed her to find a quiet place to pray that prayer if she indeed wanted to become a Christian. This she joyously did.

The cashier at a carwash was reading a book as I approached to pay. I inquired about the book and she began telling me the various subjects it covered. I was able to piggyback her response into a discussion of some of the various subjects of the Bible.

A nurse at a doctor's office taking my blood pressure commented that we shared the same birthday. I immediately responded "I have two birthdays, how about you?" She was puzzled for a moment and then replied, "You mean born-again?" "Yes," I replied and then made a witness.

10. Get into the witness with a discussion about their home.
(1) Pay a compliment to the home, its beauty, its warmth, and its décor. (2) Say, "You certainly have a beautiful home and it appears a wonderful fellowship with your family. Did you know the Bible teaches that everybody needs three homes? A person needs a Christian home, a Celestial home and a Church home. May I briefly tell you the importance of each and how you can have all three today?

11. Get into the witness by flipping a coin.
In flipping a coin ask, "How many people would it take flipping a quarter before one of them would hit heads thirty times in a row?" (The answer is a billion.) "Did you know that of the thirty recorded prophecies concerning the birth, the

death and resurrection of Jesus Christ He fulfilled them all?"[8] That's a lot of "heads in a row" isn't it? Did you know the Bible teaches that the reason Jesus came into this world was to make possible the forgiveness of mans sin, bridge mans separation from God that was created by sin and reconcile man to God through His death on the Cross?"

12. Get into the witness through expression of sympathy.
In times of sorrow the soulwinner has an open door to minister and later to present a witness.

13. Get into the witness with matches.
Give away books of matches to people in restaurants, athletic events, and gas stations.[9] Each book should have printed the church logo, address and phone number on the front cover and the gospel in a nutshell on the back. It's a great conversation jump starter.

14. Get into the witness by using a witnessing pen.
Give the prospect a witnessing pen that has printed on its side, "Look unto Me and be ye saved" (Isaiah 45:22) and say, "You are holding in your hand a pen that tells you the way to peace with God and Heaven." This immediately opens the door to share a witness. This is the text from which a layman preached a powerful sermon on a cold, snowy day in London that led to C. H. Spurgeon's conversion.

15. Get into the witness by using prayer.
In restaurant witnessing it is highly effective to offer to pray for the server. Say, "In just a moment I am going to return thanks for my meal and would like to pray for you. Is there any need of which I can specifically pray for you?" You will be amazed at how many doors to share a brief word for Jesus this approach opens. A friend of mine worked tables through college and told me that Christians were notorious for their poor tipping. What a reproach to God and poor testimony for the Christian faith! You should always tip generously but especially when you speak of Christ to the server. A good soulwinning rule is that if you testify, tip generously!

You have heard that when people come to your house you have a witness at your door; when eating out, you literally have a witness at your table. Don't neglect it; you could make a difference in a person's life. R. A. Torrey wrote, "One evening when Mr. Alexander and I were in Brighton, England, one of the workers went from the afternoon meeting to a restaurant for his evening meal. His attention was drawn toward the man who waited upon him, and there came to his heart a strong impression that he should speak to that waiter about his soul, but that seemed to him such an unusual thing to do that he kept putting it off. When the meal was ended and the bill paid, he stepped out of the restaurant, but had such a feeling that he should speak to that waiter that he decided to wait outside until the waiter came out. In a little while the proprietor came out and asked him why he was waiting. He replied that he was waiting to speak with the man who had waited upon him at the table. The proprietor replied, "You will never speak to that man again. After waiting upon you he went to his room and shot himself."[10]

16. Get into the witness with a newspaper.
Morning coffee and a newspaper go together for many people. Provide free newspapers to people entering local restaurants (secure permission from management), laundromats, hospital, and auto service center waiting rooms. Inserted in each newspaper should be an attractive brochure or newsletter of your church detailing location, directions, time of services, contact numbers and the GOOD NEWS. A possible approach in doing this would be to say, "I am from Shandon Baptist Church and today we are giving away free newspapers and information about our church. Please let us know if we can be of help to you in anyway." The soulwinner should be alert for a *permissive* response to share the gospel.

17. Get into the witness by using trigger words or phrases.
Michael L. Simpson in his book *Permission Evangelism* suggested the use of trigger words or phrases to open the door to a gospel witness. He wrote, "Trigger phrases pull a superficial conversation into a personal direction, but without force, so the other person isn't made to feel uncomfortable. A trigger phrase tells the person you are open to revealing a bit of your life if he is curious. It leaves a question hanging between you. If he asks it, you know he cares. If he doesn't care enough about you as a person to ask the question, what makes you think he will be open to you presenting the Gospel? Trigger phrases open the door that leads him toward a point of personal connection where he may or may not give you permission to share your story. Each leading statement intentionally draws them deeper so that you can move to the next step and introduce a trigger word."[11] Late one night studying I received a prank call from a teenage girl. As I answered the phone she said, "I want your bod." Immediately, I responded, "Jesus wants your soul" (trigger phrase). In that she didn't hang up I gained permission to share the Good News, which resulted in her salvation.

Permission Evangelism is like the soulwinner and the prospect chatting as they walk down a hallway toward a door; each favorite response to the believers trigger word or phrase leads them a step closer to the door wherein an evangelistic presentation is made seeking his salvation. If the prospect is unresponsive to a trigger phrase or word in asking the obvious question in this hall walk he is not ready to walk through the door and should be given a gracious way to opt out of the conversation.[12]

18. Get into the witness by feeding washers and dryers.
With a pocket full of quarters and gospel tracts Christians can hang out at local Laundromats *"feeding* washers and dryers looking for open doors to witness.[13]

19. Get into the witness by turning the telephone conversation.
Telemarketers often call saying, "May I have a few minutes to ask you several questions about…?" Turn the conversation immediately into a witnessing opportunity by replying, " I will be happy to if you first will answer just three questions for me." Upon their agreement ask these questions: "Do you know for certain that if you died today you would go to Heaven?" "In standing before God if He asked why He should let you into my Heaven how would you respond?" "May I share with you how you can be certain of Heaven?"

20. Get into the witness by *tract and treat.*
At Halloween insert in trick-or-treat bags along with candy a gospel tract, book, Bible or evangelistic movie. Include contact information and brochures about your church.

What Influence People to Salvation[14]	
Advertisement	2%
Organized visitation	6%
Contact by Pastor	6%
Friends and Relatives	86%

The Evangelistic Presentation
Once the initial contact is made and the ice is broken the soulwinner should move forward into his witnessing presentation. How? My father often took me fishing when I was a child. He was a master at it, and as a novice I earnestly looked to him for direction as to how to catch fish. He would tell me when to use crickets, earthworms, or catawbas on my hook and which kind of fishing pole or rod to use. I learned that the type of bait and pole used is all-important in catching fish. As fishers of men there is only one bait to be used and that is "Jesus Christ and Him crucified." No other bait can attract, convict and then convert the sinner. This is why our 'fishing' must be always Christo-centric. Jesus said, "If I be high and lifted up, I will draw all men to me" (John 12:32). A fishing and tackle shop posted a card that read, "Flies with which to catch fish in this locality." In fishing various types bait is necessary for different regions to catch fish but not so in fishing for men. The gospel bait is effective regardless of the locale. It need not and must not be altered. There can be and should be many different rods or poles (methods) the soulwinner uses on which to place the bait. The choice of fishing pole used is determined by the fishpond in which one is fishing (campus, community, prison, mission field), the type fish one is trying to catch (students, adults, children), and one's ability to use it to catch fish. A rod and reel in the

hands of my father could be used to catch large bass but in my hands nothing but grass.

One fishing tackle supplier boasts of its ability to access 252 different types of rods alone. They state, "Carp and pike fishing demands fishing powerful rods." There are likewise many different types of spiritual fishing poles available but "heart and soul fishing demands fishing powerful rods." Exercise spiritual discretion in their selection and use. Methods of soulwinning must never override the soulwinner's message nor hinder his effort in winning souls. In soulwinning there are no sure-fire methods. The soulwinner must take his clue from the Holy Spirit as to which method to use if he is to be productive. C. H. Spurgeon said, "We cannot make the fish bite, but we can do our best to draw them near to the killing bait of the Word of God; and once they are there, we will watch and pray till they are fully taken."[15]

Stephen Olford wrote, "It must be recognized that no rigid rule can be laid down for personal soulwinning, or, indeed, for any other form of Christian service. God is sovereign in His work and never deals with any two people in exactly the same way."[16]

Helen Smith Shoemaker wrote, "People are lost and need to be found. They search for God, ultimate reality and faith, but they cannot by themselves find 'the most important door in the world', which is 'the door through which people walk when they find God.' " Poetically, Shoemaker describes this truth,

People crave to know where the door is
and all that so many ever find
Is only a wall where a door ought to be.
They creep along the wall like blind men,
With outstretched, groping hands.
Feeling for a door, knowing there must be a door,
Yet they never find it.

Man die outside that door, as starving beggars die
On cold nights in cruel cities in the dead of winter –
Die for want of what is within their grasp.
They live on the other side of it –
Live because they have not found it."[17]

It is the task of the soulwinner to show man "the Door" (John 10:9).

1. Gospel Booklets.
There are many excellent plans of salvation outlined step by step in booklet format

simplifying the presentation of the gospel. Among these are Campus Crusade's *The Four Spiritual Laws*; Billy Graham's *Steps to Peace with God* and the Southern Baptist Convention's *Eternal Life* and *How To Have a Full and Meaningful Life.*

A sample presentation of my soulwinning booklet *False Hopes of Heaven* will serve as a pattern for each of these plans.

"I have a little booklet that I would like to give to you entitled *False Hopes of Heaven*. May I briefly share it with you? (Trigger question) It opens with this direct question, "Would you like to know for certain that you are going to heaven?" (Pause to await their reply) I know I do. The Bible makes clear that not everyone who believes they will go to heaven at death will." Continue to read slowly through the booklet occasionally pausing to ask, "Is this making sense? Do you understand what it is stating?" Stay alert not to be distracted with non-essential questions postponing dealing with them to the end of the witness. At the question, "Have you been holding onto a False Hope?" tread prayerfully and slowly. If they answer, "I have" proceed to the next question which asks, "Would you be willing to say yes to the only true hope of heaven right now?" Upon an affirmative answer continue to read from the booklet, "The only true hope of heaven is a personal relationship with Jesus Christ. Let me share how you can possess a true hope of heaven." Read slowly the next three pages. Now you are at the point to call for a decision by asking, "Would you pray with me to receive Christ into your life right now?" Upon an affirmative answer invite the person to pray the sinner's prayer recorded in the booklet.

2. Colors of Salvation Card.
This lamented card has the colors of salvation on one side and the explanation of each on the other. I have used it often with great effectiveness with all ages. This presentation could be adapted for use with the Wordless book and the Witnessing bracelet. This card is available through this ministry inclusively.

THE COLORS OF SALVATION EXPLAINED

Hello, my name is Frank Shivers and I'm visiting in behalf of Shandon Baptist Church. I have a little card of colors that I would like to give you. These colors tell of God's great LOVE and man's great NEED. May I take just a few minutes to share it with you?

BLACK COLOR
Black stands for man's sin against God that resulted in separation and condemnation. Do you know what sin is? (Give opportunity to respond) Yes, sin

is disobeying God. It is failure to keep His commandments. The Bible states, "All have sinned and fallen short of the glory of God" (Romans 3:23). All mankind is in the same boat spiritually and in need of a Savior. This sin has power to separate a person from God now and in eternity. The Bible in Romans 6:23 states, "The wages (consequences) of sin is death." Sin also hinders a person from experiencing God's best intentions for life. Jesus said, "You would not come to me, that ye might have life" (John 5:40). Man's greatest need is forgiveness of sin and reconciliation to God. But how?

RED COLOR

Red stands for the precious Blood of Jesus Christ that was shed at Calvary in response to man's desperate need and God's amazing love. There is nothing that sinful man can do to save himself from the consequences of his sin. Nothing. But Jesus Christ is able. John says, "The blood of Jesus Christ cleanses from all sin" (I John 1:7). John 3:16 declares, "For God so loved the world (you) that He gave His only begotten son that whosoever (you) believes on Him should not perish but have everlasting life." Friend, God gave His only Son to the death of a Cross to bear mans sin so that he might be reconciled (saved) to God. This same Jesus God rose from the dead! He now is seated at the right hand of God in Heaven.

WHITE COLOR

White stands for the soul's cleansing upon repentance and faith in Jesus Christ. The condition of salvation (forgiveness) is "repentance toward God and faith in the Lord Jesus Christ" (Acts 20:21). To repent is to change one's mind about both the sin of which he has committed and the place he gives God in life. The moment a person turns from sin to the Lord Jesus Christ receiving Him as Lord and Savior new life begins. The Bible states, "Come and let us reason together saith the Lord, though your sins be as scarlet they shall be as white as snow, though they be red as crimson they shall be as wool" (Isaiah 1:18). Man, in bringing his sin to Jesus Christ in repentance and faith is forgiven, made white as snow and becomes a child of God! Jesus declares, "But as many as received him, to them gave he power to become the sons of God, *even* to them that believe on his name" (John 1:12).

BLUE COLOR

Blue stands for one's confession of Christ openly in believers' baptism. Baptism does not save a person; one is baptized because of salvation. Scripture is crystal clear in its teaching that the new believer must be baptized as soon as feasibly possible. Luke admonishes, "Repent and be baptized every one of you in the name of the Lord Jesus Christ for the remission of sins" (Acts 2:38). Baptism is a bold declaration to the world that a person believes in Jesus' death, burial and resurrection; testifies of personal regeneration and submission to His Lordship. Baptism is the very first order of business for the new Christian and is an outward demonstration of an inward experience of which one ought not to be ashamed. Jesus declared, "Whosoever therefore shall confess me before men, him will I confess also before my Father which is in heaven. But whosoever shall deny me before men, him will I also deny before my Father which is in heaven" (Matthew 10:32-33).

GREEN COLOR

Green stands for the disciplines essential for spiritual growth. Once a person receives Christ as Savior and Lord he is as a "newborn babe" requiring help to "grow up" in Christ Jesus. Scripture urges the believer to "grow in the grace and knowledge of our Lord and Savior Jesus Christ" (II Peter 3:18). The Christian grows through bible study, prayer, church (worship and fellowship with the saints), mentorship and witnessing. The young believer will not be left to "make it" on his own for Christians will be at his side to "spur" him own to spiritual maturity (Hebrews 10:23-24).

PURPLE COLOR

Purple stands for the Lordship of Christ in the believer's life. Jesus is to be "Lord of all." Acts 10:36 states, "The word which *God* sent unto the children of Israel, preaching peace by Jesus Christ: (He is Lord of all)." As Lord Christ has the say-so about the use of one's time, talent and treasure and is to ever be seated in the place of authority on the throne in the citadel of the heart. Jesus declared, "Why call me Lord, Lord and not do the things, which I say?" (Luke 6:46). The person in whose life Jesus is Lord seeks to live unto His pleasure and purpose 24 - 7.

YELLOW COLOR

Yellow stands for the saint's faithful service to Jesus Christ. Christians are to be "faithful unto death" in service and stand. John admonishes, "Fear none of those things which thou shalt suffer: behold, the devil shall cast *some* of you into prison, that ye may be tried; and ye shall have tribulation ten days: be thou faithful unto death, and I will give thee a crown of life" (Revelation 2:10). Sadly more people start out as great saints then end up great saints. My friend, determine to persevere in service to Christ regardless of cost or consequence with the firm resolve to finish the race well. "These are they that follow the Lamb wherever He goes...for they are without fault before the throne of God" (Revelation 14: 4, 5). Renew your commitment to Christ declaring, "Lord, at any cost, by any road I will follow you without turning back."

GOLD COLOR

Gold stands for the believer's eternal home in Heaven. Heaven awaits the child of God at the end of life's journey. Jesus in speaking of Heaven said, "Let not your heart be troubled: ye believe in God, believe also in me. In my Father's house are many mansions: if *it were* not *so*, I would have told you. I go to prepare a place for you. And if I go and prepare a place for you, I will come again, and receive you unto myself; that where I am, *there* ye may be also" (John 14: 1 – 3). How awesome that day will be when the saved get to see their Savior, Jesus Christ face to face! It surely will not be long before this joy will be realized by all the people of God.

GRAY COLOR
Gray stands for the Valley of Decision in which you now reside. The prophet Joel cries "Multitudes, multitudes in the valley of decision in the day of the Lord" (Joel 3:14). The Lord calls on man to make a decision concerning personal sin and his relationship to Him. I ask you Pilate's question, "What will you do with Jesus?" You cannot remain neutral. Right now Jesus is "knocking on the door of your heart" seeking entrance. He says, "Behold, I stand at the door, and knock: if any man hears my voice, and opens the door, I will come in to him, and will sup with him, and he with me" (Revelation 3:20). Will you open that door by faith and repentance and receive His free gift of eternal life? Jesus promises that if you will open the door He will come in! Again the Bible states, "For whosoever shall call upon the name of the Lord shall be saved" (Romans 10:13). Is there any good reason why you could not call upon His name right now to save you? Surely there is not. Will you pray with me to receive Christ into your life as Lord and Savior?

Color of Salvation Card Hints
In witnessing to an unsaved person focus on the first three colors. Explain what each of these colors represent and then drop down to the gray color calling for a salvation decision. Once a person receives Christ share what the remaining colors represent, namely what now is expected.

In witnessing to a saved person review the first three colors making sure they have met God's condition for salvation and then deal most with the other colors that call for commitment. Next use the gray color to call for a decision of recommitment to Christ.

3. Personal Testimony.
One of the greatest methods of soulwinning is the use of one's salvation testimony. The soulwinner should take diligence in its writing to structure it for easy recall and greatest effectiveness. A personal testimony should include five specific points and easily be shared in three to five minutes.

(1) My life before meeting Christ.
(2) How I came to realize my need of Christ.
(3) What I did to become a Christian.
(4) My life since I became a Christian.
(5) Would you be willing to do as I did and receive Jesus Christ into your life as Lord and Savior?

May I share with you briefly how religion kept me from being saved?

Step 1. At an early age I was baptized and joined the church. My parents compelled me to attend at least two of the three services the church had weekly. I was a Royal Ambassador; president of the church youth group and selected as the outstanding young person in the church. Upon entering college I served as a summer youth worker and later became a student pastor at the age of 18. I worked hard at being religious and righteous in order to gain the approval of God.

Step 2. Upon entering seminary and assuming the pastorate of my third church God began dealing with me about the genuineness of my salvation. He used the Billy Graham movie *For Pete's Sake,* Jack Price's song *It's Real,* and just plain inner restlessness and doubt to open my heart eyes to the truth of my soul's need. It wasn't that I was insincere or purposely living a pretentious hypocritical life but that I was just deceived holding onto the false hope of religious knowledge and morality as meriting the favor of God. The Holy Spirit convicted me that this was so wrong and illumined my heart to the real truth of salvation.

Step 3. It wasn't easy for my selfish pride to acknowledge that I, a church pastor and seminary student, was not saved. I pondered questions like, "What would my church members think? What would my preacher friends say?" Finally after months of the Holy Spirit's dealing within my life on June 9, 1972, at 9:15 p.m. at an old fashioned church altar in South Flomaton, Alabama, I repented of my sin and received Jesus Christ into my life as Lord and Savior. I simply prayed from a heart of sorrow, doubt, and emptiness something like this, "Lord Jesus I am sorry for my sins and I do this night turn from them embracing you as my all in all. Come into my heart and be my Lord and Savior."

Step 4. I can honestly say that from that day to this moment I have had a peace and assurance about my relationship with Jesus Christ. Jesus has filled the emptiness in my heart that religion could not satisfy. I certainly can attest to the truth of the song *Everyday with Jesus is Sweeter than the Day Before.* I wish I could say that my life has always been pleasing to the Lord since I got saved but I cannot. However, He has always been faithful and loving to forgive and restore.

Step 5. Would you be willing to do as I and receive Jesus Christ into your life as Lord and Savior? This may involve you doing as I and saying no to former experiences of religion in order to say yes to the real thing. With complete assurance I can say that if with heartfelt sincerity you repent of sin and in faith look to Jesus to save you, He gloriously will! Scripture states, "For whosoever calls upon the name of the Lord shall be saved" (Romans 10:13). If you would welcome Jesus into your life please take my hand as a sign of that desire and pray with me what many call the sinners prayer. There is nothing magical about these words but if you mean them with all sincerity Christ will certainly hear, forgive and save you.

Roland Q. Leavell said, "It is experience not logic, which grips the heart of a seeking sinner. To tell one's spiritual experience is more convincing than a thousand theories."[18]

4. The Gospel Tract Ladder.
A friend introduced me to this method of soulwinning thirty years ago and it is one of which I have never forgotten. It is a simple but effective approach to sharing the gospel with tracts even for the most timid. It begins with the elementary stage in sharing the gospel and progresses to the most difficult.

Picture a ladder with five rungs.

Rung One is Leave a Tract.
This first step in witnessing through tracts requires no courage for it can be done in secrecy. It simply requires the soulwinner to distribute gospel tracts in places like restrooms, phone booths, bus stations, restaurant menus, or magazines.

Rung Two is Mail a Tract.
This rung demands some boldness but not a heaping lot. The soulwinner simply inserts in payment bills and correspondence a gospel tract.

Rung Three is Pin & Tract.
This step involves the soulwinner wearing a large bold colored badge that prompts others to inquire of its meaning. In response to this inquiry the soulwinner responds, "Oh, it is to remind me to give you this tract that tells you how much God loves you." In this method the unsaved initiates the witness making it easier for the soulwinner. This rung does require more courage than the first two.

Rung Four is Hand a Tract.
This rung involves the soulwinner simply handing a tract to a person asking him/her to read it at their leisure.

Rung Five is Lend a Tract.
More boldness will be needed to step on this rung in soulwinning than the previous ones. The soulwinner using this method actually loans a tract or book to an unsaved person asking for its return as soon as possible. This applies pressure on the unsaved to read the material and provides the soulwinner an opportunity to discuss it with that person upon its return.

Rung Six is Share a Tract.
The soulwinner utilizing this rung walks up to a stranger asking if he might give him a tract that means a lot to him. Once the person accepts it the soulwinner proceeds to share exactly what the tract states seeking to bring the person to a decision for Christ then and there.

The soulwinner should carry several different type tracts to distribute for one may not *fit all*. Choose tracts wisely. Make sure the tracts distributed are biblically sound and are spiritual dynamite.

C. H. Spurgeon began his ministry in distributing tracts. He wrote, "The very first service which my youthful heart rendered to Christ was the placing of tracts in envelopes, and then sealing them up, that I might send them. . . . I might have done nothing for Christ if I had not been encouraged by finding myself able to do a little. Then I sought to do something more, and from that something more, and I do not doubt that many servants of God have been led on to higher and nobler labors for their Lord, because they began to serve Him in the right spirit and manner. . . . I used to write texts on little scraps of paper, and drop them anywhere, that some poor creatures might pick them up, and receive them as messages of mercy to their souls. I could scarcely content myself even for five minutes without trying to do something for Christ. If I walked along the street, I must have a few tracts with me; if I went into a railway carriage, I must drop a tract out of the window; if I had a moment's leisure, I must be upon my knees or at my Bible; if I were in company, I must turn the subject of conversation to Christ, that I might serve my Master. It may be that, in the young dawn of my Christian life, I did imprudent things in order to serve the cause of Christ, but I still say, give me back that time again, with all its imprudence and with all its hastiness, if I may but have the same love to my Master, the same overwhelming influence in my spirit, making me obey my Lord's commands because it was a pleasure to me to do anything to serve my God."[19] May these words from one of the church's greatest soulwinners burn deep into our heart rekindling the passion for souls that has been retarded by the flaming missiles of Hell inciting the return to our first love for both Christ and the unsaved.

5. Evangelistic Movies.
Many have been won to faith in Christ by the viewing of professionally produced, biblically sound, evangelistic movies. I suggest the use of this means to reach some in your neighborhood or college campus. Invite two or three prospects for Christ to your home, dorm room, or apartment for "refreshments and a movie." At the conclusion of the movie do a brief recap and enter into a witness. This evangelistic method may be used on a larger scale by inviting twenty or thirty prospects to view a movie. A Christian movie played an important role in my conversion.

Evangelistic movies I recommend are *The Crossing, Without Reservation, Lay it Down, Second Glance, The Harvest, and Home Run for Rusty (Children)*. Additional evangelistic movies may be reviewed at ChristianCinema.com.

6. The Roman Road Plan.
The most often used and effective plan of soulwinning that I use is the Roman

Road method. This plan is confined to six brief passages in the book of Romans. The soulwinner should mark these verses in his New Testament in a "go to next" manner. This was the first method I ever used in soulwinning.

"May I share with you what scripture teaches a person has to do become a Christian?"

1. Romans 3:23   - The fact of man's sin.
2. Romans 6:23   - The fact of man's separation.
3. Romans 5:8   - The fact of man's substitution.
4. Romans 10: 9 -13   - The fact of man's solution.
5. Romans 10:13   - The fact of man's security

"May I share with you what the book of Romans teaches a person has to do to be saved?"

Step 1. "I want you first to look at Romans 3:23 and read it with me.
"For all have sinned, and come short of the glory of God." Do you know what sin is? It is the failure to keep the Ten Commandments and totally obey the Lord. Boy I certainly am in that category, how about you? Indeed all man is guilty, "there is none righteous, no not one."

Step 2. Now turn to Romans 6:23 and see the effect of this sin. Read it for us.
"For the wages of sin *is* death; but the gift of God *is* eternal life through Jesus Christ our Lord." The word "wages" is an old English word that simply means *salary or pay*check. It is a term used for money received for services rendered. Here it means that the consequence of our sin against Holy God is the paycheck of eternal separation from Him. God would be just to keep us out of heaven and cast us into Hell due to our sin.

Step 3. If the gospel message stopped there you and I both would be utterly lost without hope, but it doesn't. Read Romans 5:8 for us. "But God showed his great love for us by sending Christ to die for us while we were still sinners."(NLT) Man cannot bridge the chasm between Holy God and himself created by his sin. Church going, tithing, doing good things, being religious and even believing in God cannot remedy man's problem. In fact there is nothing man can do to get right with God. I have good news. What man cannot do for himself God has made possible through the Cross of His son the Lord Jesus Christ. You probably can quote John 3:16. It states, "For God so loved the world, that he gave his only begotten Son, that whosoever believeth in him should not perish, but have everlasting life." Read that verse now inserting your name in the place of *world* and *whosoever.* God loves you so much He gave His only Son Jesus to die upon a Cross to make possible your forgiveness and salvation. What awesome love!

Step 4. Next read Romans 10: 9 -13 and Acts 20: 21 for it tells the how of salvation. "That if thou shalt confess with thy mouth the Lord Jesus, and shalt believe in thine heart that God hath raised him from the dead, thou shalt be saved. For with the heart man believeth unto righteousness; and with the mouth confession is made unto salvation. For the scripture saith, whosoever believeth on him shall not be ashamed. For there is no difference between the Jew and the Greek: for the same Lord over all is rich unto all that call upon him. For whosoever shall call upon the name of the Lord shall be saved" (Romans 10:9-13).

"Repentance toward God and faith in the Lord Jesus Christ" (Acts 20:21). To become a Christian you need to repent of your sin and place faith in Jesus Christ (Acts 20:21). Repentance means to change one's mind about his sin and relationship to Jesus Christ. It is to make an "about face" spiritually and to head in the opposite direction by expressing sorrow for sin and placing trust in Jesus Christ as Lord and Savior.

Who do you think the word "whosoever" refers in Romans 10:13? Indeed you, me and everybody else. This is a promise of God regarding salvation. Right now if you will turn from sin; place faith in Jesus Christ believing in what His death, burial and resurrection accomplished for man you certainly will be saved. Isn't that Good News?

Surely there is no reason why you wouldn't want to be saved is there? If you are willing to become a Christian then take my hand as a sign of faith and pray this prayer with me from your heart. "Lord Jesus, I am a sinner in need of your forgiveness. I am sorry for breaking your Law and my disobedience. Thank you for dying on the Cross and being raised from the dead to make my salvation possible. I do invite you into my life to be Lord and Savior. Amen."

Step 5. This step is to grant security and assurance of salvation.
"My friend, what did you just ask Jesus Christ to do for you?" He will respond, "I asked Him to come into my life and forgive me." Do you believe He did? He will respond, "Yes, I do." I want you to read Romans 10:13 again and explain what Jesus is promising in this text. They will state "Jesus is promising to save all those who call upon His name in faith and repentance." You may also choose to use Revelation 3:20 to grant assurance telling the new believer that when anyone opens the door of their heart in faith and repentance to Jesus, He states, "I will come in." Share with the new believer that Paul declares that absolutely nothing can separate the saint from the Savior. He declared, "Who shall separate us from the love of Christ? *shall* tribulation, or distress, or persecution, or famine, or nakedness, or peril, or sword? As it is written, for thy sake we are killed all the day long; we are accounted as sheep for the slaughter. Nay, in all these things we are more than conquerors through him that loved us. For I am persuaded,

that neither death, nor life, nor angels, nor principalities, nor powers, nor things present, nor things to come, Nor height, nor depth, nor any other creature, shall be able to separate us from the love of God, which is in Christ Jesus our Lord" (Romans 8: 35-39).

7. Red glass and Red paper. (Children)
Take a piece of red paper and tell the child it represents the soul that is "red like crimson" (Isaiah 1:18). Explain that this phrase means that man's heart is black with sin due to disobeying God and that sin separates man from God. Secondly take a piece of red glass and tell the child it represents the blood of Jesus Christ shed for the world on Calvary. Place the red glass on top of the red paper and have the child look through it. He will see the color white. Explain that the heart washed in the blood of Jesus is made "white as snow" (Isaiah 1:18).

8. Evangelistic Sermon recordings.
At a restaurant frequented by truck drivers and tourists in Walterboro, South Carolina, one will find a tray of free sermon CDs. This is an indirect but good method of soulwinning. Attain copies of biblical evangelistic messages and make them available free in your town or community at a gas station, restaurant, or store.

9. The F.A.I.T.H. method.
In this method FAITH is an acronym that the soulwinner uses to explain how one can know for certain he/she is going to heaven. The *F* stands for Forgiveness; The *A* stands for Available (forgiveness available for all); *I* stands for Impossible (impossible for God to allow sin into heaven); *T* stands for Turn (necessity of repentance) and *H* stands for Heaven (the place of the eternally saved). The complete presentation of this plan can be downloaded at <pages.preferred.com/ ~7ofus/Faith%20Evangelism.html>.

10. Open-air evangelism.
While a student at Charleston Southern University, I was asked to speak at a Salvation Army service on a Saturday night. Upon arriving, the team and I discovered the door was locked and no one ever showed. I saw youth in the streets nearby so I took the team to that location and conducted an open-air meeting. Thirty persons made a profession of faith. The soulwinner at times needs to take it to the streets collecting a crowd through music and singing for the purpose of confronting the lost personally with the gospel. The Longridge Camp staff and I have done this on the beach with great success.

John Wesley wrote in his journal on March 31, 1731, about his first encounter with open air preaching. He said, "In the evening I reached Bristol, and met Mr. Whitefield there. I could scarce reconcile myself at the first to this strange way of preaching in the fields, of which he set me an example on Sunday; having been all my life (till very lately) so tenacious of every point relating to decency and order, that I should have thought the saving of souls almost a sin, if had it not been done in a church."[20] Whitefield's example led Wesley to become an extremely successful open-air soulwinner.

Qualifications For Open-Air Preachers [21]

1. A good voice
2. Naturalness of manner
3. Self-possession
4. A good knowledge of Scripture and of common things
5. Ability to adapt himself to any congregation
6. Good illustrative powers
7. Zeal, prudence, and common sense
8. A large, loving heart
9. Sincere belief in all he says
10. Entire dependence on the Holy Spirit for success.
11. A close walk with God by prayer
12. A consistent walk before men by a holy life.

C. H. Spurgeon declared to his preacher boys attending his college, " 'Go ye into the highways and hedges and compel them to come in' - albeit it constitutes part of a parable, is worthy to be taken very literally, and in so doing its meaning will be best carried out. We should actually go into the streets and lanes and highways, for there are lurkers in the hedges, tramps on the highway, streetwalkers, and lane-haunters whom we shall never reach unless we pursue them into their own domains. Sportsmen must not stop at home and wait for the birds to come and be shot at, neither must fisherman throw their nets inside their boats, and hope to take many fish."[22]

11. The Good News Glove (Children)
Using a large four-finger glove, color the first finger yellow, the second black, the third red and the last white. Open the witness to the child by asking, "Have you ever seen a glove like this? This glove tells a wonderful story, a story of Good News. That's why we call it the Good News Glove. Do you like to hear Good News? This glove tells 4 things which God wants you to know. These 4 things just fit on the 4 fingers of this glove and on the 4 fingers of your hand."[23] Review the complete presentation of the Good News Glove in Campus Crusade's *Good News* Tract.

12. Operation Andrew.
This method of outreach is based on soul cultivation of the unsaved with the explicit purpose to have them attend an evangelistic service. The Billy Graham Evangelistic Association has utilized this approach in their crusades for years with great effectiveness. Graham's ministry utilizes this method in the following manner.

Operation Andrew comes from John 1:40-42. Andrew met Jesus and he immediately brought his brother to meet Jesus.

LOOK AROUND — your mission field is right where you live, work, or go to school. List names of five individuals you know who need Jesus Christ, whom you will pray for regularly.

LOOK UP — because God changes people through prayer. Pray each day for those on your list that God will give you opportunities to share his love with them.

LOOK OUT — for ways to cultivate friendships with each person on your list and earn their confidence. Spend time with them. An invitation to dinner or a special event will build friendships that can open the way to talk about Christ.

LOOK FORWARD — by beginning to talk with each person on your list about attending an evangelistic event (revival, crusade, evangelistic rally) with you. Choose a specific day to attend, pray and invite them. *LOOK AFTER* — those who respond to Christ during the evangelistic event or begin to show interest in the Gospel, for they need your encouragement. Continue to love and pray for those who do not respond. [24]

13. The Testimony of others.

The sharing of a salvation testimony of someone the person to whom you witness looks up to, admires or respects can be a dynamite witness. The soulwinner should integrate within this testimony the same facts he would share in his personal testimony.

14. Evangelistic Books.

The loaning of evangelistic books is a good method to reach persons who are atheistic, agnostic or skeptical. You loan instead of give the book to a person in order to place responsibility upon them to read it as soon as possible. Upon the return of the book discussion should incur and a witness presented. I suggest specifically for this purpose Josh McDowell's book *The New Evidence That Demands A Verdict*, Lee Strobel's *The Case for Christ,* and Paul Little's *Know Why You Believe.* In 1735 George Whitfield was saved by reading the book *The Life of God in the Soul of Man, a* loan to him from John Wesley. Many years afterward he said, "I know the place...Whenever I go to Oxford, I cannot help running to the spot where Jesus Christ first revealed himself to me, and gave me the new birth."[25] A book was used to convert Whitfield and he turned thousands to Christ through his preaching and soulwinning.

15. II Kings 5:10-11

"And Elisha sent a messenger unto him, saying, Go and wash in Jordan seven times, and thy flesh shall come again to thee, and thou shalt be clean. But Naaman was wroth, and went away, and said, Behold, I thought, He will surely come out to me, and stand, and call on the name of the LORD his God, and strike his hand over the place, and recover the leper." Naaman was a very powerful and influential man who sought out the prophet Elisha for healing of his leprosy. Elisha sent word to him to wash himself seven times in the muddy Jordan River to be cured. Naaman protested believing something more fitting his dignity should be done. Finally his soldiers convinced him to do as the man of God commanded, so swallowing pride he washed himself seven times in the river and was miraculously made whole. The scripture teaches that man is infected with leprosy of the soul due to disobedience toward God and his only hope of salvation (though he may think something more or different be required as Naaman) is "Repentance toward God and faith in the Lord Jesus Christ" (Acts 20:21). Naaman didn't *feel* that taking seven dips in the muddy Jordan River would bring about healing but it did. The sinner may not *feel* that simply trusting Jesus will save him but it certainly will. Faith, not feeling is the key to heart salvation. Paul declared, "For by grace are you saved through faith, and that not of yourselves. It is a gift of God, not of works lest any man should boast" (Ephesians 2: 8-9).

16. Chat Room evangelism.
Thanks to cyber-space technology soulwinning can be done over a computer. Chat rooms are popular places for lonely, confused and hurting people who need Jesus. They also are the place for pedophiles and other sexually perverted individuals who prey upon others. The soulwinner surfer must always be cautiously alert to this danger. Students should only engage in chat room evangelism under the supervision of a church leader or parent. The same safety considerations apply in chat room witnessing as in any other chat room visit, never give your last name, phone number or address; chat only with your own sex; never agree to meet with a person you meet in a chat room and sign off immediately should the conversation drift into an area "off limits." Remember your purpose in visiting the chat room is to share Christ so be fully prepared to do so with simplicity and clarity. It is imperative you possess a firm doctrinal theological understanding in witnessing on-line always ready to give a reason for the Gospel faith.

Dawn Witherspoon, minister of missions and evangelism at a church in Nashville, Tennessee, uses her chat room password name, Connected2Him as a means to initiate a gospel witness. Dawn states when someone asks her what that means, "Bam, I have an immediate way to start talking about Jesus Christ."[26]

17. Surf Evangelism.
A second witnessing approach one can use on the internet involves going "door-to-door" visiting people's web sites, developing relationships via e-mail, and presenting a witness for Christ when the opportunity surfaces. One might call this method of soulwinning *surf evangelism*.[27] The same safety factors apply as with chat room evangelism.

18. Evangelistic letters.
Due to distance or verbal difficulty in witnessing to someone the writing of an evangelistic letter or card is a tool to use. Roland Q. Leavell wrote, "A postage

stamp is a mighty ally in soulwinning. In a letter one can write smoothly and succinctly the essential things of salvation which the unsaved man should believe and accept."[28] C.H. Spurgeon said, "Paper and ink are never better used then in soulwinning."[29] Henry Clay Trumbull was won by a letter. Dr. J.B. Gambrell was so concerned for his stenographer that he dictated an evangelistic letter to a fictitious person. In that letter he poured out his concern for that friend's salvation, outlined the way to be saved and appealed to him to be saved. The next day when the stenographer brought the letter into Dr. Gambrell's office to be signed she testified how it led to her salvation. In response Gambrell told her not to mail the letter for it had reached the one to whom it was intended.[30]

Hints in writing evangelistic letters:
1. Pray for the Holy Spirit's guidance in its writing.
2. Keep it personal and warm — don't let it smell like a form letter.
3. Share briefly your testimony or an evangelistic presentation.
4. Enclose a tract or evangelistic movie requesting feedback.
5. Couch your witness between a warm greeting and cheerful ending.
6. Pray for the letter as you mail it and upon its receipt for God to use to His glory.
7. Keep it simple, brief and non-condemnatory.

---

19. The Ten Commandments and Romans 6:23; 5: 8-10.

In clear view of the prospect use a pencil and draw a straight line down the middle of a piece of paper. Above the first column should be written, "The Ten Commandments" and above the other "You and I." The next step is contrasting each commandment with the sinners conduct, asking the unsaved if he has been guilty of violating that specific command. The unsaved must be brought to understand that one can be guilty of breaking a commandment both in deed and in thought. This type of presentation is used by the Holy Spirit to illumine the lost to their sin and thus need for a Savior (Galatians 3:24).

The Ten Commandments	You and I
No other gods before me	Placing other gods (things) before God
No carved images	False or heartless worship of God
Do not profane God's name	Using God's name in a profane manner
Keep the Sabbath day Holy	Dishonoring of God's day
Honor thy Father and Mother	Disrespect for one's parents
Do not murder	Murder or bitter hatred toward another
Do not commit adultery	Lust or sexual misconduct
Do not steal	Stolen something or ones reputation
Do not lie about others	Speaking untruth
Do not covet	Discontented with what God has provided

The Ten Commandments reveal conclusively that man is guilty before God.

The next step is to point out the consequence for breaking God's commandments (sin). Have the prospect read aloud Romans 6:23, "For the wages of sin is death." Point out that this verse indicates that he and all man deserve eternal separation from God in Hell for breaking God's law. Next show the prospect Romans 5: 8 – 10 which speaks of God's great loving intervention on man's behalf to make possible his forgiveness for this sin, "But God commendeth (demonstrates, shows) his love toward us, in that, while we were yet sinners, Christ died for us.ÿπ Much more then, being now justified by his blood, we shall be saved from wrath through him. For if, when we were enemies, we were reconciled to God by the death of his Son, much more, being reconciled, we shall be saved by his life." Make clear the fact that Jesus Christ is man's only provision for reconciliation to God and that through surrender to Him as Lord and Savior he will be saved from sin's consequences.

C. H. Spurgeon, whose conversion was rooted in conviction that he had broken God's Ten Commandments, wrote, "My hearer, does not the Law of God convince you of sin? Under the hand of God's Spirit does it not make you feel that you have been guilty, that you deserve to be lost, that you have incurred the fierce anger of God? Look here: have you not broken these Ten Commandments; even in the letter, have you not broken them? Who is there among you who has always honored his mother and father? Who is there among you who has always spoken the truth? Have we sometimes borne the witness against our neighbors? Is there one person here who has not made to himself another god, and loved to himself , or his business, or his friends, more than he has Jehovah, the God of the whole earth? Which of you has not coveted his neighbor's house, or his manservant, or his ox, or his donkey? We are all guilty with regard to every letter of the Law; we have all of us transgressed the Commandments."[31]

20. Helping "preacher-boys."
Funding the education of a promising ministerial student or financially undergirding a vocational evangelist or missionary who possesses a passion for souls is an indirect but direct way to win souls. It is my conviction that the believer who enables another to win souls at home or on the mission field is credited in heaven along with that servant for all the souls he reaches for Christ.

21. Vacation Bible School, Revival, Evangelistic Crusades or Rallies, Camps, Church.
Getting the lost to attend a service or event in which the gospel will be presented is a valid method of soulwinning. Many have been won to Christ due to this type of evangelism. At this ministry's camp in Ridgeway, South Carolina over 3, 500 professions of faith have been recorded since 1981. In the past five years, 472,707 people have made professions of saving faith in Christ through Vacation Bible School in the Southern Baptist Convention. It is yet the number one outreach tool

for Southern Baptist churches.[32] Evangelists testify of great harvests of souls in revival and evangelistic meetings especially in churches or arenas where diligent preparation is made. Sunday church services also are excellent reaping times. C.H. Spurgeon states "What can you do to win souls? Let me recommend to those who think they can do nothing, the bringing of others to hear the Word. That is a duty much neglected. Go up with the prayer that your minister's sermon may be blessed, and if you cannot preach yourselves, yet, by bringing others under the sound of the Word, you may be doing what is the next best."[33]

22. Evangelism on its knees.
Prayer is a form of soul winning. Battle the power of Satan on your knees pleading the blood of Jesus for lost souls fervently and faithfully. All can engage in this form of soulwinning, especially the shut-in, physically disabled, hospitalized, and nursing and retirement home resident.

23. Isaiah 53:6
I want to share an actual soulwinning encounter of R. A. Torrey as he used this single text. Approaching a man who had just heard him preach, he asked, "Are you a Christian?" "No sir," he replied. Torrey asked, "Would you become one if I showed you how?" The man said, "I would." Torrey said, "Let's sit down and talk it over." He opened his Bible to Isaiah 53:6 and read, "All we like sheep have gone astray. We have turned every one to his own way." "Is that true of you?" he asked the man. He said, "It is, sir." Torrey then asked, "What are you then?" The man answered, "I am lost." Torrey said, "Now listen to the rest of the verse" - "And the Lord hath laid on Him the iniquity of us all." "Do you believe that?" Torrey asked. The man answered, "Yes. I believe everything in the Bible." Torrey continued, "Do you believe that the Lord hath laid on Him the iniquity of us all? Do you believe that the Lord hath laid on Jesus your sin?" He said, "I do." Torrey said, "What then is all that is necessary for you to do in order to be saved?" "Simply to believe on the Lord Jesus Christ," he said. Torrey inquired, "Will you do it now?" The man answered, "I will." Torrey then said, "Let us tell God so" and they knelt to pray. Upon the conclusion of the prayer Torrey asked, "What are you?" He said, "I am saved. My sins are forgiven." Torrey said, "What are you going to do about it?" He said, "I am going back to my home and set up the family altar and unite with the church."[34]

John R. Rice, commenting on Isaiah 53:6, stated, "It says that all of us have sinned and are lost. It says that the heart of sin is our self-will, our wanting our own way. It says that Jesus Christ has borne all of our sins." Rice tells the story of a English preacher who upon completing a sermon rushed to the train station to catch a train back to London. A man deeply convicted of his sins followed him there and said, "I want to be saved. Please tell me how." With the final train to London about to depart for the night he said, "Do you have a Bible?" "Yes," the lost man replied, "but I do not know where to read." The preacher instructed him to turn to Isaiah 53:6 and asked, "Have you got it?" The man replied, "Yes, Isaiah 53:6." The preacher told him, "Then come in at the first 'all' and come out at the last 'all' and you will be saved." In saying that he boarded the train. The man thought this a strange way to be saved but he went home and did as the preacher instructed. He discovered that the first word in the text is 'all' – "All we like sheep have gone astray." He said to himself, "Well, I can come in there, for I have gone astray. I am a sinner." He was not finished with the preacher's instruction for now he must "come out at the second 'all.' He discovered that the last word in the text is 'all' – 'The Lord hath laid on him (*on Jesus*) the iniquity of us all.' " The man thought, "And I am one of those whose iniquities were laid on Jesus. My sins are paid for! Well, I will come out there, and so I will be saved!"[35]

24. Relationship Evangelism.

G. S. Dobbins stated, "It is a truism that as a rule, we must first win the lost to ourselves before we can win them to our Savior. If the unsaved person in whom I am interested does not believe in me, does not like me, or holds himself aloof from me, it is next to impossible to influence him to accept Christ. Someone else may do it, but I cannot. It is therefore of utmost importance that we seek to be winsome, friendly, attractive in manner and personality. If I can convince anybody that I am interested in him, that I like him for his own sake, that I believe he has possibilities; if I can get him to talk about himself, to reveal his aspirations and ambitions, to confide his hopes and fears; then he will assume toward me a friendly attitude."[36]

Lewis Drummond wrote, "The person-to-person ministry must be utilized, and members can be educated to perform it. Witnessing in the context of meeting pressing needs often opens the door for a reception of the gospel. To repeat John Stott, "A hungry man has no ears." Personal witnessing is often the most effective way to confront the post-moderns with the gospel. This calls for building relationships, which can often be done by the meeting of needs. Relatively few postmoderns are now attending church. The factory worker speaking about Christ to his coworkers, the young person giving the Good News to his or her friends – these are the ones who will make the greatest impact on contemporary society. It will take time, effort, and sacrifice. Relationships are costly. It hardly seems an overstatement to say that either the mouths of God's people will be opened and relationships established, or the church may well slip into even more serious decline."[37]

25. The EvangeCube.

The EvangeCube is a seven-panel cube that tells the story of the Gospel of Christ in pictures. A presentation of how to use the EvangeCube can be downloaded at EvangeCube.com.

Jesus' approach to the Woman at the Well   (John 4: 6 – 25)

This passage contains a step-by-step account of how Jesus actually won a woman at Jacob's Well in Sychar. *Step One.* Jesus saw this woman as a fit subject for salvation, refusing to allow neither the racial prejudice that existed between Jew and Samaritan nor her sinful lifestyle to interfere (v 7). The soulwinner must be careful not to restrict witnessing simply to those whose lives are not entrenched in some great sin (the Rich Young Rulers' and Nicodemus') but ever be ready as Jesus to share with those in the vice grip of drugs, sexual impurity, pornography and alcohol. The soulwinner must view every sinner regardless of lifestyle or race as a candidate for eternal life.

Step Two. Jesus asks this woman for a drink of water (v 7). This request for a glass of water clearly said to the woman that it was cool for Jesus to be associated with her. This was an important message to communicate especially since she was counted as an outcast in the city. In all probability this woman was at Jacob's Well at this unusual time of day drawing water to avoid the ridicule and scorn of the other women who came for water. Questions are an excellent tool to use to initiate a witness.

Obviously Jesus' request spoke volumes to her heart and created a spirit of receptivity to what He wanted to share. The psychology of allowing a person to do something in the soulwinner's behalf creates a bridge between the soulwinner and sinner over which the gospel message may be transported to their soul. The opposite approach likewise is highly effective. Giving a cup of "water" (books, tracts, food, clothing, and monetary aid) to the sinner often creates personal and gospel receptivity.

Step Three. Jesus introduces the subject of salvation by connecting it with the "well" from which she was drawing "water" (v 10 – 13). The physical was used to preach the spiritual. The use of physical "pegs" on which to hang spiritual "truths" in soulwinning is greatly effective. In scripture the apostle Paul used the *peg* of a boxer in the ring (I Corinthians 9: 26), a runner in a race (I Corinthians 9:24), a farmer in the field (2 Timothy 2:6) and of a soldier in a battle (2 Timothy 2: 3) among others to convey the gospel message. Jesus used this method often in the telling of parables.

Step Four. Jesus spoke to this woman in simplicity (v 14). He knew the entire theological *Lingo* but kept His words simple so she could clearly understand what was required to be saved. Don't assume the sinner understands even the most commonplace words relating to salvation.

Step Five. Jesus confronted her about personal sin (v 16-18). He compassionately but frankly spoke to her about her adultery. She had broken the seventh commandment and was guilty before God. To get a person saved the soulwinner must first get them lost and that happens when the truth about sin is shared. (Romans 6:23) A person must understand that he has violated God's Law for which he stands guilty and condemned.

Step Six. Jesus was sensitive to this woman's inner need. He saw her "empty heart." The water from the Well of the World satisfied momentarily causing her inner restlessness to resurface. The soulwinner needs this same perception with people in their neighborhood, apartment complex, classroom, and job. All around us are those who have drawn in vain from the Well of this World's pleasure and are yet "empty." We must tell them of Jesus who alone can give them "living water."

Step Seven. Jesus did not compromise His witness (v 20-21). He made it clear that it was not where or how a person worshipped but "whom." The soulwinner must not dilute the gospel to win a soul.

Step Eight. Jesus was not shocked or thrown off balance by this woman's lack of biblical knowledge. He took her where she was theologically and led her to balanced and saving Truth. The soulwinner must be prepared for opposing theological views and not allow such to cause "shell shock."

Step Nine. He refused to get sidetracked in His appeal (v 21). He simply used her interruption as a vehicle to usher the gospel into her heart. The lost will throw up many "smoke screens" trying to evade the real issue of salvation. The soulwinner must refuse biting this bait chasing theological rabbits that lead nowhere.

Step Ten. Jesus gave His best effort (v 22-23). He did not save His best witness for someone more promising or affluent but spoke to this woman's heart as if she was the only lost person in the world. The soulwinner must give his best effort in reaching every sinner. A parachute factory in England years ago had a banner hanging from its ceiling that read, "Make each parachute the best you can, it's the pilot's last chance." A good motto for the soulwinner is, "Make each witness the best you can for it could be the sinner's last chance to be saved."

This counsel is applicable to preachers who regularly or occasionally speak to small congregations. On Sunday morning, January 6, 1850, a young boy by the name of Charles Spurgeon was one of only fifteen present for worship at a Primitive Methodist Chapel. The speaker, a layman, preached the best he could, urging Spurgeon specifically to "Look unto Christ." Spurgeon responded to that call and was gloriously converted. One can only wonder how different Spurgeon's life may had been had this layman not done his best despite the few that were gathered that morning.[38]

Step Eleven. Jesus draws the net (v 24 – 26). The purpose in soulwinning is to win souls; it's senseless to witness and not "draw the net." Soulwinners must invite people to repent of their sin and in faith embrace Christ at the end of their presentation of the gospel message. This woman gets gloriously saved and immediately becomes an evangelist going through the city shouting, "Come, see a man, which told me all things that ever I did: is not this the Christ?"(v 29). The Dallas Theological Seminary Faculty Bible Knowledge Commentary says in relation to this verse, "She framed the question this way, in all probability, because she knew the people would not respond favorably to a dogmatic assertion from a woman, especially one of her reputation. Just as Jesus had captured her attention by curiosity, so she raised the people's curiosity." John tells us that because of the testimony of this woman many believed on Jesus (v 39).

The text states emphatically that Jesus "must needs go through Samaria" (v 4). He had to go that way plain and simple; the reason is obvious. God has prearranged Divine appointments for the soulwinner to witness to a "woman at Jacob's Well." Today that "woman" is a friend at the end of class, a waiter at the restaurant, someone in the apartment or at the game, a person on the bus, or a fellow employee at work. Often, we, too, "must needs go through Samaria" (be detoured, have plans interrupted, and end up where didn't intend) to get to that person at the right time to share the message of Christ!

How to make a door-to-door visit.
 1. Pray before the visit. Pray for Holy Spirit discernment as to who to visit; pray as you go from house to house - in the car, on the street, at the front porch.
 2. Determine prior to the visit who will take the lead in making the witness (in two-by-two visitation).
 3. Formulate a game plan mentally regarding the soulwinning approach and method.
 4. Review the prospect card and put it away before ringing the doorbell.
 5. Knock firmly four or five times on the door and then step back a few steps on the porch.
 6. Identify yourself clearly and the name of your church. Use any prior relationship the prospect or a family member may have had with your church (Worship service, Sunday School, Revival, Vacation Bible School, Christmas program) in your greeting.
 7. The person leading the witness should sit nearest the prospect.
 8. The witnessing partner should tactfully handle distractions — radio or television noise; animals and children; pray silently as the witness unfolds and be ready to witness to a second person.
 9. Engage in casual conversation (FORM or another approach) and then begin the witness relying upon the leadership and convicting power of the Holy Spirit.
10. Call for a decision.
11. Record salvation decisions. Tell the new convert what to expect now and what he should do next. Leave a tract clearly marking the way of salvation with those who choose to delay a salvation decision and pray with them if possible. Keep the door open for a follow-up visit.

THE PARABLE OF THE SOULWINNER

In the parable of the Sower (Matthew 13:18 -23) Jesus teaches that the soulwinner will meet with mixed results as he sows the seed of the gospel. Not all the seed sown will take root unto genuine salvation. He specifically teaches that soulwinners will encounter four responses in witnessing to the lost. First there is the response from the *unready heart*. "When any one heareth the word of the kingdom, and understandeth *it* not, then cometh the wicked *one*, and catcheth away that which was sown in his heart. This is he which received seed by the way side" (v 18). These individuals in hearing a witness trample beneath it with their feet for they do not see the relevancy of the gospel or its need. The "soil" in their soul is unbroken and has not been ploughed by the tiller of the Law of God and until it is their hearts will remain as hard as concrete. Cultivation of this field is imperative before one sows the seed of redeeming grace.

Second, there is the response from the *impetuous heart*. "But he that received the seed into stony places, the same is he that heareth the word, and anon with joy receiveth it; Yet hath he not root in himself, but endureth for a while: for when tribulation or persecution ariseth because of the word, by and by he is offended" (v 20-21). The response from these type hearers is one of immediate and sincere acceptance to the sower's message. These may experience euphoria accompanied with shouting and crying in their decision for Christ. All outward evidence will indicate these people got saved. However when affliction, persecution or tribulation occur due to their interest expressed in the Word these return to their former sinful lifestyle revealing they had not been saved. John declares, "They went out from us, but they were not of us; for if they had been of us, they would *no doubt* have continued with us: but *they went out*, that they might be made manifest that they were not all of us (I John 2:19). Their experience was superficial. The seed though received intellectually and emotionally never penetrated the soil of their soul. Soulwinners must be alert to such type hearts granting time for additional contact before pressing for a decision.

The third class of respondents Jesus speaks is that of the *unrepentant heart*. "He also that received seed among the thorns is he that heareth the word; and the care of this world, and the deceitfulness of riches, choke the word, and he becometh unfruitful" (v 22). These respondents to the gospel seed receive it but not with genuine sincerity. Their hearts are yet preoccupied with *thorns*, cares and love for the sinful pleasures of this world. These thorns *choke* out the gospel seed before it can germinate. This certainly was the case with the Rich Young Ruler to whom Jesus witnessed who desired to be saved but in hearing of the cost involved to follow Jesus walked away "sorrowfully for he was very rich"(Luke 18:23). The message of repentance must be sounded by the soulwinner if genuine fruit is to be harvested (Acts 20:21; Matthew 6:24).

To this point in the *parable of the soulwinner* the soulwinner has struck out three times in his effort to win a soul, but he's still at bat. Looking at the fourth type of respondent to the sowing of the gospel seed one sees the *ready heart.* "But he that received seed into the good ground is he that heareth the word, and understandeth *it*; which also beareth fruit, and bringeth forth, some an hundredfold, some sixty, some thirty" (v 23). This heart has been ploughed, broken up, fertilized and is prepared to receive the gospel message with *understanding.* Matthew Henry stated that this hearer deeply ponders what he hears, chews on it, until he understands it sufficiently to be saved. "Intelligent hearers; they hear the word and understand it; they understand not only the sense and meaning of the word, but their own concern in it; they understand it as a man of business understands his business. God in his word deals with men as men, in a rational way, and gains possession of the will and affections by opening the understanding."[39] Soulwinner be encouraged with this home run. Don't allow what appears to be a strike out to stop you from going and sowing. The psalmist gives the soulwinner a promise, "They that sow in tears shall reap in joy. He that goeth forth and weepeth, bearing precious seed, shall doubtless come again with rejoicing, bringing his sheaves *with him*" (Psalms 126:5-6). *Bringing in the Sheaves* is an old hymn of the church that sounds out this promise.

Bringing in the Sheaves

Sowing in the morning, sowing seeds of kindness,
Sowing in the noontide and the dewy eve;
Waiting for the harvest, and the time of reaping,
We shall come rejoicing, bringing in the sheaves.

Refrain:
Bringing in the sheaves, bringing in the sheaves,
We shall come rejoicing, bringing in the sheaves,
Bringing in the sheaves, bringing in the sheaves,
We shall come rejoicing, bringing in the sheaves,

Sowing in the sunshine, sowing in the shadows,
Fearing neither clouds nor winter's chilling breeze;
By and by the harvest and the labor ended,
We shall come rejoicing, bringing in the sheaves.

Going forth with weeping, sowing for the Master,
Though the loss sustained our spirit often grieves;
When our weeping's over, He will bid us welcome,
We shall come rejoicing, bringing in the sheaves.

                                        Knowles Shaw, 1874

It is the character of the person and condition of his heart that determines receptivity or not to the gospel. The incorruptible Seed of the gospel has the power to convert all who gladly receive it as illustrated in this final group of respondents. Evidence that this seed took root Jesus states is in that it "beareth fruit." The soulwinner can know with all assurance that the seed he sows has taken root when it produces fruit, "some thirty-fold; some sixty-fold and some a hundred-fold."

Questions to ask prior to a visit
1. Who can reach this person the easiest?
2. What is the best time to visit?
3. What approach ought to be utilized?
4. Does the prospect have any prior connection with our church?
5. Where is the best place (freest from distraction) to attempt the witness?
6. Has something happened in the prospect's life or family (sickness, sorrow, suicide) I need to know?
7. When was the prospect last visited?
8. What has been the prospect's response to previous evangelistic visits?

SOULWINNING AT THE ALTAR

Christians should always be prepared to give assistance in winning souls during the minister's invitational appeal at the conclusion of a sermon. How?

1. Readiness.
The soulwinner should be ready to witness 24-7, in church or out of church. The soulwinner's Bible and witnessing plan must always be in his possession. The soulwinner should make himself available to work the altar call and then anticipate being called upon for assistance during every invitation.

2. Prayerfulness.
Let the soulwinner pray prior to the invitation, "O Lord please grant others and myself the high privilege to lead some soul to saving grace during the invitation. Move upon the sinners heart with convicting power; remove every obstacle in his way to salvation and grant him courage to respond publicly."

3. Watchfulness.
The soulwinner ought to be seated on the front pew during the invitation for quick and easy assess by the minister. During the invitation he must be alert to the minister's signal for needed assistance which may be communicated through eye contact, a nod or tap on the shoulder.

4. Introduction.
The minister should always briefly introduce the soulwinner to the prospect by saying, "John, this is Billy Smith, one our counselors. He will explain to you more about what is involved in becoming a Christian."

5. Presentation.

A lengthy gospel presentation is not necessary in most cases due to the message the prospect just heard. A review of the basics of salvation should conclude with the soulwinner saying, "Would you like to pray with me to receive Jesus Christ into your life as Lord and Savior?" Upon a yes response the soulwinner should then lead the sinner in the sinner's prayer and then give assurance that Jesus keeps His promise to save all who call upon Him in faith and repentance.

6. Direction.

The soulwinner should encourage the new convert to make a decision about baptism and church membership.

7. Follow-up.

The soulwinner should place in the hands of the new believer a copy of "What to do Now?" or some other simple and concise follow up booklet that details the first steps of the Christian life.

8. Information.

A decision card must be completed by the soulwinner for each person he presents the gospel. This record should be hand printed for clarity.

9. Communication.

The soulwinner upon returning to the sanctuary with the new believer should sit on the front pew. At this point the soulwinner should wait for the right moment to communicate this decision to the minister.

10. Trouble Shooting.

There always should be a designated trained counselor available during the invitation to give any necessary assistance to the soulwinners around the altar. I find this extremely helpful during the invitations at Camp Longridge.

SEVEN

The Conquest Factor In Soulwinning

Anybody who is not doing personal work has sin in his life. I don't care who you are – preacher, teacher, mother, father – if you are not reaching definite people to a definite Savior at a definite time, or trying hard to do so, you have sin in your life.[1] Charles M. Alexander

But sanctify the Lord God in your hearts: and be ready always to give an answer to every man that asketh you a reason of the hope that is in you with meekness and fear. Peter (I Peter 3:15)

Soulwinning is about winning souls to Christ. To stop short of offering the unsaved an opportunity to be saved in witnessing is tragic. It is sad but often the case that following a good witness the soulwinner will simply invite the prospect to church or a Sunday School class failing to draw the net. How is it that one can draw the net calling for a response to God's offer of eternal life? One way is by asking the prospect "Is there any good reason why you couldn't receive Christ now as your Lord and Savior?" If they respond "No" then ask them to take your hand as a sign of faith and pray to receive Christ into their life. A second way to draw the net at the conclusion of a witness is by saying, "If you would like to receive Christ into your life as Lord and Savior please take my hand as a sign of faith and I will lead you in what is called the 'sinner's prayer.' There is nothing magical about the prayer but if you will mean it with all sincerity Christ this moment will enter into your life."

Nearly every book on soulwinning I have researched deals at length with the myriads of excuses the unsaved will throw up in the soulwinner's face as to why they cannot or will not be saved. It is so easy for the believer to look at these and at once decide there is no way he possibly can learn enough to handle them and quit soulwinning before he begins.   Don't despair. In excess of forty years in soulwinning I have never heard most of them, and probably the authors who detail them haven't either. Accordingly I chose here to include only the most common excuses cited by the unsaved for their unwillingness to be saved and scripture's rebuttal.

1. "I don't feel this is the time".
E. J. Daniels offered a good counter to this excuse when he stated, "When someone offers this excuse to me I generally quote John 3:16 and put the word 'feel' in the place of the word 'believe.' Open your Bible and begin reading like this: 'For God so loved the world that He gave His only begotten Son that whosoever 'feels like it', should not perish but have everlasting life.' Usually the person can see the inconsistency of putting feeling in the place of faith."[2] Point out that the only feeling required to be saved is one of sorrow for breaking God's Law and desire

to repent of it. (2 Corinthians 7:10) Scripture makes plain that the feeling of joy follows conversion not precedes it. (Acts 8: 39B) Salvation is a matter of *will* not *feel*.

2. "I have already been baptized."
State clearly that baptism is not synonymous with salvation (Acts 4:12). Point out that Simon Magus though baptized by Phillip yet was lost (Acts 8:13-23). Tell the sinner that salvation involves repentance toward God and faith in the Lord Jesus Christ. (Acts 20:21) and that baptism absolutely has nothing to do with becoming a Christian. Take a wedding ring and say, "The wearing of a wedding ring doesn't make one married, does it? Anybody can wear a wedding band. It is the reciting of the marital vows in a legal setting by a man and woman that consummates marriage. Baptism is to the Christian what a wedding ring is to the married. It is merely a symbol of a union. It is not that which enables the union but testifies of it. A person only becomes a Christian when he in sincerity of heart says 'I do' to Jesus Christ as his Lord and Savior through repentance and faith."

3. "I am a church member".
Occasionally when the soulwinner asks a person, "Is there any good reason why you couldn't give your life to Christ right now?" one will respond, "I am already a church member." Point out that attending and supporting a church is admirable and one ought to do that but it is not synonymous with being a Christian. Tell the prospect about Nicodemus' avid church attendance and even preaching while yet lost and how it was to this religious man Jesus said, "Ye must be born again" (John 3: 7).

Billy Graham stated that church members must be evangelized. He declared that eighty per cent of the opportunity of evangelism lies within the door of the church.[3]

4. "I will wait until later."
Respond, "I understand what you are saying but I would be less than honest not to share that you may not have another opportunity to be saved." James warned, 'Go to now, ye that say, today or tomorrow we will go into such a city and continue there a year, and buy and sell, and get gain: Whereas ye know not what shall be on the morrow. For what is your life? It is even a vapor that appeareth for a little time, and then vanisheth away' (James 4: 13-14). The uncertainty of tomorrow necessitates a decision for Christ today. A man by the name of Felix heard a witness by the Apostle Paul and though he trembled at the Word of God he delayed salvation preferring to wait for a more convenient time (Acts 24: 24 – 29). To our knowledge such a time never came and he died lost. It is so important to decide for Christ now. Tomorrow may be too late. Don't gamble with your soul. Paul

declared, 'Behold now is the accepted time; behold, now is the day of salvation' (2 Corinthians 6:2B). Will you say yes to Christ today?"

5. "I feel that I am already saved."
This excuse primarily will be heard from the unsaved who embrace another faith. Share with this person Proverbs 14:12, "There is a way that seemeth right unto man but the end thereof are the ways of death." Using the pages of Holy Scripture clarify exactly how a person is saved.

In response to this excuse from a person of the Christian faith first ask upon what bases does he believe that he is saved (2 Corinthians 13:5). Listen carefully for he may answer his own excuse. Tell him it is possible for a person to sincerely believe he is saved but all the while be lost as with Saul of Tarsus (Proverbs 14:12). Saul of Tarsus "felt" he was saved but one is not saved by what he feels but by faith. Point out that the Bible indicates the spiritual birthmarks of those genuinely saved and ask him to read them with you (I John 1:6; 2:3; 2:15; 2:29; 3:14; 3:24; 5:13; Titus 1:16; James 2:14).

6. "I have to straighten some things out first."
Some people believe they have to clean up their life before salvation is possible. Share Jeremiah 13:23, "Can the Ethiopian change his skin or the leopard his spots?" Explain that it is impossible for man to improve his condition spiritually apart from Jesus Christ. Tell the sinner that God knows all about his sin and stands ready to cleanse it through the blood of the Lord Jesus Christ (Isaiah 1:18, I John 1:7, 9). The soulwinner may share lyrics from the hymn *Just as I Am* to illustrate how one is to come to God and His readiness to receive the sinner who simply comes to Him in faith and repentance.

7. "I enjoy my sin too much."
In witnessing to a teenage boy at a gas station I asked why he was unwilling to give his life to Jesus Christ. He honestly replied, "I guess I love my sin too much." If people were honest with the soulwinner this would be the most often stated excuse for not being saved. People love their pleasure, popularity, sexual immorality, drinking and drugs, partying and self-pleasing life too much to be saved.

The sinner must give up his sin or else he will be forever damned. Jesus asked, "What shall it profit a man if he gain the whole world and yet lose his own soul? Or what shall a man give in exchange for his soul?" (Mark 8:36-37). In Luke 13:3 again Jesus declared, "I tell you, Nay: but, except you repent, ye shall all likewise perish." The Apostle Paul said, "Be not deceived; God is not mocked: for whatsoever a man soweth, that shall he also reap. For he that soweth to his flesh shall of the flesh reap corruption; but he that soweth to the Spirit shall of the Spirit reap life everlasting" (Galatians 6:7 -8). The sinner must decide between God and the World; life and death; a Savior and a sin; Heaven and Hell. He must weigh carefully the temporal pleasures of sin against the present and eternal blessings of salvation (Joshua 24:15). Press home to the sinners heart the question of Jesus, "For what is a man profited, if he shall gain the whole world, and lose his own soul? or what shall a man give in exchange for his soul?" (Matthew 16:26).

8. "I am just as good as some people I know that attend your church."
The sinner who tells the soulwinner this statement is probably right. Sadly there are hypocrites within the church. It is probably a good idea not to respond to these individuals who use this excuse in the same manner as the great Methodist evangelist Sam Jones who told one such person, "Yes, and there is always room for one more!"[4] A survey of three universities asked students, "Write out the first thing that comes to mind when you hear the word Christianity?" Out of the eight options listed students were unanimous in choosing the option that read, "I've met too many Christians who are hypocritical and stuck-up."[5] What an indictment and hindrance to the church!

How should the soulwinner tactfully handle this excuse? (1) Agree with the person about this fact. (2) Tell him the reason this is sadly true is because some have never been saved and others have not matured in their walk with Jesus. (3) Tell him to take his eyes off people and focus upon Jesus in whom there is no fault. (4) Remind him that at the Judgment he will only have to give an account for his life not others. (5) Urge him not to let the actions of others keep him from knowing the wonderful love and grace of the Lord Jesus Christ (Isaiah 45:22).

9. "I am too bad a person to be saved."
L.R. Scarborough gave clear direction in handling this excuse. "Tell them of Paul's case (I Timothy 1:15). He was the chief of sinners, and yet God saved him. Tell them of the Thief on the Cross (Luke 23:39-43), who was a criminal and a condemned sinner and yet Christ spoke words of life to him. Tell them of the harlot at Jacob's Well (John 4), who was saved and sent away as an evangel of light. Tell them of the jailer at Philippi (Acts 16: 22-33) who cruelly treated Paul and yet was saved. Tell them of David's double crime of murder and adultery (Psalms 51) and how, on his repentance and confession, God forgave him. Show God's promises of pardon and salvation covering every case, it matters not how hard."[6]

10. "I am waiting on someone else to do it first."
A common excuse for delay in being saved is for the lost to state they are waiting

on a spouse, a sibling or a friend to first make that decision. Use the story of the conversion of the Philippian Jailer to illustrate the importance of a person leading out in this decision. It was when the jailer chose to be saved that his wife and children got saved (Acts 16:31-40).

Share the account of a solitude leper who came to Jesus for healing (Matthew 8: 1-4). This man knew that his loathsome disease could only be cured by Jesus so he immediately ran down the "aisle" to where He was standing. He refused to wait on other lepers to make up their mind to join him or to discourage him in his going. Certainly following the miracle of his healing many lepers flocked to Jesus. Tell the sinner, "Please don't allow friend or family discourage you from coming to Jesus or delay coming until they decide to come. Come now. God will use the miracle He performs in your life to impact and influence others spiritually. Declare with the songwriter right now, "I have decided to follow Jesus. Though none go with me still I will follow. No turning back. No turning back." The leper was joyous in his decision and so will you be also."

11. "There are many paths to God."
To this respond, "I have heard that said before but no one has ever showed me in the Bible where that is stated." Hand the person a Bible and say, "Will you please show me?" Obviously they cannot. Taking the Bible back, share John 14:6, Acts 4:12 and John 10:9 making clear the teaching of Jesus Himself that He is the only way, the exclusive way to God.

The reason that other faiths do not lead to God is because only the Christian faith is true. Paul Little stated, "Neither sincerity or intensity of faith can create truth. Faith is no more valid than the object in which it is placed. Believing doesn't make something true, per se, and refusing to believe a truth cannot make it false. The real issue is the question of truth."[7]

12. "Why should I believe the Bible?"
Jesus is the infallible Son of God, the Savior of the world and He places His stamp of approval upon the Holy Scripture. Luke 24:27 declares, "And beginning at Moses and all the prophets, he expounded unto them in all the scriptures the things concerning himself. Again Jesus testified, "These *are* the words which I spake unto you, while I was yet with you, that all things must be fulfilled, which were written in the law of Moses, and *in* the prophets, and *in* the Psalms, concerning me. (Luke 24:44) One ought to believe the Bible because of the testimony of Jesus concerning its Divine authority.

When witnessing, ask the doubter, "How many people would it take flipping a quarter before one person hits heads thirty times in a row?" Let him make a guess. Continue by stating, "According to *Ripley's Believe It or Not! Strange*

Coincidences, in order for a coin to land on heads fifty times in a row it would take one million men flipping ten coins a minute, forty hours a week and then it would happen only once every nine hundred years. This is why I know the Bible is the Word of God. There are at least thirty prophecies about the birth, the death and the resurrection of Jesus Christ in the Bible that have come true. Wouldn't you agree that's a whole lot like tossing a coin thirty times in a row coming up heads?"[8]

Peter Stoner in *Science Speaks* further gave evidence for the Bible to be the infallible Word of God. In writing of the probability of just eight prophecies about the Messiah (place of birth, time of birth, manner of birth, betrayal, manner of death, reaction to death (mocking, spitting), sword piercing and burial) being fulfilled in any one man, Stoner stated, "We find that the chance that any man might have lived down to the present time and fulfilled all eight prophecies is 1 in 10 (10 to the 17th power). That would be 1 in 100,000,000,000,000,000." Stoner illustrated this by supposing that 10 to the 17th power) of silver dollars were laid all over Texas covering the State two feet deep; you marked one of them and then stirred the whole mass thoroughly. Next blindfold a man instructing him to travel as far across Texas as he wants but he must pick up one silver dollar and say it is the right one. What is the likelihood of him picking up the right silver dollar? Stoner states it would be the same chance that the prophets would have had of writing these eight prophecies and having them all come true in any one man, from their day to the present time, providing they wrote them according to their own wisdom."[9] This is almost absolute evidence that the Bible is what it claims to be, the inspired Word of God.

C. H. Spurgeon advised, "Truth least defended is best defended...Do not attempt to prove the existence of the sun. Pull up the blinds; throw back the shutters; let Him fill the room with His brightness. What demonstration can be more complete?"[10]

13. "I'm afraid I can't live it."
L. R. Scarborough stated, " The man, who says he cannot stem the tide and live the Christian life, fearing he will fall, needs to have explained to him the plan of salvation: that he becomes by faith a child of God and possesses eternal life and that God is able to keep his children."[11] "For I the Lord thy God will hold thy right hand, saying unto thee, Fear not; I will help thee" (Isaiah 41:13). Jude writes, "Now unto him that is able to keep you from falling and to present you faultless before the presence of his glory with exceeding joy..." (Jude 24).

Prospects need to clearly understand that in salvation it is not them holding on to God but rather God holding on to them and that His hand will never loosen its grip (John 10: 28-29). God enables the worst and weakest of sinners who come to

Christ to *live it.* Paul, who counted himself the chief of sinners, stated, "I am crucified with Christ: nevertheless I live; yet not I, but Christ liveth in me: and the life which I now live in the flesh I live by the faith of the Son of God, who loved me, and gave himself for me" (Galatians 2:20).

Removing obstacles from the pathway of the unsaved on their journey to the Cross is imperative and must be done through the use of scripture and the power of the Holy Spirit. A soul's value is worth the soulwinners mastering techniques and memorizing scripture in order to topple man's excuse for delaying acceptance of or rejecting Jesus Christ.

Hints on dealing with excuses

1. Don't argue. Never turn the witness into a theological debate.
2. Seek to discern excuses giving answer to them before they are presented. (Luke 6:7-9)
3. Use scripture to answer mans excuses. Jot down possible excuses and scripture rebuttals in your Bible.
4. Don't try to talk a person out of his excuses into the Kingdom of God. "A man convinced against his will is unconvinced still." The Holy Spirit must do the work of conviction and drawing of the lost to Christ, not the soulwinners debating skill.
5. Discern the sincerity of the prospect in stating excuses. Some have excuses and some have sincere excuses. This discernment will result in whether the visit should continue or end. "Don't cast your bread before swine." (Matthew 7:6)
6. The Holy Spirit uses the Word of God to convict of sin. Therefore the soulwinner should allow the prospect to read along with him the scripture text that combats their excuse.
7. Inasmuch as possible try to circumvent the excuse stating it will be dealt with after the presentation of the gospel. Often the excuse becomes mute at the end of the witness due to the Holy Spirit's revelation of Truth.

The Christian soulwinner is a soldier in fierce combat against the powers of darkness, and he must be fully dressed in spiritual armor if he is to be victorious. Paul speaks of the believer's armor in Ephesians 6 and his need of daily putting it on. I have written a poem highlighting both the pieces and purposes of this armor.

THE GOSPEL ARMOR

The armor of Ephesians 6 is God's mighty victory weaponry for you,
put it on daily as you battle Satan and the powers of darkness all about you.

Buckle on the Belt of Scripture Truth in all you say and do,
know how to give an answer for your faith to all that asketh you.
Hold tight to sound theological truth in this liberal day of ours,
it will be your defense against Satan's deceiving power.
Truth will lead to self-discipline in your spiritual walk,
preparing you for battles whenever they are fought.

The Breastplate of Righteousness is the holy life you live,
it protects your joyfulness, fruitfulness and usefulness to God.
Your emotions are impacted by sin in your heart,
so each morning come to Jesus for cleansing and have a fresh start.
So strap on this Breastplate through obedience each day
and go where He leads you and do all that He says.

Put on your feet the shoes of the Gospel of righteousness of peace,
to be surefooted in battle not to suffer defeat.
These shoes of assurance of Christ's love for you and His willingness to fight for you,
will spark your confidence in knowing, nothing Satan does can overcome you.
Souls about you are tossed to and fro, not knowing which way to go.
Walk in these shoes and tell one a day, the good news of Jesus and how He came to save.

The Shield of Faith is but a strong confidence in God,
believing He is capable for you to provide.
This Shield will retard the flaming missiles of Hell,
all designed to cause you to miserably fail.
Whatever the arrow of temptation shot at you, doubt, discouragement, lust or despair,
raise this shield of defense by trusting God and you will be fully prepared.
Come what may believe God over what you think, hear, see or perceive
and walk steadfastly in His calling not allowing Satan to deceive.
What is placed in His control is under His control
and that you can bank on, never has He broken a promise to take care of His own.

The Helmet of the Hope of Salvation place upon your head,
it but assures you of union with Christ and heaven ahead.
Knowing for sure that He is your Lord and Savior and you are always under His care,
is a mighty weapon in defeating times of despair.
The big picture Satan tries to hide from your view,
trying to discourage you in what you now do.
Focus on the Finish Line when this life will be o'er
and all that awaits you on that happy Kingdom shore.
To be with Christ and each other in that perfect place,
will make all these years of struggle and service well worth the wait!
So when tempted to quit and give up the fight,
remember it won't be long till its over
and you will be with Jesus in that land of delight.

The Sword of the Spirit is the living, inerrant Word of God,
mediate upon its pages, memorize its parts
and never be satisfied until you know it inside out.
This Sword is both a defensive and offensive weapon to use,
it drives Satan back in temptation and converts souls through you.

Quote scripture to Satan when with him in a fight,
and he will have no recourse but to take quick flight.
In telling others of Christ use this Sword well
and it will be the means of saving them from an eternal Hell.
Thrust it in a heart and conviction of sin will be seen,
draw it out and conversion it will bring.

There is no armor for the back you but note,
warning us never to turn it to Satan and his attack.

A Roman soldier could attach his armor to a comrade is known,
this would keep him from standing against the enemy all alone.
Whose armor might you join to help in this battle and make spiritually strong?

Each piece of this Armor daily buckle on in prayer,
and you will war a good warfare always being prepared.

EIGHT

The Cost Factor In Soulwinning

We cannot keep quiet. We must speak about what we have seen and heard.
Peter and John to the Sanhedrin (Acts 4:20,NCV)

The very etymology of the word "witness" tells of the cost its practice requires. It is derived from the Greek word *martus* from which we get the word *martyr.* Soulwinning is costly business. He that gives himself to the task of bringing others to Christ can expect suffering, persecution, hardship and even death. There have been 69,421,230 martyrs from A.D. 33 to the year 2000.[1] Granted not all of these martyrs were killed for soulwinning but all were killed for professing their faith with relentless courage. Everyday in our world Christians are being persecuted for their faith and endeavors to bring others to the saving knowledge of Jesus Christ. Soulwinners must take the witness stand of the world declaring the Truth, the whole Truth and nothing but the Truth so help them God without thought to personal comfort, possessions, inconvenience, financial cost, slight, personal lost or life itself. The soulwinner must count his life as "dung" that he may win the approval of Christ (Philippians 3:8). Jesus said, "If any *man* come to me, and hate not his father, and mother, and wife, and children, and brethren, and sisters, yea, and his own life also, he cannot be my disciple" (Luke 14:26). C. H. Spurgeon said, "Are you not willing to pass through every ordeal if by any means you may save some? If this is not your spirit, you had better keep to your farm and your merchandise, for no one will ever win a soul who is not prepared to suffer everything within the realm of possibility for a soul's sake."[2] John MacArthur wrote, "Many of us will never taste the kind of persecution that the apostles or the brothers overseas have known. But the willingness to endure sacrifice for the sake of Christ should never be far from our thinking."[3] Rachel Scott, Columbine martyr, wrote in her journal, "I have no more personal friends at school. But you know what? I am not going to apologize for speaking the name of Jesus. I am not going to justify my faith to them, and I am not going to hide the light that God has put into me. If I have to sacrifice everything, I will. I will take it. If my friends have to become my enemies for me to be with my best friend, Jesus, then that's fine with me."[4] Rachel paid the cost for sharing her faith. Every believer must.

Not only is there a cost to be paid by telling the lost of the gospel but in the mentoring or discipling those who are won. Jesus in the Great Commission clearly commands the believer not to simply "go" or "teach" or even "baptize" but to "make disciples" (Matthew 28: 18 – 19). The Greek structure of this text indicates that the purpose of the soulwinner's "going, teaching and baptizing" is in order to "make disciples." This, according to Roland Q. Leavell, is Christ's imperative commission.[5] Warren Wiersbe stated that the only command in the Great Commission is "to make disciples."[6] Robert E. Coleman wrote, " It is not enough to rescue the perishing, though this is imperative; nor is it sufficient to build up newborn babes in the faith of Christ, although this too is necessary if the fruit is to endure; in fact, it is not sufficient just to get them winning souls, as commendable as this work may be. What really counts in the ultimate perpetuation of our work is the faithfulness with which our converts go out and make leaders out of their converts, not simply more followers."[7] Sadly, that of which Coleman writes and which is our Master's Plan of soulwinning is absence from the church at large today. Soulwinners are faltering and failing in "making disciples" – in reproducing their passion for souls, thirst for righteousness, hunger for Biblical knowledge, craving for intimacy with the Almighty, Biblical integrity and holiness of life in those that they win.

Billy Graham, when asked what would be his plan of action if he were a pastor of a large church in a principal city, replied, "I think one of the first things I would do would be to get a small group of eight, or ten, or twelve men around me that would meet a few hours a week and pay the price! It would cost them something in time and effort. I would share everything I have, over a period of years. Then I would actually have twelve ministers among the laymen who in turn could take eight or ten or twelve more and teach them. ...Christ, I think, set the pattern. He spent most of His time with twelve men. He didn't spend it with the great crowd. In fact, every time He had a great crowd it seems to me that there weren't too many results. The great results, it seems to me, came in his personal interview and in the time He spent with His twelve."[8] Certainly His method of evangelism was highly effective and a worthy pattern for our adoption.

Oh, that we may win men but then take them under our protective and provisional wings to edify, educate, embolden, enlighten, establish, excite and equip in spiritual matters. I am convinced this is the greatest need of our day, the greatest work of the day. Though the work of mentoring is both joyously rewarding it also is extremely demanding and at times disappointing. It requires time, resources, sacrifice, devotion and prayers. Robert E. Coleman commented, "What perhaps is the most difficult part of the whole process of training is that we must anticipate their problems and prepare them for what they will face. This is terribly hard to do and can become exasperating. It means that we can seldom put them out of our mind. Even when we are in our private mediations and study our disciples will be in our prayers and dreams. Would a parent who loves his children want it any other way? We have to accept the burden of their immaturity until such time as they can do it for themselves."[9] Tom Landry, former coach of the Dallas Cowboys said, "The job of a football coach is to make men do what they don't want to do in order to achieve what they always wanted."[10] This likewise is the job of the spiritual coach with those he mentors: to help each discipline himself to do what the flesh does not want to do, so he may be a pleasure to the Lord Jesus Christ and live unto His purpose. I wrote the following poem based upon my mentoring experiences.

THE MENTOR

In the Apostle Paul's role to Timothy, a pattern of a real mentor we clearly see,
one that should be imitated by you and me.

Older men are to mentor younger men; through Paul's example we are told.
Revealing by their life "what a holy man looks like" and helping them reach their
    spiritual goal.
If you are blessed with such a man in your life, follow his saintly advice.

A consuming burden for your Timothy must posses your heart from the start
or else you will not last long enough to impact his heart.

Until the "fog" lifts, God's plan for him may not make sense.
Assure him that God is the God of no mistakes, spurring him to trust Him
    completely,
to proceed in following Him and not to wait.
His potential in ministry you must help him to see,
or else he will never become what God designed him to be.
Believe in him even when he doesn't believe in himself,
until he is convinced of the awesome gifts he does possess.

A "barking dog" you must be, to warn him of sin and heresy.
Bark loud and long, to prevent his failure and to keep him strong.

Correct your Timothy as Paul did his when he errs,
always in a manner in which he will not despair.
Point out weaknesses in his heart, that he may not yield and injure his walk.
For his favorite sin on you let him depend, to pray and keep him accountable lest
    he give in.

What he tells you is not to be shared, not for any reason, not even for another's prayer.
He has to trust you with the secrets of his heart, so seal your lips not letting his
    words depart.

Sacrifice is the key to help him grow, so be willing to give freely of your
time, experience, knowledge and resources to make it so.

To deposit the Word of God in his heart soundly and thoroughly is your greatest part.
Teach him to mediate upon it day and night, living out its truths with all his might.

Paul loved Timothy and let him know,
just so your love for your Timothy must grow and show.

Assure him time and again that your love will not ever alter,
regardless of times in which he may in sin falter.
You have to really love him with all you are or else you won't lead him very far.
At times he may take you for granted and just use you for personal gain,
nevertheless remain faithful to him always staying the same.

To be consistent when he retreats is the biggest of tests, not to back off
but to relentlessly keep giving him your best.
Neglect not time on your knees, day and night praying for your Timothy's need.
The time you pray for him let him know, that way your concern for him will
          clearly show.

You must encourage your Timothy that through thick and thin,
he must not ever quit, allowing Satan to win.
Ever remind him that the call of God is vitally important upon his life and it
must never be abandoned regardless of price.

To be a good mentor in another's life, you have to be there for him 'day and
          night'.
You can't stay where you are and expect to bless, so be available 24/7 to his every
          request.

Paul risked criticism by friend and foe, for ministering in Timothy's life as he did so.
Anytime you invest the gospel in a life, you must be prepared as he,
          to pay that kind of price.

In Second Timothy Four we do read, that Paul's pouring out of himself in Timothy
          the way he did,
prompted this mentoree to meet his need.
Paul indeed was called to Timothy and Timothy was called to Paul,
it made for a lifelong companionship that enabled both in Christ to stand tall.

Don't expect any return in what you invest,
except for the ways in his life and ministry God will bless.
Your greatest reward will be but to see, him becoming The Man of God he was
          designed to be.
Ingratitude may be displayed for that which you do, give and say,
never let that stop you from instructing him in The Way.
An Onesiphorus, a "breath of fresh air" to you he may become,
as a blessing from God for what you have done.
This may or may not be, it hinges on who's your Timothy.

One on one is the Pauline way to impact another in a powerful, life changing way.
Let God lead you to a life you can coach, discipling him into a Man of God
     beyond reproach.
Remember a mentor is the Lord's servant to a younger man, humbly and joyously
     'washing his feet',
and seeking his spiritual needs ever to meet.

A mentor I have sought to be, based upon Paul's role with Timothy.
It is his example I have had to depend, for I never knew the mentoring of Godly men.
No greater joy have I known or work have I performed then to invest my life,
in a Timothy mentoring task.

To turn a life on for God that along in Him will abide
and for His purpose and pleasure also ever strive,
is a ministry from your life to younger men that you must keep fully alive.

Solomon said, "Iron sharpeneth iron" (Proverbs 27:17). The Lord is counting on
His people to sharpen the iron of young believers doctrinally, devotionally, and
dutifully until they then can do the same for another. Will you take serious the
Lord's command not only to win souls but "to make disciples" regardless of cost?
Today make room on your plate to invest in a young preacher boy or new believer
allowing the mighty rivers of your spiritual knowledge and experience to flow
into them and then through them.

NINE

The Conservation Factor In Soulwinning

Is there no stopping place? After a person has been won around the church altar or beside a chair in his own home, cannot we fold our arms, sigh, and say "At last the job is finished. My work is done. Now to slumber?" Not yet, Dear hearts and Gentle people, not yet. There is work to be done. Much work. Heavy work."[1]
J. W. Ellis

The moment a person is won to Christ follow-up should begin. Sadly, the estimate is that over fifty percent of those who respond affirmatively to a gospel presentation cannot be found in a church service two years later! A study by New Orleans Baptist Theological Seminary answers in part the reason for this fall out. Encompassing the period of 1969 – 1980 this study revealed that 8,748,586 people who joined Southern Baptist Churches were not given any introduction to their faith or orientation to the new church fellowship. Discipleship training is not optional but imperative to the conservation of new believers. E. J. Daniels states that while pastors (and I add layman) may be good spiritual obstetricians they are often poor pediatricians. The soulwinner must allow God to use him in both the birthing and cultivating process. L. R. Scarborough wrote, "The evangelism that stops at conversion and public profession is lopsided, wasteful, incomplete. It should go on to teach, to train, and to develop, and utilize the talents and powers of the new convert. This educational phase of evangelism is transcendently important." He continued, "Modern evangelism finds here its greatest leakage and waste."[2] George Sweazey stated, "The second half of evangelism is less exciting than the first. Getting decisions is thrilling. It is like a game that can be scored. The results come rapidly, but bringing those decisions to fulfillment in an established Christian life is not very dramatic. It takes months instead of minutes."[3] Whether it is his preference or not, conservation of the new Christian is the soulwinner's responsibility. The Apostle Paul underlined that task in declaring, "...which is Christ in you, the hope of glory: Whom we preach, warning every man, and teaching every man in all wisdom, that we may present every man perfect in Christ Jesus" (Colossians 1:27-28).

In order to conserve and cultivate new converts several things are essential.

1. Affirmation
Applaud the convert's decision. Celebrate a person's New Birth because it's a celebration to God. Scripture attests there is a celebration in the presence of the angels when someone gets saved (Luke 15:10).

Four things among others can strengthen the convert's assurance of salvation. First, it is helpful for the new believer to affirm his decision for Christ by writing in his Bible the when, where, and how it occurred. Second, it is highly beneficial to the new Christian to affirm his decision verbally periodically. Often in the convert's early days of life in Christ I ask, "Tell me, when was it you were saved?" Third, just the plain promises of God that state He will save those who come to Him in repentance and faith in Jesus Christ will grant the new believer a stronger footing in the faith (Acts 20:21, John 6:39-40, John 10:28, Romans 10:9-13, Revelation 3:20, Acts 16:31). Fourth, instruct the new believer to tell someone immediately of his decision to follow Christ while yet in your presence either in person or by phone.

2. Adoption

Assign a Barnabas to "adopt" the convert. The Apostle Paul would not have become what he was for God had it not been for Barnabas in his early life. Barnabas took Paul while just a babe in Christ under his wings and developed him in the things of Christ. Of this, Luke wrote, "But Barnabas took him (Paul) and brought him to the apostles, and declared unto them how he had seen the Lord in the way, and that he had spoken to him, and how he had preached boldly at Damascus in the name of Jesus" (Acts 9:27). The words "took him" literally mean that Barnabas physically held on to Paul to help him. It is important that every new convert be assigned a Barnabas to "hold on to them" by supplying love, guidance and protection from spiritual harm. This assignment should be made at the end of the evangelistic witness right away and always man with man and woman with woman. Wiersbe wrote, "The term 'disciples' was the most popular name for the early believers. Being a disciple meant more than being a convert or a church member. 'Apprentice' might be an equivalent term. A disciple attached himself to a teacher, identified with him, learned from him, and lived with him. He learned, not simply by listening, but also by doing."[4]

3. Association

Induct the convert into the church by baptism (Matthew 28:19). Baptism is like a "gowning" at a graduation ceremony, which does not confer a degree upon a person but symbolizes the degree that already was earned. Believer's baptism is an outward "gowning" publicly of an inward experience of salvation through faith and repentance in Jesus Christ that has already occurred (Acts 20:21). Immediately upon baptism, if not before, the new Christian must be integrated into his new family through the church's Sunday School, worship services, outreach and social activities. In soulwinning I ask the ones won to Jesus to pray a commitment prayer telling God they will be present that night (if a revival or crusade) or Sunday morning to make their decision public and present themselves for baptism and church membership.

Jimmy Draper, president of Life-Way, believes there is "a lack of urgency" within Southern Baptist churches to baptize. "I've heard from a number of people across our denomination who say professions of faith are good enough," he said. "They are not teaching the importance of publicly identifying with Jesus through baptism, and they're ignoring His command to baptize His followers."[5] This alarming statement should incite every soul winner to obey the Lord's instruction to earnestly entreat all who are won to be baptized. Although baptism is not essential for salvation it is imperative for a new convert's submission to the authority of His Lord and Savior Jesus Christ (Luke 6:46).

4. Acquisition
Instruct the convert in the Word. Jesus exhorted, ". . .teaching them to observe all things whatsoever I have commanded you" (Matthew 28:20). Place in the new believers hand immediately a simple and concise study on the fundamentals of the faith until a more thorough study can be undertaken. My booklet *What To Do Now* was written primarily for this purpose.

5. Attestation
Equip the convert to be a soulwinner. The work of follow up is never complete until the evangelized becomes an evangel testifying of what the Lord has wrought in his life through faith and repentance. The Apostle Paul told young Timothy, "And the things that thou hast heard of me among many witnesses, the same commit thou to faithful men, who shall be able to teach others also" (II Timothy 2:2). This is known as the "ministry of multiplication" and is God's method to evangelize the world. The disciple is to take what he has learned from his godly mentor (teacher) and share it unashamedly with others.

Establish the young believer in the faith. It is a hideous sin against him and God to fail to do so. Don't simply stop with a convert at the end of the evangelistic presentation.

TEN

The Commitment Factor In Soulwinning

If I never won souls, I would sigh till I did. I would break my heart over them if I could not break their hearts. Though I can understand the possibility of an earnest sower never reaping, I cannot understand the possibility of an earnest sower being content not to reap. I cannot comprehend any one of you Christian people trying to win souls and not having results, and being satisfied without results.[1]
C. H. Spurgeon

There is an old story about Jesus' return to Heaven. He meets the angel Gabriel and tells him of His work on earth and about the price He paid to purchase man's salvation through His death, burial and resurrection. Now seated at the right hand of the Father Jesus tells Gabriel He is interceding for those who receive Him as Lord and Savior. In conclusion He tells this angel of His desire for all man to hear the message of what He had done. Gabriel asked, "And what is your plan for getting this done?" Our Lord replied, "I have left the message in the hands of a dozen or so men. I am trusting them to spread it everywhere." Gabriel somewhat surprised asked, "Twelve men! What if they fail?" Jesus responded, "I have no other plan."[2]

Jesus has left the work of telling the message of His redemptive work at Calvary in the hands of His saints. They are His plan for world evangelization. This task is so magnanimous that every Christian must urgently and faithfully "Go and Tell." Soulwinning is everyman's ordained business. Andrew Murray said there are two classes of Christians, soulwinners and backsliders.[3]

The Christian who fails to soulwin is guilty of six horrible and terrible sins.

Failure to witness first is a *Sin against the Savior.* In Matthew 28: 18-20 Jesus commands the believer to witness and win the unsaved. In Acts 1:8 the summons again is trumpeted loud and clear. He that Jesus saves He subpoenas to take the witness stand of the world and tell the Truth about who He is and what He has done to provide for man's salvation; he that Jesus converts He consigns the task to win souls and he that Jesus regenerates He expects to reproduce. There is nothing that we can do to make up for not obeying Christ in this matter – no sacrifice, service, stewardship or study is sufficient. The sin of not witnessing is a sin against the heart of Jesus.

Failure to witness is a *Sin against the Scripture.* Not to soulwin is to rebel against the Bible. Throughout the pages of the inerrant and infallible Word of God the believer is told to tell of Jesus to others. Mark 16:15 says, "And He said, Go ye into all the world and preach the gospel to every creature". Jude tells us, "And others save with fear pulling them out of the fire" (v 23). In Revelation we read,

"And the Spirit and bride say come. And let him who heareth say come" (22:17). Peter exhorted, "But you are a chosen generation, a royal priesthood, a holy nation, His own special people, that you may proclaim the praises of Him who called you out of darkness into His marvelous light" (I Peter 5:9, NKJV).

Failure to witness is a *Sin against the Sinner.* It is a sin against the value of the sinner's soul and the desperate need of his heart. How valuable is a soul? Jesus stated the soul is more valuable than the entire world (Matthew 16:26). D. L. Moody said, "I believe that if an angel were to wing his way from earth up to Heaven, and were to say that there was one poor, ragged boy, without father or mother, with no one to care for him and teach him the way of life; and if God were to ask who among them were willing to come down to this earth and live here for fifty years and lead that one to Jesus Christ, every angel in Heaven would volunteer to go. Even Gabriel, who stands in the presence of the Almighty, would say, 'Let me leave my high and lofty position, and let me have the luxury of leading one soul to Jesus Christ.' There is no greater honor than to be the instrument in God's hands of leading one person out of the kingdom of Satan into the glorious light of Heaven."[4]

Failure to witness is a *Sin against the Saved.* The believer who neglects to witness hinders the progress of his church for such disobedience grieves the Holy Spirit hindering His power to be fully manifest. The believer's disobedience also promotes complacency about soulwinning in the lives of fellow saints.

Failure to witness is a *Sin against Society.* The only cure for the moral and social ills of society is Jesus Christ. The saints' neglect of soulwinning allows the world to become bleaker and darker morally and spiritually. C. H. Spurgeon told about his fascination as a child with the gas lamp lighter. He stated that as the lamplighter lit the lamps in his community he would rush to his mother exclaiming, "Come see a man who is punching holes in darkness." The born again of God must punch holes in spiritual darkness one person at a time and in doing so will bring His Light into society's deep darkness.

Failure to witness is a *Sin against one's own Soul.* Failure to be a soulwinner hurts the saint personally. It stagnates his soul, steals his power, stunts his growth, softens his burden, and stains his hands with the blood of those he refused to tell of Jesus.

Soulwinning studies, sermons, seminars and discussions are a dime a dozen. Satan doesn't care one bit how much Christians talk and pray about soulwinning as long as they never do it. This book has clearly indicated God's heart and desire about this matter. He wants you to win souls! He has no other method or means to bring unregenerate man to the Cross but you and I. If we fail in this task, we utterly fail. No amount of bible study, praying, friendship cultivation or religious activity can make up for disobedience to His command to "Go." Satan will seek to block the believers *Going and Telling* at every turn necessitating a predetermined mindset not to be sidetracked.

Wilson Carlile voiced the task of every minister when he wrote, "I have got the biggest job I have ever tackled in my life. I am trying to open the mouths of people in the pew."[5] In a time when four souls die every second without Christ and plunge into Hell believers must be compelled to open their mouth wide and passionately, persistently, boldly declare the gospel to the lost. In a day when 187 million souls are lost in America; it takes 43 Southern Baptists to add one member to the church annually; more then 10,000 Southern Baptist Churches failed to baptize a single convert last year every Christian must care enough to share. The time for timidity is over. The time for passive evangelism is gone. You and I must be aggressive for not only is obedience to God at stake but the temporal and eternal state of friends, classmates, neighbors and family members. One day they will breathe their last and eternity will greet them. What if that happened today? Oh may we so live today as if this day was their last chance to be saved. It boils down to how much we love Jesus doesn't it? *Do you really love Jesus?* Are you willing to forgo the big game, skip class, miss work or a meal to redeem perhaps a once-in-a-lifetime opportunity to speak to a person of Christ? It may be awkward; you may stumble with your words. That's cool. Just do it for love's sake. Love covers a multitude of the soulwinner's mistakes. Risk showing and sharing God's love to someone today, everyday. God is counting on you. Heaven is counting on you. Friends and families are counting on you. Souls are counting on you. For love's sake do it.

During the time of forced consolidation of high schools, a small East Texas school joined the student body of one larger. This was to the sorrow of the cheerleaders of the smaller school. They were prepared to cheer their football team to victory. These young ladies sought out the principal of the new school and pleaded their case. He felt for them and authorized a pep rally every week just for those who came from that student body. In these rallies they would shout cheers something like, "All the way to state boys, all the way to state" and "Hold that line boys, hold that line."[6] The students would be worked up into a frenzy of excitement. The irony of the whole matter though was these cheerleaders were having pep rallies for a game that never would be played. Not once would one of those players from the smaller school ever dress out for a game. Never would anyone of these players take the ball over the goal line to score a touchdown.

I fear oft times that books and studies on soulwinning are like those pep rallies - pep rallies for a game we never get around to playing. It's high time every believer dress out for the game, heed the instruction of the Coach, utilize teamwork and hit the field with resolved determination to carry the "ball" across the goal line winning souls to Christ. D. L. Moody had posted on the exit doors of his church in Chicago the words "You are now entering the mission field of the world, go soulwinning." May each believer post such words over the doors of his home, car, and business as a reminder to actually "play in the game." It is so easy to get used to boys and girls dying and going to Hell that such reminders are imperative.

I have a four-fold challenge to every believer regarding soulwinning. First, select a method of witness and constantly rehearse it until it is burned into your mind and heart. It will be helpful to practice your witnessing presentation upon Christian friends. Never become satisfied with your witnessing skills but ever endeavor to sharpen them. Second, set a reasonable goal in soulwinning. Make a commitment to tell one person a day of Christ, just seven a week and in a years time you will have spoken to 365 people of Christ. William Borden was a young millionaire who graduated from Yale University in 1909. He determined to witness to his entire class before graduation. He would go to the rooms of his unsaved classmates, study with them, talk with them, wrestle with them and then pray with them. One by one he did this until all were saved.[7] He knew what it was not only to have a passion for souls but a goal to win souls. Formulate numeric goals in terms of how many people you will witness. A discipline to evangelize is just as necessary as one to pray or study the bible. Third, link up with a witnessing partner and together make soulwinning visits. Ask that person to hold you accountable regarding consistency in soulwinning. Fourth, determine to begin witnessing this week. Don't procrastinate. Steven Curtis Chapman has a song entitled "Live out Loud." Live out loud, refuse to be silent any longer, and boldly tell the Good News. C.H. Spurgeon challenges, "Young men, and old men, and sisters of all ages, if you love the Lord, get a passion for souls. Do you not see them? They are going down to Hell by the thousands."[8] Pray each morning at day's start for the Holy Spirit to lead you to someone who is in need of Jesus Christ.

There is no greater ecstasy than that of winning a person to Christ. Nothing even comes close in comparison. The new believer has a bond with the soulwinner (spiritual father) that produces a relationship and joy that keeps on giving throughout life. Recently I met up with Buster Jordan, a man I led to Christ over twenty-five years ago. My heart was inflamed with great joy as he spoke of the souls he had won to Christ. The soulwinner's reward in witnessing is the approval of God, the transformation of a life unto godliness, the rescuing of a person from eternal damnation unto the delight of Heaven, the enlistment of a new evangel, rapturous joy and often the life long attachment of fellowship shared with those he wins.

It was report card time and Jimmy watched intently as his father noticed he had made an *F* in spelling, an *F* in math, an *F* in history, and an *F* in English; however, he made an *A* in citizenship and deportment. He looked up to his son and said,

"Great Jimmy. It looks like you're a neat, well-mannered, stupid kid."[9] Christians I fear are making *A's* in secondary subjects while making an *F* in their primary subject, soulwinning. It's report card time. What grade has the Master Teacher given you in the subject of soulwinning?

Charles C. Luther heard Reverend A.G. Upham speak of a young man who had been a Christian only a month and was dying. This young man was sad because he had so little time to serve the Lord. He said, "I'm not afraid to die; Jesus saves me now. But must I go empty handed?" This story led Luther to write the song, *Must I Go and Empty Handed* in 1877. This song serves as both a call to serious examination about and prompt commitment unto the task of soulwinning.

"Must I go, and empty handed,"
Thus my dear Redeemer meet?
Not one day of service give Him,
Lay no trophy at His feet?

"Must I go, and empty handed?"
Must I meet my Savior so?
Not one soul with which to greet Him,
Must I empty handed go?

Not at death I shrink or falter,
For my Savior saves me now;
But to meet Him empty handed,
Thought of that now clouds my brow.

O the years in sinning wasted,
Could I but recall them now,
I would give them to my Savior,
To His will I'd gladly bow.

O ye saints, arouse, be earnest,
Up and work while yet 'tis day;
Ere the night of death o'er take thee,
Strived for souls while still you may.

On September 7, 1860, the *Lady Elgin* in route for Chicago from Milwaukee encountered gale force winds in Lake Michigan. The schooner *Augusta* seeking help from the weather attempted to pull alongside the *Lady Elgin* but rammed her instead. Believing the *Lady Elgin* was not damaged the *Augusta* sailed on to Chicago. The captain of the *Augusta* was sadly wrong in that assumption because the *Lady Elgin* within twenty minutes broke apart and sank. At daybreak between 350 and 500 passengers and crew were floating in the water holding onto anything

they could.[10] Word came to a local college about this wreck and students hurried
to the shores of Lake Michigan. Ed Spencer, a famous swimmer stripped down to
the bare essentials, tied a rope to his waist and tossed the other end to fellow
students on the shore and swam out to the wreck. Grasping a drowning person he
would then give the sign for the students to pull him ashore. Spencer did this time
and again rescuing person after person until he had brought to shore ten people.
Exhausted, scarcely able to stand he warmed his body by a fire others had ignited.
As he looked back into the waters toward the *Lady Elgin* he saw men and women
still drowning. He said to fellow students, "Boys, I am going in again." They
replied, "No, no, Ed. It is utterly vain to try; you have used up all your strength,
you could not save anybody; for you to jump into the lake again will simply mean
for you to commit suicide." "Well," he cried, "boys, they are drowning, and I will
try, anyhow." As Spencer walked toward the cold waters of Lake Michigan his
friends said, "No, no Ed, no, don't try." His reply was, "I will." This young man
battled the currents and breakers bringing person after person to the shore until
they counted fifteen. In pulling him in to shore he could hardly stand by the fire to
warm himself due to intense fatigue. Looking back out into the waters Ed
exclaimed, "Boys, there's a man trying to save himself"; "Boys, there's a man
trying to save his wife." He then declared, "Boys, I am going to help him." "No,
no, Ed they exclaimed, "you can't help him. Your strength is all gone." Saying, "I
will try anyway" he dove back into the waters summoning all of his remaining
strength rescuing the man and woman.

Later Ed asked his brother, "Will, did I do my best?" Will responded, "Why, Ed,
you saved seventeen." Ed replied, "I know it, I know it, but I was afraid I didn't
do my very best. Will, do you think I did my very best." Will said, "Ed, you saved
seventeen" to which Will responded, "I know it, Will I know it; but oh, if I could
have saved just one more."[11]

Do you see the unsaved drowning in the ocean of eternal darkness at work, school,
neighborhood, marketplace and home? Are you doing your best – very best to
win as many as possible? As Ed, let's not count our life dear to us for the sake of
rescuing souls. Oh believer, keep soulwinning, keep going back into the water
time after time to rescue more and more even when strength has all but been
exhausted, and when as death opens the portals of Heaven for your entrance with
weeping eyes wail, "Oh, if I could have saved just one more." May God help us to
do our very best, win all we can and "save just one more" before its time to go
Home.

In a sermon prior to C. H. Spurgeon's death he said concerning his funeral, " . . .
you see my coffin carried to the silent grave, I should like every one of you,
whether converted or not, to be constrained to say, 'He did earnestly urge us, in
plain and simple language, not to put off the consideration of eternal things. He

did entreat us to look to Christ. Now he is gone, our blood is not at his door if we perish.' "[12] May lost souls testify to the same about you and me upon our departure. "I pray that the sharing of your faith may become effective when you perceive all the good that we may do for Christ" (Philemon v 6, NRSV).

ELEVEN

Soulwinning Sermons and Talks

The composition and delivery of effective sermons or talks on soulwinning is a great need of our day. In this chapter will be shared nineteen soulwinning outlines that may be used as a *lumber yard* for the gathering of material for construction of sermons or talks upon the subject.

1. Soulwinning Sermon Outline by R.A. Torrey.[1]

Why Every Christian Should Make Soulwinning His Life's Business
Matthew 4: 19

These words set forth two great thoughts: first, that if one would be a follower of Jesus, he must be a fisher of men and, second, that all that is really essential as a condition of success in being a fisher of men is that one be a true follower of Jesus. We are concerned here with the first thought: our Lord Jesus distinctly tells us that if we follow Him, He will make us fishers of men. If, then, we are not fishers of men, we are not following Jesus. The Greek word translated "fishers" is a peculiar word; it indicates a man whom fishing is his business – a *fisherman*– not merely one who fishes occasionally as a pastime or sport.

Six Reasons Why Every Christian Should Make Soul Winning His Life's Business.

1. This is the Work our Lord has commanded us to do. (Matthew 28: 18,19)
This commandment was not given merely to the apostles but to the rank and file of the church. So any Christian who is not leading others to be Disciples of Christ is disobeying his Commanding Officer.
2. It was the Business of life with our Lord Himself.
What is it to be Christian? Some will reply, "To be a follower of Jesus." Very well, but what is it to be a follower of Jesus? Again they will reply, "To have the same purpose in life that the Lord Jesus had." Very well, but what was our Lord's purpose in life? He has told us in the most explicit terms what His purpose in life was in Luke 19:10, "For the Son of man is come to *seek* and to *save that which* was lost.
3. This is the Work in which we enjoy the unspeakable blessing of the personal fellowship of Christ Himself. (Matthew 28: 18)
Here we see clearly the promise of our Lord to be with us always is conditioned upon our making disciples. Those who are not are constantly trying to appropriate this promise to themselves, which they have no right to do. The personal, conscious companionship of our Lord is dependent upon our having fellowship with Him in His work of saving souls.
4. In that Work alone we enjoy the fullness of the Holy Spirit's presence and power.
The Holy Spirit is given to the individual believer for the definite purpose of

witnessing for Christ (Acts 1:8). God does not give us the Holy Spirit merely that we may be happy, or even that we may be personally holy; He gives us His Holy Spirit for the specific purpose that we may be fitted for witnessing.

5. The Work that produces the most beneficent results.

This is made perfectly clear in James 5:20, "He that converts a sinner from the error of his way shall save a soul from death." Three words here need especial emphasis: "save" and "soul" and "death."

6. The Work that brings the most abundant reward.

A verse in the book of Daniel should sink into the heart of every young Christian – yes, and of every older Christian, too – Daniel 12:3: "And they that be wise shall shine as the brightness of the firmament, and they that turn many to righteousness as the stars for ever and ever." It does not pay to shine down here. But they that shine up yonder shall shine as the stars *forever and ever.* We could not most of us shine down here if we wished to; but we can all shine up there by turning many to righteousness, by winning others to Christ.

Will you make this the business of your life? Will you bear it in mind each day, shaping your business and your social engagements and your personal habits and everything else with the view of bringing as many as possible to a definite acceptance of the Lord Jesus Christ?

2. Soulwinning Sermon Outline by L.R. Scarborough.[2]

The Model Winner Under Temptation

Never has there started out any men or women in this world to do good and seek to lift up fallen humanity that the devil did not besiege them and seek to divert their service from the paths of truth and the cause of spiritual victory. Of Jesus Christ himself…He was no exception. The devil puts all of us into the testing crucible of his vigorous and aggressive temptation, if we head our lives towards the salvation of men. Immediately after Christ's baptism, the devil took him in charge and tried to destroy him by perilous temptations. They were all in the realms of the heights, on the top of the mountains, on the top of the temple. He tempts the ministry in the high places and tries to cause them to fall the farthest and the heaviest. Christ's deliverance was meant as a model of escape for us. It is a warning to all and yet an encouragement to all. Christ seems to have been delivered from these temptations with the same source of power by which we ourselves can be delivered, that is, by the use of the Word of God and the power of the Holy Spirit.

1. He was tempted in the line of food.

He was hungry and needed bread and the devil tried to tempt him on the bread line. In the realm of provision for one's self and one's family the bread question, the clothes question, the home question, the money question, is a line along which the devil tempts every one of us. Many a man has fallen where Jesus stood erect on this bread question.

2. The second temptation was on the question of promotion and protection. The devil sought to get Christ to promote and protect himself by presumptuous dependence on God, and this is a very great temptation to many preachers. Most of us at one time or another in our lives hunger for promotion, if we do not openly seek it. We want a larger place, a bigger church, a wider field, more recognition, some denominational place, some new titles, new honors, some further promotion with men.

3. The other temptation was in the line of advanced power, both with men and God. The devil told him that if he would worship him, he would give him authority, possession and control of all the world. There is a great danger that we who seek to win men will be tempted in the line the devil failed with Jesus, that is, for power, personal and denominational power. Jesus did not yield...He would not take anything out of the hands of the devil; and we lesser soulwinners should remember the vital point of this temptation in Christ's early ministry and turn away from it in our ministry as Jesus did in his.

4. Jesus answers the devil.

When Jesus Christ faced the devil in these three soul-testing temptations, his answers were positive, with conviction, and in the same line in which we can answer. His reply each time to the devil was scriptural.

It is necessary for us, as Jesus was, to be armed with the truth, hid away in our hearts, that we may have wherewithal to answer every fiery temptation of the evil one.

5. Modern temptations to soulwinners.

(1) Commercialism or the money-heart.

(2) Social evil.

It is very easy for soulwinners and evangelists to gain the confidence of women and it is tremendously tempting to them to sidestep and imperil and cripple and forever ruin their testimony to Christ by this tragic temptation.

(3) Other temptations are debts, dishonesty, and looseness in obligations.

The road of the truth through the past ages has piled out on either side the wrecks of many a useful preacher, because he allowed his expenditures to be greater than his receipts.

(4) Sensationalism, the spectacular in religion.

This is a very dangerous allurement. All sorts of antics and catchy methods and vaudeville stunts and appeals to curiosity will make their appeal through the influences of the devil to a popular-turned evangelist. If he follows these allurements his ministry will be meteoric. He will flash and fall. Sanity, common sense, the simplicity of the gospel, the track of the old truth, had better be followed by all of us who seek to win souls and put into our evangelism the constructiveness of the Kingdom of God.

(5) Professionalism is another danger.

There are many calls. The soulwinners who would build and succeed must study, seek new fields of thought, take time for recreation, save their nerves, fill up the fountains of their soul, and seek constantly to go deeper with God and deeper into the mines of truth.

Conclusion

There are many other temptations that come to the soulwinner, but these are the main ones. We should seek, as Christ did, to avoid and resist these temptations by a constant appeal to God's Word and a constant dependence upon the Holy Spirit, thus making our ministry fresh, rich, triumphant and constructive. We need to live very close to God if we resist the wiles of the devil and quench on the shield of faith all the fiery darts of the evil one whose poisons would seek to destroy our ministry and to stop us from the great work of winning men to Christ.

3. Soulwinning Sermon Outline by James Smith.[3]

Rescue Work by Angels
Genesis 19:1

"There came two angels to Sodom." Angels in Sodom! What a contrast to see the brightest and holiest of servants in the darkest and wickedest cities. Even slum work may become angelic. These messengers of mercy and of judgment are examples to all who desire to rescue the perishing. Notice –

1. Where they Went.

They went to "Sodom" (v 1). A city reeking with iniquity, and they were conscious that their eyes and ears must see and hear things that would pierce their souls with an agony of pain and distress, but they were prepared to suffer, they were willing even to "abide in the street all night" (v 2). Those who would seek the salvation of others must be ready to sacrifice their own comfort and ease.

2. Why they Went.

They went because the Lord sent them (v 13). They did not go because they felt that the wickedness of the city demanded that *something* should be done, or because they had nothing else more urgent to do. No. They went with a definite commission at the bidding of the Lord. They realized that the work was not theirs, but God's. They had come in His name, and in His strength, to do His will among them, and it would be done. The servants of Christ will soon grow weary in well-doing if they have not this perfect assurance, that they are in the very place and doing the very work He has sent them to do.

3. What they Went to do.

They went to preach instant salvation and coming judgment. "Up, get you out of this place, for the Lord will destroy this city" (v 14). They had no scheme of social reform to propose. Those Sodomites were condemned already. There was no alternative left them but to escape or perish. The eyes of these Heaven-sent messengers were wide awake to the real facts of the case, so that thy could do nothing else but press home their one message of warning and hope. They spoke and acted as those who believed in the "wrath to come," and who saw the peril of those who were disposed to "linger" through indecision (v 16). There was no time like *"now"* to them: "Behold, now is the day of salvation." So urgent were these evangelists that they literally laid hold of Lot, his wife, and his two daughters (v 16). *Personal* dealing they felt was a pressing necessity if such were to be rescued from the approaching doom. Why should preachers of the Gospel not be as earnest and as urgent as these two heralds were? Have they not as definite a message to deliver? Is there not the same danger of destruction awaiting those who believe not, nor obey the Gospel? (I Thessalonians 5:3). "This one thing I do" which characterized these "sent ones" is a special feature in all those who have been called of God and sent. He maketh His ministers a *flame* of fire.

4. Soulwinning Sermon Outline by E.J. Daniels.[4]

The Mission of the Church
Matthew 28:19

1. First, What is the Mission of the Church?

I think you will agree with me that Christ, the founder and head of the Church, alone has the right to tell us what the real mission of the Church is. You will find the mission as He gave it in various commissions Christ gave to the Church. I would like to sum up the mission of the church by using three words that a former Mississippi pastor gave to me last week.

(1) The Mission of the Church is Introduction.

The primary business of every Church is to introduce men to Jesus. The big job of every member of the church the world around is to tell men about Jesus and His power to save. We are to win men to Christ. I care not what else we may do; if we fail here, we have UTTERLY failed.

(2) The Mission of the Church is Induction.

Not only are we to introduce men to Christ, but we are to induct them into the church through baptism when they are saved. Our marching orders are to make disciples and baptize them. I have had people come up to me in revivals, and express amazement that I, an evangelist would stress baptism. How can any evangelist or pastor say that it does not matter whether we obey Christ.

(3) The Mission of the Church is Instruction.

The third facet of the mission of the church is instruction. We are "to teach them whatsoever I have commanded you." This is the part of the mission that requires the most patience and time. This is caring for babies after we get them born. I know a lot of preachers, especially some evangelists, who believe in obstetrics, but not in pediatrics. What are we to teach them? Teach them absolute obedience to the Word and Will of God.

2. May God help each of us to be Missionary in Person.

(1) We are to be Missionary in Purity.

Dr. Vance Havner has often said that the curse of our day is that we have too many preachers preaching a dynamite gospel while their people are living firecracker lives. The way people live gives the lie to the claims we make for the gospel.

(2) We are to be Missionary in Purse.

Preachers, it is our duty unto God to seek to show our people that they are robbing God and damning souls when they fail to be missionaries in purse. I know that many of them will get angry when we preach to them about their duty in money matters. Nevertheless, it is our duty unto God to preach the truth taught in the Bible concerning tithing.

(3) We are to be Missionary in Prayer.

I do not need to tell you that the Bible teaches that prayer has real power getting men saved. In Matthew 9:38 the Lord Jesus appeals to us to "Pray ye, therefore, the Lord of the harvest, that He will send forth laborers into the His harvest." We are to pray for missionaries to go abroad. We are to pray for them after they enter the field. We are to pray that lost men might be saved. We can have a real part in the winning of souls at home and abroad by our fervent, believing prayers. We are powerless because we are prayerless.

(4) We are to be Missionary in Passion.

By this I mean that we must have a love for souls of men everywhere. It is my honest conviction that the greatest need of every preacher and Christian is a greater burden and passion for lost souls. I know that I personally cry out to God more for a deep burden for souls than for any other thing, unless it be for the filling of the Holy Spirit.

(5) We are to be Missionary in Person.

Each individual member is to be daily about the work of winning the lost, seeking to get them to obey Christ in baptism, and obey Him in all things. The curse of our day in our Baptist churches, as I see it, is that we have too many who are willing to "let George do it." We have too many shirkers and not enough workers.

Conclusion

I want to close this simple message on "The Mission of the Church" by stressing the fact that the fields are white unto harvest and that tomorrow may be too late.

5. Soulwinning Sermon Outline by Francis Dixon.[5]

Paul: A True and Effective Witness
Acts 26: 13 – 29

This study has a very special application to every Christian, for every Christian is to be an effective witness (Acts 1:8). The Apostle Paul was a good, an effective and a true witness who delivered souls (Proverbs 14:25), and as we read through the book of Acts and Paul's letters we are impressed with his tremendous passion for souls which resulted in his being a mighty witness for his Lord. Look at him as he is presented to us in Acts 26: 22-23, and note some of the marks of a true and an effective witness.

1. A True and Effective Witness is one who Speaks.[2]

Notice the word "saying" (v 22), "spake" (v 24), "speak" (v 25), "speak" (v 26) – and look up Psalms 107:2! Of course, the most effective testimony we can bear before the world is that of a consistent, Christ-like life, but the testimony of the life must be expressed also with the lips – notice the difference between Mark 5:9

and Luke 8:39. We are all very good talkers when it comes to speaking on our favorite topics, our problems or our joys, and should we not speak of our dearest Friend, our loving Savior, the Lord Jesus? Are you an effective witness, one who speaks for the Lord, or do you say, "I can't..." (Jeremiah 1: 6-9)?

2. A True and Effective Witness is one who Speaks to All and Sundry.
In verse 22, the apostle tells us that he was constantly "witnessing both to small and great." Wherever he went he talked to others about his Lord; whether his audience consisted of one or many, rich or poor, young or old, educated or illiterate, Jews or Gentiles, kings or commoners, soldiers or sailors – always, in every place, he was an effective witness. See him at work in the synagogue (Acts 13:5); by the riverside (Acts 16:13); in prison (Acts 16: 25 -32); in the market place (Acts 17:17); going from house to house (Acts 20:20); at home (Acts 28:30-31); and in the palace (Philippians 1: 12 -13). Everyone whom Paul met was a soul for whom Christ died and was therefore a potential Christian.

3. A True and Effective Witness goes on doing the Job in spite of setbacks, discouragements, and even calamities.
In verse 22, the apostle says, speaking now twenty years after his conversion, "I continue unto this joy"; or, as the Revised Version renders it, "I stand firm!" He had the grace of continuance - stickability; he had grace and grit in spite of tremendous trials, persecutions, oppositions, setbacks and threatening – look at Acts 26:21 and 24, and 2 Corinthians 11: 23-28, and see some of the things with which he had to contend.. An effective witness must have a set purpose and an unflinching objective.

4. A True and Effective Witness is unflinchingly loyal to the Word of God.
Look again at verse 22 – "saying none other things than those which the prophets and Moses did say should come...." Paul believed the testimony of Moses and the prophets. He was quite sure about the absolute reliability of the scriptures; he knew they were fully inspired (2 Timothy 3:16), and that the Holy Ghost was their author (2 Peter 1:21), and he fully realized the solemn responsibility to accept God's revealed Word (Revelations 22: 18-19), and to proclaim it all (Acts 20:27).

5. A True and Effective Witness is one who has a working knowledge of the Bible.
Paul not only knew the scriptures but knew how to use them – verses 22 -23 imply this – compare 2 Timothy 2:15. From your Bible, can you lead a soul to Christ? Can you show all have sinned (Romans 3:23); that all need to be saved (Romans 6:23); that the Lord Jesus is the only Savior (Acts 4:12); and that salvation is by faith in Him (Acts 13:38-39)? An effective witness should be able to do this.

5. A True and Effective Witness is one who makes much of the Lord Jesus.
Read verse 23 again. It is full, not of Paul, but of the Lord Jesus Himself. We are not to witness to ourselves, our church, our denomination, but to the Lord Himself – look up Acts 1:8 again, and compare Acts 8:5 and 35. The Holy Spirit always points to and magnifies Him – look up John 16:14 and Acts 19: 17; and an effective witness will do likewise.

6. A True and Effective Witness is one who has obtained help from God.
Verse 22 tells us this. Here was Paul's secret – and here is ours! No one can be an effective witness without His help. What is this "help of God"? It is spiritual power, the enduement of the Holy Ghost, the anointing of the Spirit of God for which there is absolutely no substitute – look up Zech 4:6. This is the greatest need of all who would effectively witness for the Lord. When did Paul "obtain" this help? (Acts 9:17; Acts 1:8)

6. Soul winning Sermon Outline by C.H. Spurgeon.

Obstacles to Soul Winning

1. Indifference.
2. Unbelief.
3. Delay.
4. Carnal Security.
5. Despair.
6. Love of sin.
7. Self-righteousness.
8. The habits and company of unbelievers.

7. Soulwinning Sermon Outline by Curtis Hutson.
(Sermon notes from a sermon the author heard Hutson preach)

The Importance of Soulwinning

Is it scriptural to soulwin? Why don't we? It is because we don't see the importance of it.

1. Soul Winning is important because of the Peril of Souls.
Sinners are condemned, sentenced to Hell (John 3:18).
2. Soulwinning is important because of the Price of Souls.
A French chemist claimed that the soul weighed 21 grams. He weighed the terminally ill on very sensitive scales and then again at the moment of death. The body weight dropped 21 grams, thus his conclusion the soul weighs 21 grams. I don't know how much a soul weighs, but I do know its value. Jesus stated , "What shall a man gain if he gain the whole world and lose his own soul?" One's soul is more valuable the whole world.
3. Soulwinning is important because of the Payment Jesus made for Souls.
Two thousand years ago Jesus bore the sins of the world suffering at the hands of man, God and the devil.
4. Soulwinning is important because of the Products of Soul Winning.
Soulwinning produces everything a pastor wants in his church. "He that soweth sparingly, reapeth sparingly." If you are reaping sparingly than you must be sowing

sparingly. Basically you do the reaping of what you sow.

(1) Produces attendance

(2) Produces joy among the members

(3) Produces love for each other

Nothing makes one anymore happy than winning souls. One never sees any unhappy people at a hospital nursery.

(4) Produces additional support for the church

8. Soulwinning Sermon Outline by Frank Shivers.

The Soulwinner
Acts 20: 17 – 38

Soulwinning is the monumental task of bringing the lost to Christ at every cost and was the great work of Paul all through his ministry. Unraveled in our text are seven traits of the New Testament soulwinner as revealed in Paul's life.

1. The Soulwinner's Purity (v 18).

No man could accuse Paul of unethical or immoral conduct. They knew what manner of persons he was in private and public. The first law of spiritual harvest therefore revealed in Paul's life is holiness of life in the soulwinner.

A. L.R. Scarborough said, "Holiness must be on the skirts of God's spiritual priests today."

B. Praying Hyde said, "Holiness precedes soulwinning."

C. Murray Downey said, "It is more important to be Clean than Clever."

D. Robert M. McCheyne said, "A holy man is an awesome weapon in the hands of God."

E. Our own Commander-in-Chief stated, "Be thou clean that bear the vessels of the Lord." (Isaiah 52:11)

F. It has been said that God can use a tall vessel or a small vessel but He will not use a dirty vessel.

Illustrate with the Ralph Connors account of the football player named Cameron and his being found unfit to help the team (included in Chapter Three).

How often in confronted with an opportunity to win a soul we fail because of being spiritually unfit.

2. The Soulwinner's Passion. (v 20, 31)

The holiest of saints will not win souls unless consumed with a deep burning passion for them like that of Paul's. Paul testified, "I have kept back nothing that was profitable unto you but have showed you, and have taught you publicly, and from house to house" (v 20). Verse 31 states, "Therefore watch, and remember, that by the space of three years I ceased not to warn every one night and day with tears." In Romans Paul allowed us again look deep inside his heart as he cried, "Brethren, my heart's desire and prayer to God for Israel is, that they might be saved" (10:1) and "I have great heaviness and continual sorrow in my heart. For I could wish that my self were accursed from Christ for my brethren, my kinsman according to the flesh" (9: 2-3). Paul was a man of consuming passion for the eternally damned. Oh, that such a passion will be manifest in the saints of God.

A. Oh, for a passion for souls like that of George Whitefield, who said, "Lord give me souls, or take my soul.

B. Oh, for a passion for souls like that of William Burns, who said, "The thud of Christless feet on the road to Hell is breaking my heart."

C. Oh, for a passion for souls like that of David Brainerd, who declared, "I cared not how I lived or what hardships I might go through, as long as I might win souls."

D. Oh, for a passion for souls like that of L.R. Scarborough who said, "I want to win all the lost ones I can to Christ and then as death opens the gates to glory win some lost soul to Christ."

E. Oh, for a passion for souls like that of William Booth who in response to the King of England VII for his good work wrote in the Kings autograph album, "Your Majesty, some men's passion is for art, some men's passion is for fame, some men's passion is for gold. My ambition is the souls of men."

F. Oh, for a passion for souls like John Wesley who declared that he was "out of breath pursing souls."

G. Oh, for a passion for souls like that of the prophet Jeremiah who wished his heads waters and his eyes a fountain of tears that he may weep for the salvation of Israel.

H. Oh, for a passion for souls like that of Moses who was willing for his name to be blotted out of God's record book for the salvation of Israel.

What is your consuming passion? It is that which exhausts and expends your time, talent and treasure.

3. The Soulwinner's Proclamation. (v 21)
As vitally important as purity of heart and passion of soul are in soulwinning they will avail little good apart from the soulwinner declaring the right message. The message of Paul to all he met was simply "repentance toward God and faith in the Lord Jesus Christ" (v 21). Bailey Smith well said this is the kind of proclamation that not only will keep men out of Hell but keep Hell out of men. This biblical message must not be watered down, compromised or neglected in our effort to win souls.

A magazine carried a cartoon during the 1960 Olympics depicting a marathon runner rushing into the palace of a King. Fatigue and anguish was written all over his face. As he falls before the King he is shown looking up to him saying, "I have forgotten my message." I fear many believers when they go soulwinning have forgotten their primary message. The message the King of Kings has charged the believer to tell the eternally damned is not one dealing with baptism, church membership, tithing, doing right, religious reform or 'quit your meanness' but "Ye must be born again."

4. The Soulwinner's Power (v 23).

How are the saved to accomplish the magnanimous task of telling the entire world of the Good News of Jesus Christ? More specifically and personally how are you to win friends, relatives and acquaintances to Jesus Christ? It is through the same person and power in which the apostle Paul did. Let me first hasten to state what this power source is not God has made available for the work of soulwinning.

A. It is not intellectual power.

B. It is not oratory power.

Men may speak with the golden tongue of a Chrysostom causing people to be spelledbound but one's flowery vocabulary and oratory ability cannot convict or save.

C. It is not debating power.

A man convinced against his will is unconvinced still.

D. It is not salesmanship power.

Saturn automobile dealerships build their business on letting the *Saturn* car sale itself, not a salesman. GMC believes this product is so great that once a prospect seriously considers it they will buy. The Christian's task is to present Christ in all His beauty and glory to the unsaved and let Him *sale* Himself. In reality Christ is the soulwinner, we are just His *agent or representative*.

E. It is not booklet power.

Mere mental assent to words of Truth printed in a *booklet* fail to genuinely convict or convert the sinner.

F. It is not Personality power.

Oswald Chambers stated, "When we say "What a wonderful personality, what a fascinating person, and what wonderful insight!" then what opportunity does the gospel of God have through all that? It cannot get through, because the attraction is to the messenger and not the message. If a person attracts through his personality, that becomes his appeal. If, however, he is identified with the Lord Himself, then the appeal becomes what Christ can do."[6]

What is the power source of the soulwinner in his effort to win men? It is that of the Holy Spirit. Jesus promised that the Holy Spirit would infill the believer enabling him in this great task (Acts 1:8). The reason why so few believers are soulwinning or soulwinning with results is due to the lack of Holy Spirit control. The infilling of the Holy Spirit is a pre-requisite to soulwinning (Ephesians 5: 18).

5. The Soulwinner's Petition (v 36).
"He kneeled down, and prayed." In Romans 10:1 Paul declared, "My heart desire and prayer for Israel is that they be saved." All scripture regarding Paul makes clear that he was a man who travailed over souls in fervent prayer.

The soulwinner should have a Ten Most Wanted Prayer List of souls he prays for to be saved. Right now write down in your Bible or on the bulletin ten names of people you know are lost and commit to pray for their salvation. Stephen Olford said, "Before you talk to man about God, talk to God about man." Pray for the sinner before you confront him with his need of salvation.

6. The Soulwinner's Practice (v 20).
Paul did not merely talk about soulwinning. He did it! Sermons, songs, studies on soulwinning are a dime a dozen. The church needs men and women who actually do as Paul and knock on doors seeking the lost. Billy Graham stated, "There are many preachers but few soulwinners."[7] John Bunyan said, "The heart of Christianity is in the practice part." D. L. Moody was attending a conference on soulwinning when he decided to walk outside to the street and actually witnessed to the unsaved. He practiced soulwinning while those in the church proclaimed it. In his church in Chicago he had written above each exit, "You are now entering the mission field of the world - go soulwinning." May these words be inscribed above the doors of every Sunday School, worship center and saints home door. W. A. Criswell said, "We are found to find others; we are won to win others; we are told to tell others and we are saved to save others."

The illustration in Chapter Ten about Jimmy's report card should be used here, followed by asking, "What grade has the Master Teacher given you in the subject of soulwinning?"

7. The Soulwinner's Product (v 37 – 38).
I would like to think that the "they" that "wept sore and fell on Paul's neck, and kissed him" were people his ministry had touched for Christ. In this number I hear one say, "Thank you Paul for taking time to come to my home to tell me of Christ for I would yet be lost had you not." I hear yet another with joy cry, '"Thank you Paul for winning my daughter to Christ for she was on the road to suicide." Another I hear say, "Thank you Paul for telling me of Jesus who has filled my life with great peace, joy and purpose." O the ecstasy of winning a lost person to Christ!

At a can recycling factory in Atmore, Alabama, a man responded to my witness in saying, "I have fallen down so many times that the last time I did I almost decided not to get back up." It was so great to tell Harold of Jesus who could satisfy his every need filling his heart with purpose and hope. In Florence, South Carolina a teenage boy was saved in a revival meeting. Upon my return to that church sometime later he pulled me to the side and said, "Thank you for telling me about Jesus." Wow. Oh the joy of soulwinning. The psalmist is exactly right in stating, "Those that sow in tears shall reap in joy" (Psalms 126: 5) D. L. Moody said, "If we only lead one soul to Jesus Christ, we may set a stream in motion that will flow on when we are dead and gone."

The soulwinner will not win all he confronts but oh what joy it is to win some and evidence the change of life God brings about in ones life, home, marriage and work. It has to be the greatest, most satisfying work on earth. Let's go soulwinning!

Conclusion (The story of the tornado warning referenced in Chapter One)

9. Soulwinning Sermon Outline by Stephen Olford.[8]

The Successful Soulwinner
Matthew 12: 18-21

What, then, are the characteristics of the soulwinner? Let us turn again to Matthew 12: 18-21 and notice what is said of the Lord Jesus. God sets Him forth with the words, "Behold my servant." Let us, then, behold these characteristics of the Servant of the Lord.

1. His Appointment.
"Behold my servant, whom I have chosen" (v 18).
All true soulwinners are divinely appointed. In the counsels of eternity the Lord Jesus was appointed to be Seeker and Savior of men. What was true of the Lord Jesus applies also to us.

2. His Approbation.
"Behold...my beloved in whom my soul is well pleased..." (v 18).
Before a life can be a power to God, it must be a pleasure to God. This was also true of our Savior as evidenced by the Father's words of approval at the baptism and transfiguration of His well-beloved Son. (See Matthew 3:17; 17:5) We can merit that approval only by complete surrender to the Father's will.

3. His Anointing.
"Behold my servant...I will put my Spirit upon him" (v 18).
This is the anointing for service and soulwinning.

4. His Announcement.
"Behold my servant...He shall show (proclaim) judgment to the Gentiles" (v 18).
So our message, in personal conversation or public discourse, must be that of righteousness made available through our Savior, who is just and the Justifier of all who believe in Him (Romans 3:26).

5. His Approach.
"Behold my servant, whom I have chosen; my beloved, in whom my soul is well pleased: I will put my spirit upon him, and he shall shew judgment to the Gentiles. He shall not strive, nor cry; neither shall any man hear his voice in the streets. A bruised reed shall he not break, and smoking flax shall he not quench, till he send forth judgment unto victory" (v 18-20).

These words describe the pervading calmness and composure that characterized our Savior's approach to man in His work of soulwinning.

6. His Assurance.
"Behold my servant, whom I have chosen; my beloved, in whom my soul is well pleased: I will put my spirit upon him, and he shall shew judgment to the Gentiles. He shall not strive, nor cry; neither shall any man hear his voice in the streets. A bruised reed shall he not break, and smoking flax shall he not quench, till he send forth judgment unto victory."

The Lord Jesus was never a pessimist or a defeatist. He was confident of the ultimate victory of God's purpose of grace. This secret assurance gave Him poise and a positive response in dealing with men and women. Such assurance must also characterize us if we would succeed in the work of soulwinning.

7. His Acceptance.
"Behold my servant, whom I have chosen; my beloved, in whom my soul is well pleased: I will put my spirit upon him, and he shall shew judgment to the Gentiles. And in his name shall the Gentiles trust" (v 18,21).

In our contact and conversation with people we, as soulwinners, must be characterized by a reality and radiance of faith if we would have acceptance with souls who are hungry for God.

Conclusion
If truly born again, we, too, have with us the wonderful secret of successful soul winning. God's perfect Servant and Soulwinner lives in our hearts and longs to express Himself through our lives.

10. Soulwinning Sermon Outline by B.H. Carroll.[9]

Conditions of Success in Soulwinning
Acts 11: 22-24; Psalms 51: 11-13

Upon these two passages of Scripture I wish to set forth briefly some of the qualifications and characteristics of either preacher or layman who likely is to be successful in leading souls to Christ. It is said here of Barnabas that he possessed four of these qualifications or characteristics:

1. First, he was glad when he saw evidence that Gentiles were converted at Antioch. There was no envy excited in his heart by the display of the divine power toward the Grecians, although it contravened all his race prejudices. I put this, then, as one of the first things – the kind of a spirit that rejoices, that is glad at the display of the divine power in the salvation of men. I am sure that it is impossible for anyone to be influenced in leading another to Christ whose entire heart is not made glad by the display of the divine grace in the conviction and conversion of sinners.

We may examine our hearts upon this point and may measure our readiness for a word of this kind by asking a question: Would we be glad tonight if God should commence a work of grace in this house, or would we regard it as so great an inconvenience to us that we could not take pleasure in this display of the divine power?

2. The second characteristic possessed by Barnabas as stated here, was that "he was a good man."
I shall never attempt to set a limit to the means employed by the Spirit of God in dealing with men, but may say this: That unless a man is a good man, unless he has the reputation of being a good man, unless in the estimation of people that are without he is what is ordinarily called a good man, he cannot be very efficient in leading them, through any influence he may bring to bear, into an interest in the Christian religion.

The term "good man" covers the whole ground of moral action, in the common acceptation of that word: veracity, honesty, kindness, mercy, and all kindred qualities.

3. The third qualification possessed by Barnabas is far more important: "He was full of the Holy Spirit."
But what means the phrase, "full of the Holy Spirit?" It does not mean that you should be a converted man, though that is implied. It means far more than that. A great many genuinely converted men are not full of the Holy Spirit. When we say that a man is full of the Holy Spirit, that means that the divine indwelling governs his actions, furnishes his motives, giving him his power, as when on the day of Pentecost they were all filled with the Spirit and so induced with power.

4. His fourth qualification is thus expressed: "He was full of faith."
This, though implying it, does not refer to personal saving faith because every Christian who personally receives and appropriates Jesus Christ has that faith. To be "full of faith" means something more than and different from that. One "full of faith" fully assures his heart that what God has spoken He will surely bring to pass, and so sets his mind and stays his soul upon the promises of God that you cannot scare him, you cannot shake him from his foundation. And so with great confidence and assurance he goes out into the world.

To be "full of faith" then means that every word God of God is not only "yea, yea and nay, nay," but that you see it to be so, and you feel it to be so, and you risk your life upon its being so. Indeed, you go out and do things in your confidence that to the unspiritual would make you appear to be a fool.

Conclusion
Such being the character of Barnabas, what followed? It is said that "much people were added to the Lord."

(Part II of this sermon is based on Psalms 51. Carroll presented in this part of the message the negative aspects – the disqualifications of a person being a soulwinner.)

11. Soulwinning Sermon Outline by W. Stanford Reid.[10]

God's Feeble Witnesses
I Corinthians 1: 26-31

Every member of Christ's Church ought to be a witness for Him. Today, as at all other times, the crying need of the Christian Church is for witnesses. In our day and generation the Christian message often seems to be outmoded, outdated, and generally irrelevant. Consequently, in self-conscious weakness we refrain from speaking the word that God would place in our mouths.

1. God's Call of Feeble Witnesses.
First of all, and of fundamental importance, is the fact that God calls these feeble witnesses. Paul begins by saying that the early Christians did not appoint themselves. It was God that determined that they should bring Christ to the world and this must always be the case. Paul assures the Corinthian Christians, however, that if they indeed know Christ as their Savior and Lord they also have a call from God to tell others about Christ. The Apostle is not here writing his letter to a few select Corinthian leaders, such as the pastors and elders of the congregation. He is speaking to all of the believers in Christ, and pointing out that God has called each of them to bear witness.

Thus, whether we are rich or poor, wise or foolish, in the eyes of the world, we must continually remind ourselves that as Christians God has chosen us to be His witness and that from the world's point of view we are silly, even moronic, in bearing testimony to such a simple gospel. That is the high call of every Christian.

2. God's Power for Feeble Witnesses.
In the second place the Apostle points out that with their call from God to be His witnesses, the Corinthian Christian have also received His power. The same truth hold good for us today.

3. God's Triumph through Feeble Witnesses.
In the third place, the Apostle speaks about the triumph of God's feeble witnesses. Because the power of God makes the testimony of Christians effective, this witness wins the victory (I Corinthians 1:28-29). Here is the triumph of God through His feeble witnesses, ...the triumph that throughout the world today is manifesting itself in hosts of humble hearts and lives who have been transformed through God's feeble witnesses. In all such triumphs no one feels more astonished then the Christian witness himself. Through the feeblest of the saints the Spirit of God brings to Christ as Savior and Lord those who have been His enemies. Through feeble witnesses He has won the victory (II Corinthians 2:14A).

Conclusion
Again and again Christian history has illustrated the truth of our text. In the Early Church God's feeble witnesses often came from among slaves and other social outcasts. Through such lowly agents, many of whom encountered persecution, torture, and death, the church conquered large parts of the Roman Empire. During the Reformation Luther, Calvin, and other men on whom the Roman Church looked down, won for the evangelical cause large portions of Europe. In Victorian England such a scholar as William Robert Dale stood amazed at the outpouring effects of the Gospel as spoken by such an unlearned man as Dwight L. Moody. Likewise in our own century, with all its materialism, sophistication, and secularism, the Lord blesses personal work by countless inconspicuous saints.

Many times the believer may feel that his testimony is feeble, foolish, and ineffective. Still he is to continue bearing witness, knowing that he is not the one to decide whether or not his words will win a soul for Christ.

12. Soulwinning Sermon Outline by C.H. Spurgeon.[11]

The Making of Men-Catchers
Matthew 4:19
Conversion is most fully displayed when it leads converts to seek the conversion of others: we must truly follow Christ when we become fishers of men.

1. Something to be done by us. "Follow Me."
A. We must be separated to Him that we may pursue His object.
B. We must abide with Him that we may catch His spirit.
C. We must obey Him that we may learn His method.
Teach what He taught. (Matthew 28:20)
Teach as He taught. (Matthew 11:29; I Thessalonians 2:7)
Teach such as He taught, namely, the poor, the base, children, etc.

2. Something to be done by Him. "I will make you."
A. By our following Jesus He works conviction and conversion in men; He uses our example as a means to the end.

B. By His Spirit He qualifies us to reach men.

C. By His secret working on men's hearts He speeds us in our work.

3. A Figure Instructing Us. "Fishers of Men."
The man who saves souls is like a fisher upon the sea.
A fisher is dependent and trustful.
He is diligent and preserving.
He is intelligent and watchful.
He is laborious and self-denying.
He is daring, and is not afraid to venture upon a dangerous sea.
He is successful. He is no fisher who never catches anything.

13. Soulwinning Sermon Outline by Porter M. Bales.[12]

The Last Question Ever Asked
Psalms 142:4

Some years ago, in Jacksonville, Florida, a policeman served for twenty years as a traffic officer. His business was to keep traffic in that great city moving, by directing and signaling the many tourists and travelers who passed his street intersection constantly. During these twenty years, he was asked all sorts of questions about all sorts of matters by thousands who passed that way. He was asked the direction and mileage to thousands of places; his opinion about hundreds of questions; about his own personal health; the welfare of this personal family and a multitude of other things. One day, after spending twenty years directing traffic and being quizzed by thousands of people, one man came and asked if he was a Christian.

This question, asked concerning his soul's welfare by one who cared, made him think. As he thought, his soul was aroused and moved toward God. He confessed his Lord, followed him in baptism, and was a faithful and loyal deacon in the great Main Street Baptist Church of that city. Yes! The last question one is ever asked is that about his soul. No wonder David cried out in his distress, "No man cared for my soul."

There are so many reasons why we should care for the souls of men.

1. The Kingdom workers have come from homes where a sympathetic interest and a sincere care for their souls were manifested.
A study of the biographies of one hundred twenty-eight missionaries some years ago revealed the fact that one hundred twenty-one came from homes that were deeply and manifestly religious – homes that magnified Christ, homes that were loyal to the program of the church, faithful in the work of our Lord, and reverent in spirit; homes where it was easy in youth to find God.

2. A second reason for caring for the souls of men is because many men are anxious and will respond to the proper interest in their souls.
Down deep in the hearts of all men there is a heart hunger for God. They may try to hide it and suppress it and conceal it; they may try to cover it with all sorts of excuses, but it is there and, like Banquo's Ghost, it will not down. They care for their souls because they know that life is uncertain. None knows when the brittle cord of life will be snapped and his soul thrust into a godless eternity. If men would think on their evil ways and on the uncertainty of life, earnestly and seriously, there would be no trouble reaching people for God.

3. Another reason is because of the reality of God's saving grace.
Christ Jesus, God's only begotten and beloved Son, can change the hearts of men. He saves with an everlasting salvation. He turns men about and starts them on the road to right living. He effects a transformation in their lives. It makes a great deal of difference when one comes to die whether he has made it right with God or not. There is reality in the saving power of Jesus.

4. Again, we should have a care for souls of men because of the impressions made on us in early youth by those who have asked about *our* souls. There are the impressions that last down through life's long day. These are the ones that are imperishable. These are they that never fade away. Some of you can feel yet the hand that rested on your head and hear yet the appealing voice that spoke about your soul long years ago.

The one supreme care of every child of God should be an interest, an abiding, everlasting interest, a heart-hungering interest, a soul-longing interest in the spiritual welfare of man. No preacher can give to every member of his church a job. If we are saved, if we are alive and interested in the ongoing of the church, we will not wait until the preacher or some church official assigns to us a task; we will go out and seek others for Jesus. There are a thousand ways to show your care for the souls of men. The spoken word, the labor of love, some kindness manifested, moving your church membership, attendance on the worship of God, earnest prayer in their behalf, and loyalty to the services of your church.

5. We should care for the souls of men because Jesus Christ and him crucified is the world's only hope.
The world is sick and feverish and restless and tossing. There are many remedies prescribed for the world's ills. The teacher says that more knowledge is the remedy, but we will never know enough. The artists say that more beauty is the remedy, but a bouquet of flowers will not ease the cutting pains of blood poison. The philosopher says we need a new theory of life, but do not now live perfectly the theories we have. The supreme need of the world is Jesus. He will cure every ill of every individual, of every home, of every community anywhere. He will cool the fever of the restless world, soothe its nerves, bring order out of chaos, and peace to a troubled soul. He and he alone, is the remedy for the world's ills.

14. Soulwinning Sermon Outline by Frank Shivers.

The In and Out of Soulwinning

1. The Exhortation of Soulwinning – Matthew 28: 18-20
Jesus commands the saved to witness.
2. The Expectation of Soulwinning - I John 2:3: I Peter 3:15
Jesus expects the saved to witness. Soulwinning should be second nature.
3. The Energy of Soulwinning – Acts 1:8
Jesus empowers the saved to witness.
4. The Equipment of Soulwinning – Ephesians 6:13-18
Jesus equips the saved to witness.
5. The Ease of Soulwinning – John 1:40 – 42A
It is simple for the saved to witness.
6. The Earnestness of Soulwinning – Jude 22; Acts 20:31; Romans 9: 1-3
The great requirement of the saved to witness is burning compassion.
7. The Ecstasy of Soulwinning – Psalms 126:5; Luke 10:17
The joy of the saved in witnessing is indescribable.
8. The Effect of Soulwinning – Psalms 126: 6; John 4:39; Jude 23
The soulwinner snatches *"brands from the burning."*
9. The Enemy of Soulwinning – Matthew 10:28; 2 Timothy 1:7
A primary obstacle hindering the saved to witness is fear.
10. The End of Soulwinning – Luke 19:13
The saved (*stewards*) are to witness until Jesus (*Master*) returns.

15. Soulwinning Sermon Outline by Hyman J. Appelman.[13]

The Soulwinner's Promise
Psalms 126:6

This is the soulwinner's text – the simplest, the most definite in the world. Its directions are positive; its assurances encouraging. God, Christ and the Holy Spirit are behind it. The testimony of nineteen hundred years supports its assertion. The witness of the great soulwinners through the ages sustains its direct promise. It is universal, unqualified, to be accepted and made concrete by all who have made soulwinning the ultimate aim of their Christian experience and existence.

Clearly, easily read, on the very face of the verse, are its three stirring thoughts.

1. The Passion of the Soulwinner.
The passion of the soulwinner is two-fold: a burning passion of love for the blessed Redeemer; a burdening compassion of longing for the souls of men. Jesus kept sweet in our souls will strengthen us in sorrows, sustain us in toil, supply us with the peace of God which passeth all understanding. Our passion for Christ will generate within us a compassion for the souls of men. The two are inseparable. They ever go together.

Dry-eyed, dry-hearted, dry-tongued preaching, praying and personal work will never win souls for Christ. Someone has well said, "It takes a broken heart to preach a bleeding Cross." Cry unto God, beloved. Cry unto God for the gift of passion, the gift of tears. Compassion for souls must be developed, or our work will become matter-of-fact and mechanical. A passionless Christian is a bitter anomaly. A passionless Christian is the heartache of heaven. A passionless Christian is the laughing stock of hell.

2. The Program of the Soulwinner.
Let Jesus be our great example in this. Let Paul's life and pursuits guide us, challenge us, instruct us. What did Jesus do to win the lost? What did Paul do to rescue the perishing? Two things signalize the lives of both Jesus and Paul. Intensive prayer was one of them. Extensive witness bearing, publicly and from house to house, was the other element in their success. We can do no better than follow in their steps. We cannot improve upon their procedure.

Prayer will convict and convert the lost about us. Prayer will bring the Spirit down upon us. Prayer will lead us into the pathway of duty. The second part of the soulwinner's program is this: he must *go into all the world, and preach the gospel to every creature.* This Christian generation lacks "going" Christians. There is seed to sow. I am aware that much of our witness-bearing is futile because we do not use the proper seed, the Word of God. The very essence of sowing is often left out. There is not a word about sin and salvation.

3. The Promise to the Soulwinner.
"Shall doubtless come again with rejoicing, bringing his sheaves with him."
This is the guarantee of God. God's promise has never failed. The "going," weeping, sowing Christian will become the reaping Christian. Where Jesus goes, there is joy. Where Jesus goes, there is victory. Where Jesus goes, there is fruitfulness. This promise has never fallen short of fulfillment. Our going, our weeping, our sowing shall not be in vain. All the power in heaven and earth is at the command of those who do the will of God in this most sacred task to be performed by the children of God.

The joy of the soulwinner is beyond description. It outstrips and outweighs any and every other benediction and pleasure that comes to the human heart. Nothing on earth can compare with it. To know that you have been instrumental in the hands of the Holy Spirit in rescuing a brand from the burning will compensate for every tear, for every toil, for every trial, for every trouble that may come your way in this greatest of all pursuits.

Conclusion
This very day, this very hour, this very moment let us determine in our hearts that we shall be in the ranks of the soulwinners. Let us dedicate ourselves to the task

with all that we are and have. Let us count no cost too great, no sacrifice too extensive, no toil too arduous, no task too exacting to accomplish this great duty.

16. Soulwinning Sermon Outline by L.R. Scarborough.[14]

Evangelism in the Life of Jesus

The examples of Jesus in soulwinning sweep the whole gamut of types of evangelism. Practically every expression of soulwinning in all the kingdom of God today finds in the ministry of Jesus a great outstanding illustration and tremendous emphasis. I want to sum up and set out the different ways in which he expressed his love-longings for a lost world in his effort to win men to life everlasting.

1. Personal Evangelism.
Jesus was a great believer in carrying the gospel to men one by one, face to face, in personal approach.
2. Domestic Evangelism.
Jesus believed in our reaching for life everlasting every one in our home circle.
3. Commercial and Professional Evangelism.
I mean by this the obligation of one businessman or one professional man to win to Christ his business and professional friend. The saved employer ought to lead to Christ the unsaved employee; and the saved employee ought to lead to Christ the unsaved employer.
4. Educational Evangelism.
Jesus in his great commission married in a holy union education and soulwinning. The soulwinner is the forerunner of the teacher; and evangelism is preparation for the school. They must go hand in hand if the world is to be won and trained and cultured for Christ. This means every teacher ought to be a soulwinner and that every school, certainly religious schools, should be hotbeds for evangelism.
5. Wayside Evangelism.
The example of Christ in the matter of picking up souls wherever he found them is a great encouragement to all those who would testify for Christ by the waysides, roadsides, seasides, everywhere.
6. Outdoor Evangelism.
The gospel is an outdoor religion. It likes free air, the health-giving ozones of the open places. The first preacher of the gospel – John the Baptist- was an outdoor, country preacher.
7. Church Evangelism.
He organized his church and churches to be the mighty agencies of soulwinning the world around.
8. Pastoral Evangelism.
Jesus himself was the great shepherd of souls; and, as the shepherd, he set the example for all pastors in soulwinning. He put the pastor in the churches as God's big man, his key man in soulwinning. The pastor ought to love it, believe in

it, study it, prepare for it, practice it, preach it, and major in it.

9. Layman Evangelism.

Jesus was a great believer in utilizing the men and women in the ranks of his disciples for soulwinning. He used more than apostles. He used the seventy who, as far as we know, were laymen.

10. Evangelist Evangelism.

The New Testament recognizes the evangelist and makes special mention of him and his work and bids him God-speed and honors and recognizes him as having an important place in the constructive and aggressive forces of the kingdom of God. These men go about winning the lost to Christ, holding revivals, and creating pentecosts of soulwinning power. Jesus and the New Testament give honor and place to such men.

11. Singing Evangelism.

There are no records in the New Testament of the singing evangelist, but there is nothing in the New Testament to forbid such glorious work; the grave work of singing evangelists with their marvelous leadership in song has come up out of the very heart of the New Testament and the work of Christ.

12. Perennial Evangelism.

Jesus believed in soulwinning in season and out of season. It was the master passion of his life, the primal task of his ministry. He believed in it everywhere.

Conclusion

In these and in other ways, Christ and the example He gave through his ministry show us today the importance, the necessity, and the call to a life of evangelism.

17. Soulwinning Sermon Outline by Frank Shivers.

"Shall We Sit Here?"
Numbers 32:6

The children of Gad and Reuben preferred to remain in their comfort and safety zone at home while their "brethren" went to war. Moses calls their hand on this great sin. I choose to adapt this question to apply to the battle for souls of which many saints neglect by asking, "Shall other believers engage in the battle for souls, and shall ye sit here while they do?" Concerning this question note:

1. It is a Personal Question.

It was directed specifically to the children of Gad and Reuben. It was these believers who refused to join other saints in the *war* opting to stay where they were. The question of the hour is for saints who are Gadites and Reubenites who neglect soulwinning. It doesn't apply to those who are passionately and faithfully soulwinning leaving the place of their comfort zone making sacrifices and taking risks. Are you a Gaddite and Reubenite relying upon others to go to the front line for Jesus at your school or job while you stay where you are?

2. It is a Pointed Question.

There was no way for the Gadites or Reubenites to misunderstand the question.

Moses didn't try to dress it up in user-friendly terminology. Note the specificity of the question, not a question about stewardship, church attendance, or even devotional life but about joining the battle against the enemy. This clear, unmistakable question must be asked of saints who neglect battling for souls.

3. It is a Pertinent Question.

The question is relevant because God did not exempt these two tribes from fighting in the battle for His cause and glory. The church has too few soulwinning workers and too many soulwinning shirkers. No more pertinent question deems to be asked among the Gadites and Reubenites of our churches regarding soulwinning than this one. "Shall your brethren go to war, and shall ye sit here?"

4. It is a Priority Question.

This question was asked urgently. The battle was about to begin. Help on the frontlines was needed. It could not be delayed until later. In a day when 92 percent of Southern Baptists will die without ever witnessing to one soul about Christ this question must be addressed passionately, urgently and quickly of God's people.

5. It is a Perennial Question.

This question demands *preaching* continuously until every saint joins in the battle for souls or every lost person is saved. Sunday school teachers, pastors, evangelists, student ministers, missionaries, musicians and soulwinners at large must ever pose this question elevating the need in the eyes of the saved of the need to win souls.

6. It is a Profitable Question.

This question led to the Gadites and Reubenites declaring to Moses, "We will build sheepfolds here for our cattle, and cities for our little ones: But we ourselves will go ready armed before the children of Israel, until we have brought them unto their place: and our little ones shall dwell in the fenced cities because of the inhabitants of the land. We will not return unto our houses, until the children of Israel have inherited every man his inheritance. For we will not inherit with them on yonder side Jordan, or forward; because our inheritance is fallen to us on this side Jordan eastward (v 16 – 19). "And the children of Gad and the children of Reuben spake unto Moses, saying, Thy servants will do as my lord commandeth (v 26). Moses' question obviously accomplished profitable results. Such a question regarding soulwinning is intended to accomplish the same – the prompting of saints who have been negligent in soulwinning to make commitments to join in the battle for souls.

Conclusion

"Shall your brethren go to war, and shall ye sit here?" How shall you answer this paramount question?

18. Soulwinning Sermon Outline by Frank Shivers.

Rescuing Souls
Jeremiah 38: 1 – 13

Jeremiah was in a dungeon pit. Upon learning of the plight of this prophet Ebed-Melech takes steps to rescue him. Unraveling this narrative, one discovers what it takes for a Christian to become a soulwinner.

1. It takes Information (v 7).

It was not until Ebed-Melech "heard that they had put Jeremiah in the dungeon" that he took immediate steps to rescue him. Christians will not make any serious soul rescue attempt until they are clearly and convincingly made aware of man's hopeless and helpless estate apart from God. Throughout scripture God seeks to inform saints of the sinners' dire and urgent need of salvation (Isaiah 53:6; Romans 3:10; Revelation 20:15).

2. It takes Intercession (v 9).

Ebed-Melech boldly, courageously enters the King's presence to plead for the salvation of Jeremiah. The soulwinner must boldly enter into the throne room of the Thrice-Holy God and plead vigorously for the souls of the eternally damned by name wherein that is possible. Soulwinners ought to have a *Ten Most Wanted List* of souls of those he is regularly and fervently praying.

3. It takes Co-operation (v 10 – 11).

The King authorized Ebed-Melech to recruit thirty men to assist in the rescue of Jeremiah. A portion of these men would prevent interruption from opposition while the remaining number would actually participate in the rescue.

(1)Partnership in soulwinning is advantageous. Jesus sent the seventy out witnessing two-by-two. This approach in soulwinning allows one partner to make the *rescue* (presentation) while the other provides protection from interruption.

(2) The point also can be made here for joint co-operation among saints in evangelistic crusades, revivals and harvest days in the rescue effort of lost souls.

(3) The soulwinner has the authority of the King of Kings to rescue the eternally damned all over the world.

4. It takes Authentication (v 11).

Look with me and see Ebed-Melech making a rope out of "old cast clouts" and yanking on each section to make certain its strength. The soulwinner must be certain of the means of which he employs to win the lost. He must from personal experience (salvation) and scripture know that the sinners' only hope is "repentance toward God and faith in the Lord Jesus Christ" (Acts 20:17). No other rope but this one can deliver the soul from the pit of sins captivity.

5. It takes Compassion (v 12).

"And Ebed-Melech, the Ethiopian said unto Jeremiah, Put now these old cast clouts and rotten rags under thine armholes under the cords." Matthew Henry makes the point that it was an act of great tenderness and compassion on Ebed-Melech's part to provide soft rags for Jeremiah to put under his armpits to prevent them from being irritated by the rope. Additionally note that Ebed-Melech does not recklessly throw the rope into the pit but with care lowers it down. The soulwinner in his rescue attempts must ever be respectful, courteous, considerate and compassionate making it as easy as possible for the sinner to be saved. He must not be a spiritual psycho throwing out the rope haphazardly or uncompassionately.

6. It takes Instruction (v 12).

"And Ebed-Melech the Ethiopian said unto Jeremiah, Put now these old cast clouts and rotten rags under thine armholes under the cords." Ebed-Melech instructed Jeremiah in exactly what he needed to do to be saved. It is expedient and imperative the soulwinner know how to win a soul. This pastor and staff will provide soulwinning instruction to each and everyone who seek it. One simple and often used soulwinning method that can be used is the Roman Road.

7. It takes Determination (v 13).

Ebed-Melech did not rest until Jeremiah's feet were out of the miry clay and upon solid rock. The soulwinner must be tireless in his effort to rescue the perishing and care for the dying. Experience teaches some souls will be saved when first presented the gospel for others it may take years. It is essential that the soulwinner refuse to quit in the rescue effort.

8. It takes Volition (v 12b).

Ebed-Melech did not and could not force Jeremiah to do as he instructed and thus be rescued. The decision was up to Jeremiah. The soulwinner can only make his best effort in seeking to win souls. Ultimately it's up to the sinner whether he will be saved or not. Jesus allowed the Rich Young Ruler to walk away from him unsaved.

19. Soulwinning Sermon Outline by Junior Hill.

"Lessons About Sowing Seed"
Luke 8:5-15

1. We must never misunderstand the soils.

Just as those seed fell into different soils, so there will be different responses to witnessing. Some will hear, and some will not.

2. We must never misjudge the seasons.

The Bible says, "Be not weary in well doing for in due season ye shall reap." There are established times and seasons and we have to honor them as we witness. Some will respond now, and some perhaps later.

3. We must never misinterpret success.

Our success is in sowing the seed. It is our business to sow the seed, and it is God's business to make it come up.

TWELVE

Soulwinning Stories and Illustrations

Illustrations abound in multiplied books on the subject of the Christian's role in soulwinning. In lieu of this I choose here only to share 33 soulwinning stories and illustrations that may be helpful in motivating others to witness and in making the soulwinning presentation.

1. Who is holding the rope?
In a fishing village that was located at the mouth of a turbulent river a scream was heard, "Boy overboard!" The strongest swimmer in the village tied a rope around his waist and threw the other among the crowd gathered and plunged in the river. He gallantly fought the tide until he reached the young boy and a great cheer went up when he grasped him into his arms. He then shouted, "Pull in the rope!" Each upon the shore looked one to the other inquiring, "Who is holding the rope?" Sadly no one was. In the excitement of watching the rescue effort the rope slipped into the water. Unable to help they watched two lives drown because no one made it their business to hold the end of the rope. Are you willing to hold the shore end of the rope for others as they seek to rescue the unsaved at home and around the world?

2. Neglect to witness at church
A major New York life insurance company invited all of its agents to its corporate office for a conference. In the midst of that conference one of the company's agents insured the elevator man, barber and a waiter all of which had been employed at the corporate office for many years. No one thought to seek to sale a policy to these men in the home corporate office![1] Soulwinning begins at our own doorsteps, within our own homes and churches.

3. The rope
A medical missionary performed surgery on a poor blind man that restored his sight. The man disappeared for a few days and then appeared at the missionary's door. In opening the door the missionary saw this man holding one end of a rope. On that rope were ten more blind people. If Jesus has opened your spiritual eyes to the Truth about salvation and saved you it is imperative you find a *rope* and bring as many blind people to the Cross possible.

4. The rope's too short; throw me a longer rope
(See the Foreword for this illustration.)

5. He didn't know of the souls he won.
In one of Francis Dixon's revivals in Australia a young man stood up and testified. He stated that as he walked down George Street in Sydney a white-haired man approached him and said, "Excuse me, Sir, I wonder if you might let me ask you

a question. If you were to die today, where would you spend eternity? The Bible says it will be either heaven or hell. Think about it." This led the young man to church where he discovered how he could trust Christ as His Savior and Lord. Dixon shared this testimony with congregations all over the world and was astonished to learn that people on five continents had come to know Christ as a result of that white-haired man on George Street. Determined to meet this man, Dixon made his way to Sydney to his resident. The man at this time was bed-ridden. As Dixon told him of the testimonies he had heard all over the world of his soul winning efforts, the man began to weep. In all of his years of faithfully witnessing on George Street, this was the first time he had learned of anyone being saved as a result of his witness! Sometimes the greatest decisions the soulwinner has for Christ are those he knows nothing about until he reaches heaven. Keep sowing despite unseen conversions.

6. Talking fishing without fishing
There was a group of fishermen who met every week, month after month, year after year to discuss when, where, and how to fish successfully. These men constructed large, beautiful buildings to serve as their fishing corporate office. They enjoyed and loved fishing so much their goal was to have everyone become a fisherman. However, they were so consumed with writing, talking and reading about fishing that they neglected to do the one essential thing: to fish. How like these fishermen most Christians are!

7. He gave up his freedom for lost souls
Stephen Olford told the story of a 19th Century missionary in the West Indies who worked tirelessly night and day seeking to win the natives with no avail. This man's passion was so intense for the souls of the people he in desperation sold himself into slavery to become one of them. Though he forfeited his freedom, working side by side these natives he won many to Christ. What price are you willing to pay to win souls?

8. Why didn't we join hands sooner?
A child was lost in a vast wheat field. Friends and rescue helpers searched diligently until the dark forced them to halt for the night. The next morning as they resumed their search the suggestion was made that they join hands and form an unbroken human chain across the field in search for the child. In doing this they found the lost child but tragically it was too late. The child's mother with the wringing of her hands walked back and forth crying, "Why didn't we join hands sooner? Why didn't we join hands sooner?" The lost are all about us. It is high time believers join hands in rescuing them before it is eternally too late. Will you join hands with others in our church in this soul saving rescue attempt?

9. One more for Jesus
Rick Warren in his classic book *The Purpose Driven Life* tells of the final hours of his father's life. His dad had been in a semi-conscious state nearly twenty-four hours a day talking aloud of church building projects. One night as he tried to get out of bed Rick's wife asked him, "Jimmy, what are you trying to do?" He replied, "Got to save one more soul for Jesus.! Got to save one more soul for Jesus! Got to save one more soul for Jesus!" He repeated that phrase probably a hundred times over the next hour. As Rick began to thank God for his dad's faith, his father placed his frail hand upon his head and said, as if commissioning him, "Save one more for Jesus! Save one more for Jesus!" May we all be on the lookout to "Save one more for Jesus!"[2]

10. Throwing stones while people perish
(See Chapter One for this illustration.)

11. Tell me how to be saved in three minutes
An England minister made application to serve as an army chaplain. In an effort to test him to ascertain his qualification for such service the Chaplain General with his watch in hand said, "All right, just imagine that I am a soldier dying on the battlefield. I have only three minutes to live. Can you tell me how to be saved?" The preacher squandered the first two minutes, floundering around the matter. At that point the Chaplain General said, "I have one minute left. What have you to say to me?" Sadly, all the minister could do was pull out his prayer book. The Chaplain General said, "No, that won't help in an hour like that."[3] Confronted with a real situation like that of this preacher could you tell the dying man how to be saved in three minutes? Do you know clearly the message of salvation that a lost and dying world needs so desperately to hear? I've got my stopwatch out. Ready, set, go.

12. I meant to tell her of Christ but never got around to it
S. D. Gordon tells the story of a pastor visiting a home where a young woman had just died. This pastor asked his assistant who met him at the home and who was over the chapel that the young woman attended if the young lady died a Christian. He answered, "No, I had a strong impulse to speak to her about the matter, but I never got around to it." Next he asked the lady's Sunday School teacher the same question and received a similar answer. Finally he asked the girl's mother about her daughter's salvation. She said, "A voice within me told me to talk to her about salvation, but I didn't do it." The assistant at the chapel, the Sunday School teacher and this mother though all saved failed to share a witness with the young woman and as a result she died unsaved.[4] How many souls are in Hell today due to Christians who never quite got around to telling them of Jesus Christ and His offer of salvation? Oh Christian get around to this task today and tell someone, anyone of Jesus' awesome love and grace.

13. Others
It is said that when General William Booth lay dying, he was asked for a message to send around the world. With his dying breath he uttered that the message should be – others. This one word message summed up the life and ministry of this great soulwinner.[5] Others need our witness. Others need to be reached for Christ. Others need to hear the gospel of the Lord Jesus Christ. Others need cleansing of sin. Others need peace with God. Others need meaning and fulfillment in life. Others must be warned about the reality of Hell. Others must be told of the hope of heaven. It is when we shift our eyes from self to others that God can use us to win souls.

14. Hunting for souls now
Kim, a native African, hunted tigers for years. One day he heard the gospel and was saved. Later a missionary met him on a trail and inquired what he was carrying in his bag. "Ammunition," he replied and opened it for the missionary. Seeing only a New Testament and a hymnal the missionary said, "You can't hunt tigers with those things." "That's right," said Kim, "but I'm hunting for souls now!"[6] At the moment of conversion the Christian ought to be "hunting for souls now!" Are you?

15. That's simple; I just needed someone to explain it
While I was leading a revival in Augusta, Georgia, a 14-year-old boy was attending church for the first time in his life. In the aftermath of the service I asked permission to talk to him about his need of salvation. Upon conclusion of my presentation the boy looked up to me and said, "That's simple. I just needed someone to explain it to me" and then received Christ into his life. There are people all about us who would be saved if we would take the time to "explain it" to them.

16. Charlotte Elliot and the hymn "Just As I Am"
Charlotte Elliot was visiting some friends in West London where she met a minister named Cesar Malan who at supper told her that he hoped she was a Christian. Charlotte took great offense in what he said. The preacher apologized and told her he hoped one day she would become a worker for Christ. The Lord orchestrated a meeting between these again three weeks later at a friend's home. Charlotte told Malan that she had been trying to find the Savior ever since he last spoke to her and wanted him to tell how she might be saved. He told her, "Just come to him as you are." This she did and was gloriously saved. Twelve years later Charlotte Elliot wrote the beloved hymn, "Just As I am." My friend that's the way every sinner must come to Christ including you. Come to Him with your doubts, questions, and your baggage of sin. He stands eagerly awaiting to forgive and save you even as He did Charlotte Elliot.

17. "Is It Well With My Soul"
The great Chicago fire in 1871 left three hundred dead and one hundred thousand

homeless. A friend of D. L. Moody, Horatio Gates Spafford assisted the homeless, grief stricken, and needy for two years. Spafford and his family then decided join the Moody team on one of their evangelistic crusades in Europe. Horatio Spafford was delayed departing with his wife and four daughters on the ship *Ville du Havre* due to business. He would meet up with them later on the other side of the Atlantic. Their ship collided with the English sailing ship the *Loch Earn* and sunk within twenty minutes. Spafford's wife, Anna, was the only survivor of his family (one of only forty seven total). Upon reaching Europe she sent her husband a message that consisted of two words, "Saved Alone." He boarded the next ship to England and asked the Captain to let him know when they came to the spot where his children perished. It was about midnight when he received word they were at that spot. It was on this voyage that Horatio Spafford comprised the hymn "It is Well." Listen to the words he wrote after viewing the spot where his four daughters died: "When peace, life a river, attendeth my way, When sorrows like sea-billows roll; Whatever my lot, Thou hast taught me to say, It is well, it is well with my soul. My sin-oh the bliss of this glorious thought – my sin not in part but the whole-is nailed to the Cross and I bear it no more, Praise the Lord, praise the Lord O my soul. It is well with my soul, It is well, it is well with my soul." My friend, can you say with Spafford "It is well with my soul?" Have you repented of your sin and received Christ Jesus into your life as Lord and Savior? If death would greet you this night or Christ return for His church can you say without a doubt, "It is well with my soul?"

18. The wheelbarrow illustration

"Believe on the name of the Lord Jesus Christ and thou shalt be saved" (Acts 16:31). Perhaps a better translation for the word "believe" in this text would be trust. Years ago the great Blondie cautiously pushed a wheelbarrow across a tight rope stretched across the roaring Niagara Falls. The crowd applauded that great feat. He asked, "Who of you believe I can push someone in this wheelbarrow across the falls?" The crowd replied in the affirmative. Then he stunned them by asking, "Who of you are willing to be that person?" There were no takers. The people believed with their head that he could successfully do this but none were willing to trust him with their heart. It is one thing to believe my friend that Jesus Christ is the Son of God; that He can forgive your sin and save you from its penalty and give you heaven one day and something else for you to sit down in the wheelbarrow trusting Him to do just that. Scripture states that, "the demons believe and tremble." Salvation involves more than merely head knowledge, mental assent. It involves heart trust, repentance and faith. Will you sit down in the wheelbarrow – trust Jesus Christ – to do as He promised for those who call upon His name in faith and repentance?

19. The chair illustration

I see before me a chair. Immediately my subconscious tells me it is a chair; that its purpose is to hold a person up and that it has fulfilled its purpose time and again. However, I can stand here by this chair believing it is a chair; its purpose is to hold a person up and that indeed it has accomplished its purpose numerous times until I collapse due to fatigue and it can do me no good until I act upon what I know. Just so it is the same with Christ my friend. Acknowledging Jesus is Lord and Savior and that He can save you from the penalty of sin and give you both life abundant and eternal will do you no good until you act in faith and repentance upon what you know and *sit down in the chair.* Wouldn't you be willing to do that now?

20. The New Testament illustration
The soulwinner says he has in his hand a copy of the New Testament and wants to give it to the person to whom he is witnessing at no cost. He asks the person what is it that he must do to receive it? The person responds, "Reach out and take it." The soulwinner says, "That's exactly right. You don't have to do anything for it to become yours except accept it. Salvation is a free gift of God that He makes available through His only son Jesus Christ. You cannot merit it, earn it or become deserving of it. It is a loving gift that must simply be accepted through the expression of faith and repentance."

21. Recline on the Lord Jesus Christ and thou shalt be saved
Billy Graham told of a missionary who sought to communicate the gospel to a tribal village but had great difficulty finding a word in their language that expressed the meaning of the word *faith.* He worked hard at finding this one word for months. One day he noticed a tribal member reclining on a bed that supported his whole weight and immediately rejoiced, knowing he had finally found that word. The missionary then shared John 3:16-17 in an understandable fashion by stating, "For God so loved the world that whosoever reclineth upon Him with all his weight shall not perish but whosoever reclineth not upon Him with all his weight shall perish. For whosoever reclineth upon Him with all his weight is not condemned but whosoever does not recline upon Him with all his weight is condemned already for he has not reclined upon the Lord Jesus Christ."

This word they could readily understand, making clear what was necessary for salvation. Will you *recline* (trust absolutely, inclusively) upon Jesus Christ for the salvation of sin? Reclining on church membership, baptism, or morality will not save you but only reclining upon Jesus.

22. I know who I am but do not know where I am going
Billy Graham, when being honored at a Charlotte, North Carolina, event, related the following story about Dr. Einstein. Einstein on once occasion when traveling by train couldn't find his ticket. The conductor said, "I know who you are" and told him not to worry about it. The conductor then passed to other passengers requesting tickets. Upon looking back in the direction of Einstein he saw him down on all fours searching for the ticket. He again told Einstein the ticket wasn't important because he knew who he was. Einstein looked up at the conductor and

said, "I know who I am. I just don't know where I am going." It is important for a person to know who he is but even more important to know where he is going. Do you know where you are going at death?

23. Paul's level of pain for the lost

The Apostle Paul experienced pain for the unsaved. He cried, "Brethren, my heart's desire and prayer to God is for Israel to be saved" (Romans 10:1). He labored for souls night and day (Acts 20). When speaking to his team about losing a game, NBA coach Hubie Brown said, "When your level of pain reaches my level of pain then we can do something." It is only when the Christian's level of pain for the lost reaches Paul's level that we will engage in soulwinning passionately and persistently. Each Christian should ask how deep his pain for the eternally damned really is.

24. Laughing at the Clown

In England, a man was to be hung. His mother interceded on his behalf before the king, and she prevailed in getting a pardon. The page commissioned to deliver the pardon stopped to watch a clown performing and then hurried to fulfill his errand. He arrived minutes too late. While accounting to the king, he said, "I laughed with the crowd at the clown, and the time slipped away." Many Christians are laughing at the clown and enjoying life and its pleasures as time slips away and souls die without Jesus.

25. I failed him

A college student approached me with concern about a best friend's soul. He wanted to share Christ with him but didn't know how. I mentored this student in the basics of soulwinning, including approaches, plans, praying, the writing of evangelistic letters, and handling excuses. This encompassed most of a summer.

However, sadly before he shared Christ with his friend news came he was killed in an auto accident. Oh the sorrow of that hour for both him and me. He knew how, but now it was eternally too late to share Christ with his friend.

The blood of this friend is not upon his hands but mine. As his mentor, I should have encouraged him to confront his friend immediately after his first soulwinning lesson. I worked hard at sharpening this student's ability to win his friend and prayed fervently with him for his friend's salvation, but I failed them both.

Saints should study hard at being great soulwinners but ever be encouraged in the midst of such training to witness passionately and urgently to those about them who are unsaved, fearing that for some soul they may wait one day too late to tell!

26. Reflective Mirrors

The 455 residents in the Austrian mountain village of Rattenberg suffer from a lack of sunshine in the winter, and this is responsible for the mild-to-severe depression some experience. To rectify this problem, scientists are installing thirty eight-foot mirrors in a sunnier spot across the valley. These bounce sunlight back to a rocky outcrop near Rattenberg, where a second bank of mirrors will reflect it down upon the people sitting in darkness. The mayor of this city stated, "Just across the river, we can see the sun shining in its full glory, but here in the village during these months we get no direct sunshine and it takes the pleasure out of life for many people." Markus Peskoller, a scientist at the Bartenbach Light Laboratory in Aldrans, believes the system will serve as a model for other cities. He states, "We could help many other mountain villages see the light."[7]

Spiritually, the inhabitants of our world are like those at Rattenberg. They live in darkness without hope and peace. They can see the Sun of Righteousness (Malachi 4:2) shining "in full glory just across the river" but need help in receiving it for themselves. It is every Christian's task to be a reflective mirror of Jesus Christ, the Light of the World, relaying His "true light" unto the ends of the earth. Scientists state it will only take 30 mirrors to accomplish the Rattenberg project. To accomplish the Acts 1:8 mission, every Christian is needed. "You shall be witnesses unto me." Clean the dirt and dust of sin off your mirror through repentance unto God and start reflecting His love to lost people. Can you imagine the bright Sonshine that would be evidence across our dark world if the millions who profess Christ began mirroring His message? Today we can "help many mountain villages (sinners) see the light."

27. Looking for loop-holes

W.C. Fields tells the story of an atheist who was discovered on his death bed reading a Bible. When asked why he was doing this, he replied, "I'm just looking to see if I can find any loop-holes." He was unsuccessful in finding any, and so will anyone else who tries. The only way to be saved and gain Heaven is through the finished work of Jesus Christ upon the Cross.

28. John Harper's last convert

Just four years following the tragic sinking of the Titanic a young Scotsman in a meeting in Hamilton, Canada testified, "I am a survivor of the Titanic. When I was drifting alone on a spar that awful night, the tide brought Mr. John Harper, of Glasgow, also on a piece of wreck, near me. 'Man,' he said, 'are you saved?' 'No,' I said, 'I am not.' He replied, 'Believe on the Lord Jesus Christ and thou shalt be saved.'" "The waves bore him away; but, strange to say brought him back a little later, and he said, 'Are you saved now?' 'No,' I said, 'I cannot honestly say that I am.' He said again, 'Believe on the Lord Jesus Christ, and thou shalt be saved,' and shortly after he went down; and there, alone in the night, and with two miles of water under me, I believed. I am John Harper's last convert."[8]

29. Keep your axe sharp
There was a rookie lumberjack who was determined to beat his company's average of cutting down fifteen trees a day. On the first day he cut down ten trees and counted it a grand start. On the second day he managed only to cut ten trees again showing no progress toward his goal. On day three he cut down seven trees. On day four he doubled his effort to reach his goal but surprisingly only fell five trees. Every day the number of trees he cut down grew less and less despite his hard work swinging the axe. At the end of two weeks of falling fewer and fewer trees each day he approached a veteran lumberjack asking, "I don't understand what's going on. I work hard every day, swinging my axe from dawn to dusk, but I keep doing worse and worse. What can I be doing wrong?" "Young fella," the old man replied after a long pause, "I can see them calluses on your hands and bigger muscles in your arms, to prove you been swingin' your axe. But let me ask you somethin' - When was the last time you sharpened your axe?"[9] To win souls the soulwinner must keep his axe sharp by the means of purity, prayer and Bible study.

30. Is this the sign?
Norman Cates shared the humorous story of a guy who prayed this prayer every morning: "Lord, if you want me to witness to someone today, please give me a sign to show me who it is." One day he found himself on a bus when a big, burly man sat next to him. The bus was nearly empty but this guy sat next to our praying friend.

The timid Christian anxiously waited for his stop so he could exit the bus. But before he could get very nervous about the man next to him, the big guy burst into tears and began to weep. He then cried out with a loud voice, "I need to be saved. I'm a lost sinner and I need the Lord. Won't somebody tell me how to be saved?" He turned to the Christian and pleaded, "Can you show me how to be saved?" The believer immediately bowed his head and prayed, "Lord, is this a sign?"

"Are you looking for a 'sign' to start witnessing? It can be found in Matthew 28:19-20 and Acts 1:8."[10]

31. Witnessing with a razor in his hand
Warren Wiersbe in his book Wycliffe Handbook of Preaching and Preachers shared the following story about a member in William Sangster's church.

"When he pastored the Methodist church in Scarbrough, William Sangster had an eccentric member who tried to be a zealous Christian. Unfortunately, the man was mentally deficient and usually did the wrong thing.

While working as a barber the man lathered up a customer for a shave, came at him with the poised razor, and asked, "Are you prepared to meet your God?" The frightened man fled with the lather on his face."[11]

32. If
J. Wilbur Chapman declared:

- If to be a Christian is worthwhile, then the most ordinary interest in those with whom we come in contact would prompt us to speak to them of Christ.
- If the New Testament be true — and we know that it is — who has given us the right to place the responsibility for soul-winning on other shoulders than our own?
- If they who reject Christ are in danger, is it not strange that we, who are so sympathetic when the difficulties are physical or temporal, should apparently be so devoid of interest as to allow our friends and neighbors and kindred to come into our lives and pass out again without a word of invitation to accept Christ, to say nothing of sounding a note of warning because of their peril?
- If today is the day of salvation, if tomorrow may never come, and if life is equally uncertain, how can we eat, drink and be merry when those who live with us, work with us, walk with us and love us are unprepared for eternity because they are unprepared for time?
- If Jesus called his disciples to be fishers of men, who gave us the right to be satisfied with making fishing tackle or pointing the way to the fishing banks instead of going ourselves to cast out the net until it be filled?
- If Jesus himself went seeking the lost, if Paul the Apostle was in agony because his kinsmen, according to the flesh, knew not Christ, why should we not consider it worthwhile to go out after the lost until they are found?
- If I am to stand at the judgment seat of Christ to render an account for the deeds done in the body, what shall I say to him if my children are missing, if my friends are not saved, or if my employer or employee should miss the way because I have been faithless?
- If I wish to be approved at the last, then let me remember that no intellectual superiority, no eloquence in preaching, no absorption in business, no shrinking temperament or no spirit of timidity can take the place of or be an excuse for my not making an honest, sincere, prayerful effort to win others to Christ.[12]

33. Conduits for the King's Message
King George V was about to give a speech at a London Arms conference (1930) that was to be carried around the world when it was discovered that a cable accidentally had been severed. Harold Vidian picked up one end of the cable in one hand and then the other end with his other hand and allowed the electrical current flow through him. In doing this he became a conduit through which the King's message was carried to the world. Christians are to be the King's conduit through which His saving message is proclaimed to the entire world.

Appelman, Hyman J. The Saviour's Invitation and other Evangelistic Sermons. Baker Book House: Grand Rapids, MI, 1981.

Autrey, C. E. Basic Evangelism. Zondervan Publishing House: Grand Rapids, MI, 1968.

Autrey, C. E. You Can Win Souls. Broadman: Nashville, TN, 1961.

Bales, Porter M. Revival Sermons. Broadman Press: Nashville, TN, 1938.

Barber, Fred. Travail for Souls. Sword of the Lord: Murfreesboro, TN, 8 Oct. 2004.

Blackwood, Andrew. Evangelical Sermons of Our Day. Harper & Brothers: New York, NY, 1959.

Bonar, Horatius. Words to Winners of Souls. P & R Publishing: Phillipsburg, NJ, 1995.

Booth, General William. "Who Cares" pamphlet of Last Days Ministries. Pretty Good Printing: Lindale, TX, 1994.

Bright, Bill. How To Introduce Others To Christ. Campus Crusade for Christ International, Arrowhead Springs, San Bernardino, CA, 1972.

Bright, Bill, Editor. Ten Basic Steps Toward Christian Maturity: Teacher's Manual. Campus Crusade For Christ, International, Arrowhead Springs, San Bernardino, CA, 1965.

Bronson, Michael. BibleHelp.org. 2000.

Bryan, Dawson C. A Workable Plan for Evangelism. Abingdon-Cokesbury Press: Nashville, TN, MCMXLV.

Careaga, Andrew. E-vangelism: Sharing the Gospel in Cyberspace. Vital Issues Press: Lafayette, LA, 1999.

Carroll, B. H. Revival Messages. 1939.

Chambers, Oswald. My Utmost for His Highest. Discovery House Publishers: Grand Rapids, MI, 1992.

Coleman, Robert E. The Master Plan of Evangelism. Fleming H. Revell Company: Old Tappan, NJ, 1988.

Comfort, Ray. The Evidence Bible. Bridge-Logos: Gainesville, FL, 2002.

Compolo, Tony and Gordon Aeschliman. 50 Ways You Can Reach the World, InterVarsity Press: Downers Grove, IL, 1993.

Crawford, Perry. The Art of Fishing for Men. The Mutual Press: Philadelphia, PA, 1935.

DC Talk. Jesus Freaks Vol. II. Bethany House Publishers: Minneapolis, MN, 2002.

Daniels, E. J. Dim Lights in a Dark World. Daniels Publishers: Orlando, FL, 1971.

Dixon, Francis. Bible Study Notes, Series Fifteen. Word of Life Ministries, Eastbourne, England.

Dobbins, G. S. A Winning Witness. The Sunday School Board of the Southern Baptist Convention: Nashville, TN, 1938.

Douglas, J.D., Ed. The Work of an Evangelist. Worldwide Publishers: Minneapolis, MN, 1984.

Dorsett, Lyle W. The Life of D.L. Moody: A Passion for Souls. Moody Press: Chicago, IL, 1997.

Downey, Murray W. The Art of Soulwinning. Baker Book House: Grand Rapids, MI, 1976.

Drummond, Lewis A. Reaching Generation Next. Baker Books: Nashville, TN, 2002.

Edwards, Gene. How To Have a Soul Winning Church. Soulwinning Publications: Tyler, TX, MCMLXII.

Edwards, Jonathan. The Life of David Brainerd. Baker Book House: Grand Rapids, MI, 1978.

Ellis, J. W. Fishing For Men. Western Baptist Publishing Co: Kansas City, MO, 1945.

Ellis, J. W. We Are Witnesses. Beacon Hill Press: Kansas City, MO, 1956.

Engstrom, Theodore W. Sermon Outlines & Illustrations. Zondervan Publishing House: Grand Rapids, MI, 1942.

Fabarex, Michael. Preaching that Changes Lives. Nashville, TN, 2000.

Fay, William. Share Jesus Without Fear. Broadman and Holman Publishers: Nashville, TN, 1999.

Finney, Charles. How To Experience Revival. Whitaker House: Pittsburgh, PA, 1984.

Finney, Charles. "Preacher, Save Thyself." Sword of the Lord Publishers: Murfreesboro, TN, 5 Nov. 2004.

Florida Baptist Witness. <www.floridabaptistwitness.com>. 30 Sept. 2004.

Ford, Herschel W. Simple Sermons for Sunday Evening. Zondervan: Grand Rapids, MI, 1968.

Ford, Herschel W. Simple Sermons on Conversion and Commitment. Baker Book House: Grand Rapids, MI, 1972.

Gage, Freddie. "Where Are the Tears?" sermon. James Robinson Conference, 1979.

"Good News" tract. Campus Crusade for Christ, Inc. New Life Publications: San Bernadino, CA, 1970.

Good Steward.com. Barna Research, 13 Sept. 2002.

Graham, Billy. 2004 Calendar.

Harrison, E. M. How To Win Souls. Van Kamper Press: Wheaton, IL, 1952.

Hayden, Eric. The Unforgettable Spurgeon. Emerald House Group: Greenville, SC, 1997.

Hunter, George G. III. How to Reach Secular People. Abingdon Press: Nashville, TN, 1992.

Hutson, Curtis, Editor. Great Preaching on Soul Winning. Sword of the Lord Publishers: Murfreesboro, TN, 1989.

Knight, Walter. Knight's Illustrations. Moody Press: Chicago, IL, 1970.

"Lady Elgin." Knowledgerush.com., 2005.

Leavell, Roland Q. Evangelism: Christ's Imperative Commission. Broadman Press: Nashville, TN, 1951.

Leavell, Roland Q. Winning Others To Christ. The Sunday School Board of the Southern Baptist Convention: Nashville, TN, 1936.

Little, Paul E. Know Why You Believe. Victor: Colorado Springs, CO, 2003.

Little, Paul E. How To Give Away Your Faith. InterVarsity Press: Downers Grove, IL, 1973.

MacArthur, John. Follow Me. Countryman: Nashville, TN, 2004.

MacArthur, John. Making Disciples: John MacArthur's Bible Studies. Moody Press: Chicago, IL, 1991.

McDowell, Josh. The New Evidence That Demands A Verdict. Thomas Nelson Publishers: Nashville, TN, 1999.

Martin, Gerald, Editor. Great Southern Baptist Evangelistic Preaching. Zondervan Publishing House: Grand Rapids, MI, 1969.

Matthews, C. E. Every Christian's Job. Broadman Press: Nashville, TN, 1951.

Miller, Basil. Praying Hyde. Ambassador: Greenville, SC, 2000.

Moyer, R. Larry. How-To Book on Personal Evangelism. Kregal Publications: Grand Rapids, MI, 1998.

Murphrey, Buddy. Drawing the Net. Undated with no publication data.

Olford, Stephen. The Secret of Soulwinning. Moody Press: Chicago, IL, 1974.

Piper, John. The Supremacy of God in Preaching. Baker Books: Grand Rapids, MI, 1990.

Reid, Alvin. "Get Real" sermon. Baptist Fire.com, 2005.

Reid, Alvin L. Radically Unchurched. Kregel: Grand Rapids, MI, 2002.

Rice, John R. John R. Rice Commentary: Acts. Sword of the Lord Publishers: Murfreesboro, TN, 1963.

Rice, John R., Ed. The Sword Scrapbook. Sword of the Lord Publishers: Murfreesboro, TN, 1969.

Rice, John R. "Personal Soul Winning." Sword of the Lord Publishers Pamphlet: Murfreesboro, TN, <www.calvary-baptist.org/soulwin.html>.

Rice, John R. Soul Winner's Fire. Moody Bible Institute: Chicago, IL, 1941.

Rogers, Adrian. Sermon: "The Sin of Silence." <sermonhelp.com>.

Scarborough, L. R. How Jesus Won Souls. Sunday School Board of the Southern Baptist Convention: Nashville, TN, 1926.

Scarborough, L. R. A Search For Souls. Sunday School Board of the Southern Baptist Convention: Nashville, TN, 1925.

Scarborough, L. R. With Christ after the Lost. Broadman Press: Nashville, TN, 1952.

Servant Magazine. Issue 72. Shelby, MT, 2005.

Simpson, Michael L. Permission Evangelism. NexGen: Colorado Springs, CO, 2003.

Sjogren, Steven, Dave Ping and Doug Pollock. Irresistible Evangelism. Group: Loveland, CO, 2004.

Smith, Bailey. Real Evangelism. Broadman Press: Nashville, TN, 1978.

Smith, Glen C., Editor. Evangelizing Youth. Tyndale House Publishers: Wheaton, IL, 1985.

Smith, Sheldon, Editor. The Sword of the Lord. Sword of the Lord Publishers: Murfreesboro, TN, 5 Nov. 2004.

Spurgeon, C. H. Evangelism. Emerald House: Greenville, SC, 1998.

Spurgeon, C. H. Lectures to My Students. Zondervan Publishing House: Grand Rapids, MI, 1970.

Spurgeon, C.H. Morning and Evening. Christian Focus Publications: Great Britain, 2000.

Spurgeon, C. H. Only A Prayer Meeting. Christian Focus Publications: Great Britain, 2000.

Spurgeon, C.H. The Pastor in Prayer. Banner of Truth in Trust: Carlisle, PA, 2004.

Spurgeon, C. H. The Soulwinner. Whitaker House: New Kensington, PA, 1995.

Spurgeon, C. H. The Soulwinner. Wm B. Eerdmans Publishing Co: Grand Rapids, MI, 1972.

Spurgeon, C.H. Spiritual Disciplines for the Christian Life. Navpress: Colorado Springs, CO, 2002.

Spurgeon, C.H. Spurgeon Archives. www.spurgeon.org/heathbio.htm.

Spurgeon, C. H. Spurgeon's Sermons Volume 4. Baker Books: Grand Rapids, MI, 1999.

Spurgeon, C.H. Spurgeon's Sermons Volume 8. Baker Books: Grand Rapids, MI, 1999.

Spurgeon, C. H. Spurgeon's Sermons on Soulwinning. Kregal Publications: Grand Rapids, MI, 1995.

The State (newspaper). Columbia, SC, 18 Sept. 2004.

Stewart, James. "The Gospel Message," Evangelism. Way of Life Literature: Port Huron, MI.

Studd, Mrs. C.T. "Men on Fire." Sword of the Lord Publishers: Murfreesboro, TN, 5 Nov. 04.

Sweazy, George E. Effective Evangelism. Harper & Row Publishers: New York, Evanston, IL, 1953.

Tan, Paul. Encylopedia of 7700 Illustrations. Assurance Publishers: Rockville, MD, 1979.

Tapia, Andres. Campus Evangelism Handbook. InterVarsity Press: Downers Grove, IL, 1987.

The Telegraph (London). "Mountain Village Sees the light," 27 Jan. 2005.

Torrey, R. A. Anecdotes and Illustrations. Fleming H. Revell Company: London & Edinburg, 1907.

Torrey, R. A. How To Bring Men to Christ. Fleming H. Revell Co: New York, NY, 1910.

Towns, Elmer. Winning the Winnable. Church Leadership Institute: Lynchburg, VA, 1986.

Walvood, John F. and Roy B. Zuck, Editors. The Bible Knowledge Commentary. Chariot Victory Publishing: Colorado Springs, CO, 1999.

Warren, Rick. The Purpose Driven Life. Zondervan: Grand Rapids, MI, 2002.

Weatherford, W. D. Introducing Men to Christ. Association Press: New York, NY, 1918.

Whitney, Donald S. Spiritual Disciplines for the Christian Life. NavPress: Colorado Springs, CO, 2002.

Wiersbe, Warren W. Bible Expository Commentary. Victor Books: Wheaton, IL, 1989.

Wood, Frederick P. Studies in Soulwinning. Marshall, Morgan & Scott: London, undated.

Hyman Appelman

Appelman was a Russian-born Jew who was converted to Christ at age twenty-eight. He was graduated from Southwestern Baptist Theological Seminary in 1933. His ministry was global, traveling around the world eight or nine times preaching the gospel. Appelman entered into eternal rest with the Almighty in 1983.

Horatius Bonar

Bonar, a Scottish Presbyterian, lived from 1808 – 1889. He was a preacher, author and hymn writer, but above all a passionate soulwinner.

B. H. Carroll

Carroll was founder and the first President of Southwestern Baptist Theological Seminary, located in Fort Worth, Texas. He made a profession of faith at age thirteen but later stated it was not real. Years later, upon his mother's constant urging, he attended a camp meeting and was saved minutes after it had ended. Carroll was influenced greatly by C. H. Spurgeon and paid tribute to him in a memorial service following his death.

One day, a young man brought a note to Carroll that he said had to be delivered personally. The young man had no idea what the note detailed. Carroll read the note, and the young man was immediately given a room in his house to stay and a place at his table. He accompanied Carroll to one of his classes. Before the class Carroll opened the note and read these words, "Dear Father, the bearer of this letter is Ed Solomon. Here at Southern, Ed has taken me into his room and shared with me in everyway to help me. As he earnestly desires to study under your instruction, I am sending him to you. Please receive him as you would receive me, for he is a true brother. Your son, Harvey." Carroll then set the letter on his desk and as tears flowed down his face he said to the class, "One day I will stand in the presence of our Heavenly Father, and He will, because I received His Son on earth, receive me into His glory even as He would receive His only begotten Son." That echoes the love this man had for the Savior! This theological giant, author of some 33 volumes, and soul winner, as he lay upon his deathbed, gave a word of guidance to L. R. Scarborurgh, his predecessor at Southwestern that speaks volumes of his doctrinal conservatism. "Lee, keep the Seminary lashed to the Cross. If heresy ever comes in the teaching, take it to the faculty. If they will not hear you then take prompt action, take it to the trustees of the Seminary. If they will not hear you, take it to the Convention that appoints the Board of Trustees, and if they will not hear you, take it to the great common people of our churches. You will not fail to get a hearing then." Just as God would receive His only begotten Son, He received Carroll on November 11, 1914.

E. J. Daniels

E. J. Daniels was one of the world's greatest "saw dust" evangelists. In crusade tent meetings, he preached with fire and passion in his soul as he called lost men to Christ. God used four of his sermons over a period of twenty-five years to reach 750,000 souls. The hand of God was mighty upon this man.

Charles Finney

Finney was saved at age 29. He had never been in a church or a Sunday School to hear the gospel, though, which makes his conversion even more miraculous. This lawyer turned evangelist and revivalist immediately won 20 people to Christ. The morning after his conversion, he said to a client, "I have a retainer from the Lord Jesus to plead His cause, and you must go and get someone else to attend to your law suit. I cannot do it." Plead His cause, Finney did—before the jury of the world and determined to win the verdict on each occasion. His grandson, speaking at his memorial service, said, "He wanted a verdict from every audience he faced, and if he did not get it he felt his sermon was wasted. He aimed at producing conviction, confession, repentance, restitution, submission, prayer for forgiveness, and self dedication, to God's service." This pastor, evangelist, revivalist, author, and soul winner went home to be with the Lord in Oberlin, Ohio, in 1875.

Junior Hill

Junior Hill is a Southern Baptist evangelist who, for 36 consecutive years, has had a full schedule each year in revival, crusade, conference, and teaching ministry. To many Southern Baptist pastors he is their "pastor." Junior has led over 1400 revivals across America and abroad. He resides in Hartselle, Alabama, with his wife, Carole.

Dwight L. Moody

A Sunday School teacher was concerned about an 18-year-old youngster who attended his Sunday School class. After some hesitation, the teacher built up enough courage to walk into the shoe store where this boy worked to tell him of Christ. Locating him in the back of the store wrapping shoes, Mr. Kimball looked at D. L. Moody and said, "I want to tell you how much Christ loved you." God had prepared Moody for this witness and he received Christ. It is said that Moody in his ministry won one million souls and established three Christian schools. During a YMCA conference in 1870, God brought Ira Sankey and Moody together. Hearing Sankey sing, Moody said to him, "I want you to help me with my work in Chicago. I have prayed for you for eight years!" Sankey would remain by Moody's side the rest of his ministry as a musician, composer, and singer. Many count Moody to be the greatest evangelist of the nineteenth century. He died in 1899.

Stephen Olford

Olford was born in Zambia March 29, 1918, and was promoted to Glory into the presence of the Savior he loved to proclaim on August 29, 2004. Many proclaimed him to be the "The Preacher's Preacher" due to his powerful exposition of scripture and his role as mentor and model to thousands of ministers. Olford founded the Institute for Biblical Preaching in 1980 and in 1988 The Stephen Olford Center for Biblical Preaching.

John R. Rice

John Richard Rice was an author, evangelist, radio host, and editor who touched millions in his eighty-five years on earth. He authored more than 200 titles and was the founding editor of <u>Sword of the Lord</u>. Rice died in 1980.

Alvin L. Reid

Reid is a professor and the Bailey Smith Chair of Evangelism at Southeastern Baptist Theological Seminary, Wake Forest, North Carolina. He is the author of several books, including *Light the Fire, Introduction to Evangelism, Evangelism for a Changing World,* and *Raising the Bar.*

L. R. Scarborough

From a cow-camp preacher to the presidency of a great theological seminary, Lee Rutland Scarborough had few equals as an evangelist. He served as professor of evangelism at Southwestern Theological Seminary from 1908 until 1915, when he became its President. He served in this position until 1942. He influenced many in the classroom, church pew, and crusade arena by his lectures and sermons to win souls.

He was "promoted to Glory" on April 10, 1945.

Bailey Smith

Smith left a 20,000-member church to enter vocational evangelism. In that pastorate he baptized 2,000 people in only twelve months. He presently hosts Real Evangelism Conferences across America and leads in evangelistic crusades. Smith has authored several books, including <u>Real Evangelism</u>.

Charles Haddon Spurgeon

Spurgeon's name is recognized by most ministers with various volumes of his sermons housed upon their library shelf. Known as the "Prince of Preachers," he began preaching at age sixteen and at age twenty became pastor of the New Park Street Chapel in London. Shortly after his ministry began in this church, attendance grew so much that work began on the construction of a 6,000-seat sanctuary. In 1861 Spurgeon and his church family moved into the Metropolitan Tabernacle.

His heart for ministers is keenly seen in his formation of a Pastor's College, which yet continues. His **passion** for the unsaved is felt in his many volumes of sermons. Spurgeon greatly influenced men who became giants for God in America, including B. H. Carroll and John R. Rice. He died in 1892.

Ruben A. Torrey

Torrey was a Bible scholar and evangelist. D. L. Moody was used by the Lord to set a fire in his heart for souls that led him to engage in wide spread crusades calling men to Christ. In his campaign that took him around the world, some 100,000 souls were saved! Moody handpicked Torrey to be the president of Chicago's Moody Bible Institute and pastor of Moody Memorial Church in 1899. He authored forty books on evangelism, soul winning, and theology. He died in 1928.

George W. Truett

In September of 1897 George W. Truett became pastor of the First Baptist Church of Dallas, Texas, where he served for forty-seven years. He was the predecessor to Dr. W. A. Criswell. Under his leadership the church saw 18,124 additions and 5,337 baptisms and its Sunday School soar to 4,000, making it the largest church in the world. His book A Quest for Souls pulsates with this great man's passion for God and heartbeat for souls. He was a man on fire who always preached for a decision.

John Wesley

Founder of Methodism, Wesley was born in Epworth, England, and died in London in 1791. He preached often on the subject "You Must Be Born Again" and when asked why he replied, "Because you must be born again!" His sermons display his passion for lost souls and how he would plead with them to be saved

George Whitfield

Whitfield paid his way through Oxford University waiting tables. His preaching brought him to the United States, where he founded the first American orphanage. In the Cambuslang Revival he preached at noon, again at 6, and once again at 9. During his ministry of thirty-four years he averaged speaking ten times a week with a voice that was said could be heard clearly a mile away. From a balcony less than an hour before his death, he preached to 2,000 people giving an invitation for them to repent and be saved. John Wesley conducted his funeral in 1770.

Foreword

1. Florida Baptist Witness. <www.floridabaptistwitness.com>. 30 Sept. 2004.
2. Sjorgren, Ping, and Pollock. Irresistible Evangelism. p 38.
3. Michael Bronson. BibleHelp.org. Chapter 13:09.
4. C.H. Spurgeon. Spurgeon's Sermons on Soulwinning. p 18.
5. L.R. Scarborough. With Christ after the Lost. p 3.

Chapter One: The Compulsion Factor in Soulwinning

1. C.H. Spurgeon. The Soulwinner. p 45.
2. Bailey Smith. Real Evangelism. pp 163-164.
3. C.E. Autrey. Can You Win Souls. p 6.
4. L.R. Scarborough. With Christ after the Lost. pp 43-44.
5. Buddy Murphrey. Drawing the Net. p 16.
6. Charles G. Finney. The Sword of the Lord, "Preacher, Save Thyself!" p 4.
7. Billy Graham 2004 Calendar, February entry.
8. Billy Graham 2004 Calendar, August entry.
9. Mrs. C.T. Studd. The Sword of the Lord, "Men on Fire." p 4.
10. John MacArthur. Follow Me. p 25.
11. John MacArthur. Making Disciples. pp 70-71.
12. Curtis Hutson, Ed. Great Preaching on Soulwinning. p 28.
13. Curtis Hutson, Ed. Great Preaching on Soulwinning. p 31.
14. Billy Graham 2004 Calendar, December entry.
15. Curtis Hutson, Ed. Great Preaching on Soulwinning. p 165.
16. Bill Bright. "How To Introduce Others to Christ" tract.
17. Horatius Bonar. Words to Winners of Souls. p 4.
18. Freddie Gage. "Where Are the Tears?"
19. Freddie Gage. "Where Are the Tears?"
20. Freddie Gage. "Where Are the Tears?"
21. Billy Graham 2004 Calendar, November entry.
22. Paul Little. How To Give Away Your Faith. pp 23-24.
23. Freddie Gage. "Where Are the Tears?"
24. William Booth. Who Cares. p 6.
25. Frederick P. Wood. Studies in Soulwinning. pp 74-75.
26. Horatius Bonar. Words to Winners of Souls. pp 23-24.
27. R.A. Torrey. Anecdotes and Illustrations. pp 156-157.
28. C.H. Spurgeon. Spurgeon's Sermons Vol. 4. p 265.
29. Bill Bright. How To Introduce Others to Christ. pp 9-12.
30. Lewis A. Drummond. Reaching Generation Next. pp 35-36.

Chapter Two: The Content Factor in Soulwinning

1. E.M. Harrison. How To Win Souls. p 24.
2. Paul E. Little. How To Give Away Your Faith. pp 57-58.
3. Charles Finney. How To Experience Revival. p 99.
4. Horatius Bonar. Words To Winners of Souls. p 6.
5. John MacArthur. Follow Me. p 61.
6. C.H. Spurgeon. Evangelism. p 199.
7. Ray Comfort. The Evidence Bible. p 411.
8. Ray Comfort. The Evidence Bible. p 615.
9. Ray Comfort. The Evidence Bible. p 521.
10. C. H. Spurgeon. Lectures To My Students. p 338.
11. James Stewart. Evangelism.

Chapter Three: The Character Factor in Soulwinning

1. W.D. Weatherford. Introducing Men to Christ. p 102.
2. E.M. Harrison. How To Win Souls. p 11.
3. L.R. Scarborough. With Christ After the Lost. p 12.
4. J.D. Douglas. The Work of an Evangelist. p 73.
5. C.H. Spurgeon. Spurgeon's Sermons on Soulwinning. p 33.
6. Murray Downey. The Art of Soulwinning. p 17.
7. Bill Bright, Ed. Ten Basic Steps Toward Christian Maturity: Teacher's Manual. p 207.
8. Michael Fabarex. Preaching That Changes Lives. p 72.
9. Eric Hayden. The Unforgettable Spurgeon. p 212.
10. L.R. Scarborough. A Search for Souls. p 15.
11. Alvin I. Reid. Radically Unchurched. p 51.
12. Fred Barber. Travail for Souls. p 201.
13. C.H. Spurgeon. Evangelism. p 201.
14. C.H. Spurgeon. The Pastor in Prayer. p 26.
15. Fred Barber. Travail for Souls. p 21.
16. Fred Barber. Travail for Souls. p 21.
17. E.J. Daniels. Dim Lights in a Dark World. p 23.
18. L.R. Scarborough. With Christ After the Lost. p 30.
19. John R. Rice. Soul Winner's Fire. p 41.
20. E.M. Harrison. How To Win Souls. p 23.
21. E.M. Harrison. How To Win Souls. p 14.
22. Horatius Bonar. Words to Winners of Souls. pp 4-5.
23. C.H. Spurgeon. When the Preacher Has No Burden for the Souls of Men. pp 5-6.
24. Buddy Murphrey. Drawing the Net. p 47.

24. Buddy Murphrey. Drawing the Net. p 47.
25. Lewis A. Drummond. Reaching Generation Next. p 113.
26. Lewis A. Drummond. Reaching Generation Next. p 113.
27. L.R. Scarborough. With Christ After the Lost. pp 22-23.
28. Donald S. Whitney. Spiritual Disciplines for the Christian. p 102.
29. Dick Lincoln sermon, October 3, 2004.
30. Robert E. Coleman. The Master Plan of Evangelism. p 173.
31. Elmer Towns. Winning the Winnable. p 13.
32. Flavil Yeakley, 1976 (by personal correspondence with Elmer Towns, 29 Sept. 2004)
33. Elmer Towns, personal correspondence, 29 Sept. 2004.
34. Curtis Hutson, Ed. Great Preaching on Soulwinning. p 64.
35. Walwood and Zuck, Eds. The Bible Knowledge Commentary, Vol. 2. p 378.
36. Herald of His Coming. Vol. 64, Number 5, May 2005.
37. Jonathan Edwards. The Life of David Brainerd. p 111.
38. Michael Fabarez. Preaching That Changes Lives. p 71.
39. L. R. Scarborough. With Christ After the Lost. p 36.
40. John R. Rice. John R. Rice Commentary: Acts. p 48.
41. Bill Bright. How To Introduce Others To Christ. p 7.
42. <www.preceptaustin.org>. Jehovah-Nissi: The Lord our Banner.
43. L.R. Scarborough. A Search for Souls. p 1.
44. Lyle W. Dorsett. The Life of D.L. Moody: A Passion for Souls. pp 388-399.

Chapter Four: The Caution Factor in Soulwinning

1. Bailey Smith. Real Evangelism. p 118.
2. Charles Finney. How To Experience Revival. p 79.
3. George Sweazey. Effective Evangelism. p 122.
4. G.S. Dobbins. A Winning Witness. p 84.
5. The Mike Gallagher Show. Radio production by Mike Gallagher, 19 Oct. 2004.
6. Dawson C. Bryan. A Workable Plan for Evangelism. p 124.
7. C.H. Spurgeon. Spurgeon Sermons: A Time for Finding Lost Sheep, Vol 4. p 121.
8. C.E. Autrey. Basic Evangelism. p 91.
9. C.E. Autrey. Basic Evangelism. p 89.
10. Gerald Martin, Ed. Great Southern Baptist Evangelistic Preaching. p 88.
11. Frederick P Wood. Studies in Soulwinning. p 120.
12. Oswald Chambers. My Utmost for His Highest. June 28 entry.
13. Basil Miller. Praying Hyde. p 34.
14. Michael Fabarez. Preaching That Changes Lives. p 70.

15. John R. Rice. Personal Soul Winning. p 6.
16. Eric Hayden. The Unforgettable Spurgeon. p 187.
17. R.A. Torrey. How To Bring Men To Christ. p 100.
18. J.W. Ellis. We Are Witnesses. p 92.
19. Gene Edwards. How To Have a Soulwinning Church. p 118.
20. J.W. Ellis. We Are Witnesses. p 93.
21. R.A. Torrey. How To Bring Men To Christ. p 95.
22. Glen C. Smith, ed. Evangelizing Youth. p 63.
23. C.E. Matthews. Every Christian's Job. p 67.
24. Frederick P. Wood. Studies in Soulwinning. pp 121-122.
25. C.E. Autrey. Basic Evangelism. p 88.
26. J.W. Ellis. We Are Witnesses. p 123.
27. George Sweazey. Effective Evangelism. p 122.
28. Murray W. Downey. The Art of Soulwinning. p 57.
29. Eric Hayden. The Unforgettable Spurgeon. p 164.
30. G.S. Dobbins. A Winning Witness. p 120.
31. William Fay. Share Jesus Without Fear. p 143.
32. Curtis Hutson, Ed. Great Preaching on Soulwinning, Vol. 12. p 97.
33. The Good Steward.com. Barna Research, 13 Sept. 2002.
34. The State, Columbia, SC, Section A7, 18 Sept. 2004.
35. Charles Finney. How To Experience Revival. p 80.
36. C.H. Spurgeon. Evangelism. p 60.
37. C.H. Spurgeon. Spurgeon's Sermons on Soulwinning. p 25.
38. Michael L. Simpson. Permission Evangelism. p 89.
39. Michael L. Simpson. Permission Evangelism. p 89.
40. George E. Sweazey. Effective Evangelism. p 25.
41. Roland Q. Leavell. Evangelism: Christ's Imperative Command. p 157.
42. Stephen Olford. The Secret of Soul-winning. p 44.
43. Stephen Olford. The Secret of Soul-winning. p 44.
44. C.E. Autrey. You Can Win Souls. p 5.
45. C.E. Autrey. You Can Win Souls. p 5.
46. Lyle W. Dorsett. The Life of D.L. Moody: A Passion for Souls. p 399.
47. Lyle W. Dorsett. The Life of D.L. Moody: A Passion for Souls. p 399.
48. Buddy Murphrey. Drawing the Net. p 26.
49. C.H. Spurgeon. Morning and Evening. June 20, 2000 evening entry.
50. John MacArthur. Follow Me. p 65.
51. G.S. Dobbins. A Winning Witness. p 86.
52. John R. Rice. The Sword Scrapbook. p 77.
53. C.H. Spurgeon. Spurgeon's Sermons on Soulwinning. p 10.
54. Sjogren, Ping, and Pollock. Irresistible Evangelism. p 29.
55. Alvin Reid. "Get Real" sermon.
56. Curtis Hutson. Look People in the Eye. p 5.
57. C.H. Spurgeon. Evangelism. pp 198-199.
58. Buddy Murphrey. Drawing the Net. p 19.

59. Buddy Murphrey. Drawing the Net. p 44.
60. Oswald Chambers Quotes. <webmaster@cybernation.com>.
61. John MacArthur. Follow Me. p 42.
62. Oswald Chambers. My Utmost for His Highest. May 5 entry.
63. Lewis Drummond. pp 100-101.
64. Elmer Towns. Winning the Winnable. cover page.
65. Florida Baptist Witness. <www.floridabaptistwitness.com/2991.article>.
66. C.H. Spurgeon. Only a Prayer Meeting. p 161.
67. John MacArthur. Follow Me.
68. Charles Finney. How To Experience Revival. p 4.
69. Lewis A. Drummond. Reaching Generation Next. p 30.
70. Lewis A. Drummond. Reaching Generation Next. p 102.
71. Lewis A. Drummond. Reaching Generation Next. p 115.
72. John Piper. The Supremacy of God in Preaching. p 94.
73. C.H. Spurgeon. Spurgeon's Sermons, Vol 8. p 233.
74. Walter Knight. Knight's Illustrations for Today. p 73.
75. Dick Lincoln sermon. 30 Jan. 2005.
76. Heralds of His Coming. Vol. 64, Number 5, May 2005. p 4.

Chapter Five: The Coward Factor in Soulwinning

1. Alvin I. Reid. "Get Real" sermon. Baptist Fire.com.
2. C.E. Autrey. Basic Evangelism. p 80.
3. Roland Q. Leavell. Evangelism, Christ's Imperative. p 162.
4. Roland Q. Leavell. Winning Others To Christ. p 25.
5. R. Larry Moyer. How-to Book on Personal Evangelism. p 79.
6. E.J. Daniels adaptation. Dim Lights in a Dark World. pp 100-101.
7. Freddie Gage sermon. "Where are the Tears."
8. W.D. Weatherford. Introducing Men to Christ. p 100.
9. John MacArthur. Follow Me. pp 101-102.

Chapter Six: The Confrontation Factor in Soulwinning

1. The Evidence Bible. p 214.
2. John R. Rice. Personal Soul Winning. p 1.
3. Bill Bright, Ed. Ten Basic Steps Toward Christian Maturity, Teacher's Manual. p 352.
4. E.J. Daniels. Dim Lights in a Dark World. p 102.
5. C.H. Spurgeon. Only A Prayer Meeting. p 160.
6. E.M. Harrison adaptation. p 38.
7. E.M. Harrison adaptation. p 38.
8. William Fay. Share Jesus Without Fear. p 5.
9. Sjogren, Ping, and Pollock. Irresistible Evangelism. p 187.
10. Paul Tan. 7700 Illustrations: Neglect of Soulwinning.

11. Michael L. Simpson. Permission Evangelism. p 93.
12. Michael L. Simpson. Permission Evangelism. p 94.
13. Alvin Reid sermon. "Get Real." Baptist Fire.com.
14. Elmer Towns. Winning the Winnable. p 6.
15. C.H. Spurgeon. Only A Prayer Meeting. p 160.
16. Stephen Olford. The Secret of Soulwinning. p 57.
17. George Hunter. How To Reach Secular People. pp 53-54.
18. Roland Q. Leavell. Winning Others to Christ. p 39.
19. Spurgeon Archives. <www.spurgeon.org/heathbio.htm>.
20. C.H. Spurgeon. Lectures to My Students. p 246.
21. C.H. Spurgeon. Lectures to My Students. p 269.
22. C.H. Spurgeon. Lectures to My Students. p 256.
23. "Good News" tract. Campus Crusade for Christ. p 3.
24. Billy Graham Evangelistic Association.
25. <holytrinitynewrochelle.org>.
26. Alvin I. Reid. Radically Unchurched. p 169.
27. Andrew Careaga. E-vangelism: Sharing the Gospel in Cyberspace. p 95.
28. Roland Q. Leavell. Winning Others to Christ. p 94.
29. C.H. Spurgeon. Spurgeon's Sermons on Soulwinning. p 19.
30. Roland Leavell. Winning Others to Christ. pp 94-95.
31. Ray Comfort. The Evidence Bible. pp 613-614.
32. <www.lifeway.com/lwc/article_main_page>.
33. C.H. Spurgeon. Spurgeon's Sermons on Soulwinning. p 17.
34. R.A. Torrey. Anecdotes and Illustrations. p 64.
35. John R. Rice. Personal Soulwinning. calvary-baptist.org/soulwin.html
36. G.S. Dobbins. A Winning Witness. pp 83-84.
37. Lewis Drummond. Reaching Generation Next. p 150.
38. Eric Hayden. The Unforgettable Spurgeon. p 15.
39. Matthew Henry. Matthew Henry Commentary on the Whole Bible.

Chapter Seven: The Conquest Factor in Soulwinning

1. Bailey Smith. Real Evangelism. p 161.
2. E.J. Daniels. Dim Lights in a Dark World. p 114.
3. C.E. Autrey. Basic Evangelism. p 59.
4. Dawson C. Bryan. A Workable Plan for Evangelism. p 125.
5. Andres Tapia. Campus Evangelism Handbook. pp 16-19.
6. L.R. Scarborough. With Christ After the Lost. pp 203-204.
7. Paul Little. How To Give Away Your Faith. p 70.
8. William Fay. Share Jesus Without Fear. p 89.
9. Josh McDowell. The New Evidence That Demands A Verdict. p 193.
10. Eric Hayden. The Unforgettable Spurgeon. p 209.
11. L.R. Scarborough. With Christ After the Lost. p 205.

Chapter Eight: The Cost Factor in Soulwinning

1. DC Talk. <u>Jesus Freaks Vol. II</u>. p 352.
2. C.H. Spurgeon. <u>The Soulwinner</u>. p. 180.
3. John MacArthur. <u>Follow Me</u>. p 72.
4. Ray Comfort. <u>The Evidence Bible</u>. p 799.
5. Roland Q. Leavell. <u>Evangelism: Christ's Imperative Commission</u>. p 3.
6. Warren Wiersbe. <u>Bible Exposition Commentary</u>. Matthew 28:18.
7. Robert E. Coleman. <u>The Master Plan of Evangelism</u>. pp 109-110.
8. Robert E. Coleman. <u>The Master Plan of Evangelism</u>. pp 199-120.
9. Robert E. Coleman. <u>The Master Plan of Evangelism</u>. pp 123-124.
10. Donald S. Whitney. <u>Spiritual Disciplines for the Christian Life</u>. p 18.

Chapter Nine: The Conservation Factor in Soulwinning

1. J.W. Ellis. <u>We Are Witnesses</u>. p 113.
2. L.R. Scarborough. <u>With Christ After the Lost</u>. pp 107-108.
3. George E. Sweazey. <u>Effective Evangelism</u>. p 216.
4. Warren W. Wiersbe. <u>Bible Expository Commentary</u>. Matthew 28:20.
5. <u>Florida Baptist Witness</u>. <www.floridabaptistwitness.com>, 30 Sept. 2004.

Chapter Ten: The Commitment Factor in Soulwinning

1. C.H. Spurgeon. <u>Spiritual Disciplines for the Christian Life</u>. p 111.
2. Robert E. Coleman. <u>The Master Plan of Evangelism</u>. p 168.
3. Adrian Rogers sermon "The Sin of Silence."
4. Bill Bright, Ed. <u>Ten Basic Christian Steps to Maturity Teacher's Manual</u>. p 342.
5. Lewis A. Drummond. <u>Reaching Generation Next</u>. p 150.
6. Bailey Smith. <u>Real Evangelism</u>.
7. Roland Q. Leavell. <u>Winning Others to Christ</u>. p 81.
8. <u>The Evidence Bible</u>. p 811.
9. Bailey Smith. <u>Real Evangelism</u>. p 163.
10. "The Lady Elgin." Knowledgegerush.com.
11. R.A. Torrey. <u>Anecdotes and Illustrations</u>. p 166.
12. Spurgeon Archives. <www.spurgeon.org/heathbio/htm>.

Chapter Eleven: Soulwinning Sermon and Talk Outlines

1. R.A. Torry. <u>Great Preaching on Soulwinning</u>. pp 61-70.
2. L.R. Scarborough. <u>How Jesus Won Souls</u>. pp 34-39.
3. James Smith. <u>Handfuls of Purpose</u>. pp 269-270.

4. E.J. Daniels. Fervent, Soul-Stirring Sermons. pp 103-119.
5. Francis Dixon's Bible Study Notes, Series 15, Study 8.
6. Oswald Chambers. My Utmost for His Highest. November 9 entry.
7. Stephen Olford. The Secret of Soulwinning. Foreword.
8. Stephen Olford. The Secret of Soulwinning. pp 15-23.
9. B.H. Carroll. Revival Messages. pp 37-38.
10. Andrew Blackwood. Evangelical Sermons of our Day. pp 272-278.
11. Theodore W. Engstrom. Sermon Outlines and Illustrations. pp 40-41.
12. Porter M. Bales. Revival Sermons. pp 57-67.
13. Hyman J. Appelman. The Saviour's Invitation and Other Evangelistic Sermons. pp 35-42.
14. L.R. Scarborough. How Jesus Won Souls. pp 209-211.

Chapter Twelve: Soulwinning Stories and Illustrations

1. Paul Tan. Signs of the Times - Encyclopedia of 7700 Illustrations. #5902.
2. Rick Warren. The Purpose Driven Life. pp 287-288.
3. Herschel Ford. Simple Sermons for Sunday Evening. pp 93-94.
4. Herschel Ford. Simple Sermons on Conversion and Commitment. p 25.
5. Porter M. Bales. Revival Sermons. p 172.
6. Walter Knight. Knight's Illustrations. p 315.
7. Servant Magazine. London Telegraph. 27 Jan. 2005. p 6.
8. Paul Tan. Signs of the Times — Encyclopedia of 7700 Illustratios #5875
9. www.jesussite.com/illustrations/living.htm.
10. (http://www.sermonillustrator.org/illustrator/sermon3a/is_this_a_sign.htm)
11. www.bible.org
12. www.bible.org